MILTON'S GOD

A

By the same Author

*

SEVEN TYPES OF AMBIGUITY

SOME VERSIONS OF PASTORAL

THE STRUCTURE OF COMPLEX WORDS

COLLECTED POEMS

MILTON'S GOD

William Empson

GREENWOOD PRESS, PUBLISHERS
WESTPORT, CONNECTICUT

Library of Congress Cataloging in Publication Data

Empson, William, 1906-
Milton's God.

Reprint of the ed. published by New Directions, Norfolk, Conn.
Includes index.
1. Milton, John, 1608-1674--Religion and ethics.
2. God--History of doctrines--17th century. I. Title.
[PR3592.R4E55 1978] 821'.4 78-14409
ISBN 0-313-21021-7

Reprinted with the permission of New Directions Publishing Corporation.

Reprinted in 1978 by Greenwood Press, Inc.
51 Riverside Avenue, Westport, CT 06880

Printed in the United States of America

P

In order to keep this title in print and available to the academic community, this edition was produced using digital reprint technology in a relatively short print run. This would not have been attainable using traditional methods. Although the cover has been changed from its original appearance, the text remains the same and all materials and methods used still conform to the highest book-making standards.

CONTENTS

To
Hetta Empson

PREFACE

In quoting Milton's verse, I have modernized the spelling except where it tells us whether to pronounce "-ed" or to emphasize "me" and suchlike, which seems better than what we do and not at all distracting. Line-references are to the nearest factor of five, because factors of ten are usually given in the margin of the text, and the eye can then find the place without further calculation. The show of scientific accuracy about literary quotations has reached a point which feels odd to anyone who knows how numbers are really used in the sciences. I have tried to avoid cluttering the index with things nobody could want to look up; but I aimed at including all bits of evidence, for example all references to the Bible and the *De Doctrina*.

The book carries many obligations, as it largely consists of reporting the ideas of previous critics and then using them; but I tried to make all such acknowledgments as I went along.

W. E.

Chapter 1

CRITICS

THE extremely thorough reconsideration of *Paradise Lost* during this century, beginning with Sir Walter Raleigh's splendid handbook (1900), has made the poem more interesting and beautiful by greatly advancing our understanding of it; but the general reader has not been much encouraged to regard the contestants in this co-operative light, and may well suppose that the fighting has merely died down out of exhaustion. In trying to bring the results together I am inherently offering to act as mediator, though the position may only invite brickbats from all sides. The opinions of both attackers and defenders of the poem have evidently corresponded to their various theologies or world-views; most of them have not cared to drive their argument to the point of saying so, but the subject cannot be viewed in a purely aesthetic manner, as Milton himself would be the first to claim. His God is somehow 'embarrassing'; indeed, almost all the contestants have used that coy word, with its comforting suggestion of a merely social blunder. Professor C. S. Lewis let in some needed fresh air (*A Preface to Paradise Lost*, 1942) by saying, "Many of those who say they dislike Milton's God only mean that they dislike God" (p. 126); speaking as an Anglican, he decided that the poem merely uses beliefs which are central to any Christian theology, except for some minor and doubtful points; but even he was ready to grant that Milton might sometimes describe God 'imprudently' (p. 93). I am anxious to make my beliefs clear at the outset, because the revival of Christianity among literary critics has rather taken me by surprise. A number of young people nowadays, as one can readily understand, feel that 'modern' ideals and programmes, a very mixed bag of them, have worked out so badly that the traditional ones may be better; but how badly those used to work out too seems to have been successfully kept hidden. Thus young people often join a Church because they think it is the only way to avoid becoming a Communist, without realizing that a Renaissance Christian State was itself usually a thorough-going police terror. 'Dislike' is a question-begging term here. I think the traditional God of Christianity very wicked, and have done since I was at school, where nearly all my little playmates thought the same. I did not say this in my earlier literary criticism because I thought it could be taken for granted, and that to fuss about it would do no good (like anyone else, I have sometimes expressed a solemn interest in the ancient craving for human sacrifice and its protean reappearances, but this does not imply Christian belief); and it seems that nowadays the gap often makes a reader find my position evasive or illogical. Having had ten years teaching in Japan and China, and having only been interested in propaganda during the war, halfway through them, I am still rather ill-adjusted to the change of atmosphere. Lecturing at Government universities in the Far East, which means firmly non-missionary ones, was not likely to prepare me for it; I gathered that those of my students who became interested in *Paradise Lost*, though too polite to express their opinion to me quite directly, thought "Well, if they worship such a monstrously wicked God as all that, no wonder that they themselves are so monstrously wicked as we have traditionally found them." Most Christians are so imprisoned by their own propaganda that they can scarcely imagine this reaction; though a missionary would have to agree that to worship a wicked God is morally bad for a man, so that he ought to be free to question whether his God is wicked. Such an approach does at least make Milton himself appear in a better light. He is struggling to make his God appear less wicked, as he tells us he will at the start (I. 25), and does succeed in making him noticeably less wicked than the traditional Christian one; though, after all his efforts, owing to his loyalty to the sacred text and the penetration with which he makes its story real to us, his modern critics still feel, in a puzzled way, that there is something badly wrong about it all. That this searching goes on in *Paradise Lost*, I submit, is the chief source of its fascination and poignancy; and to realize that it is going on makes the poem feel much better at many points, indeed clears up most of the objections to it.

I thus tend to accept the details of interpretation which various recent critics have used to prove the poem bad, and then try to show that they make it good. The essay is by no means a complete survey; the field of Milton criticism has become very large, and maybe a man who had covered it all would not have much energy of judgement left; but I have tried to follow up the lines which seem to me important. Nor can I claim to digest all of the objections, and this first chapter is mainly concerned with points of radical disagreement. Thus I cannot agree with the following statement of Dr Leavis: that a man who writes in the style of Milton

> whatever he may suppose, is not really interested in the achievement of precise thought of any kind; he certainly hasn't the kind of energy of mind needed for sustained analytic and discursive thinking.

It is understandable to dislike the mind of the later Milton, but he was an experienced propagandist, very capable of deploying his whole case so as to convince his readers of what he had already decided they should believe. Certainly, his poetic style does not let us watch him in the process of deciding, but we happen to be able to do that in the *De Doctrina*, and his prose style there does not have the qualities which Dr Leavis finds to entail a contemptible mind in *Paradise Lost*. Dr Leavis seems to assume that Christianity must be at worst a neutral literary topic, so that anything ugly or confused in the poem must be the fault of the author; it strikes me that Dr Leavis is the one who failed to do the analytic and discursive thinking here. However, I recognize that many present-day Christians cheerfully agree with him, and would insist that Milton makes God bad by getting into muddles. My chief difference from them is that I do not believe the religion can so easily be reformed; I warmly agree so far as they regard the poem as an awful warning. Milton is a kind of historian here, recording a large public fact; this is so well recognized that many people agree on it while disagreeing about what the fact was. An enlightened view often held is that he expressed a large part of the public mind of Europe during his period, both Reformation and Counter-Reformation; in some damaging way they were both making God 'legalistic', and the poem illustrates the bad effects. This is probably the main thing a teacher should say on the question, as it is almost uncontroversial and yet enough to make a student feel free to read the poem intelligently (to point out the marks of Milton's Arianism helps the same purpose). My objection is that it uses the Renaissance thinkers as scapegoats, whereas really they were going back to the intellectual roots of the religion. Whether this is so or not, the poem enlarges the experience of most readers in an important way; it is an impressive example of one of the more appalling things the human mind is liable to do.

The recent controversy about the poem, on the other hand, has largely been conducted between attackers who find it bad because it makes God bad and defenders who find it all right because it leaves God tolerable, even though Milton is tactless about him. Surely this is an absurd spectacle; the poem is not good in spite of but especially because of its moral confusions, which ought to be clear in your mind when you are feeling its power. I think it horrible and wonderful; I regard it as like Aztec or Benin sculpture, or to come nearer home the novels of Kafka, and am rather suspicious of any critic who claims not to feel anything so obvious. Hence I also expect that most of the attackers would find their minds at rest if they took one step further and adopted the manly and appreciative attitude of Blake and Shelley, who said that the reason why the poem is so good is that it makes God so bad.

The chief reason why they don't is that the intelligence of the Romantic authors has been held in contempt since the last bold literary revolution, spearheaded by Mr T. S. Eliot. When the young Empson got a university job in Tokyo in 1931 his advice was kindly asked by a wise old Japanese professor about some proposed appointment for another Englishman. There was a suspicion that this man held excessively 'liberal' views, which were very much unwanted of course—Japan had just begun her swing towards Manchuria and Pearl Harbour; and the old professor said, "We gather he isn't quite sound on Shelley." If he admired the revolutionary Shelley, that would mean he was a reliable old-school reactionary, whereas an anti-Shelley man might hold advanced political ideas. I found this very entertaining, and have thought our current literary orthodoxy a very confused body of doctrine ever since. An idea hangs around that Shelley thought nobody was wicked, because he was romantic and did not understand the Fall of Man; but he was incessantly denouncing tyrants, and most of his sturdy eighteenth-century rationalism was the same as that of Voltaire, whom nobody has dared to accuse of being ignorant of human evil. The main European revolt against Christianity does not date from the Romantic Movement but from more than two centuries earlier, and the first name that occurs to one is Montaigne; the Wars of Religion so disgusted sensitive and intelligent people with the cruelty of all Christian sects that, after about a century of effort, they managed to prevent the religion from burning people alive any more. A person aware of this tradition (and it deserves that name quite as much as the opposing tradition) is not likely to be 'embarrassed' by the wickedness of Milton's God, but rather to decide that some of the English figures in this long controversy have only drawn attention to their blushes by pretending to hide them behind their flirting fans.

Recent American critics, however, who have had much influence on the younger English ones, certainly cannot be laughed at for any uneasy delicacy. Thirty or forty years ago, American literary critics went through a much more agonizing reappraisal of 'humanism' than English ones did, and they are still rather startlingly determined not to have minds 'rotted away with humanitarianism'. Maybe the debate did something useful in its time, but it has become an incubus. Contempt for the opinions of Shelley has become automatic, if you are at all in the movement, and it is assumed that author before his time were simply brutes, as God meant us to be. Only by grasping this curious trend can one understand how Professor R. M. Adams, for example, in his book on Milton called *Ikon* (1956), came to remark that "the price of almost any system of abstract justice is alienation of the sentimentalists" (can *almost* be meant to exclude a just system?), so that he rejected "the frustrated anarchist, ignorant of his premises and terrified of his conclusions (which is the basic picture of Milton the liberal)". Like most Englishmen, I never know what Americans mean by a liberal; the story goes that the only way for an academic American to be quite safe from this smear, which would cost him his employment, is to give the secret police documentary proof that he has beaten one of his slaves to death with his own hands. 'Why, that settles it; that's American freedom; he *can't* be a liberal'; but nothing less than that is enough. We in England should feel grave sympathy for the predicament of our American brothers, but need not I think puzzle our heads a great deal over its intellectual effects. Milton was against burning people alive. During the Commonwealth he backed Cromwell's Independents against the minor attempts at persecution by the Presbyterians of the Rump; so he was consistent when he printed in 1659, well knowing that it would make him yet more likely to be executed at the Restoration, a book called *The System of Church Government; proving that no power has the right to persecute for religion.* I grant that he had reservations about the Catholics, on the ground that they would merely make use of liberal institutions to start persecuting again when they got power; an exact and one would think a reassuring parallel to the modern dilemma about Communists. Even so, Milton's liberality about religion involved so much politics that to present him as a patron saint of American reaction is a bit quaint.

On one point Shelley was wrong, as can be seen in the following statement from the preface to *Prometheus*

Unbound; though it also tells a fundamental truth about *Paradise Lost*:

> Milton has so far violated the popular creed (if this shall be judged a violation) as to have alleged no superiority of moral virtue to his God over his Devil. And this bold neglect of a direct moral purpose is the most decisive proof of Milton's genius.

He takes for granted that Milton secretly despised the popular myths which were the material of his art. This was not an unreasonable idea, because the later Milton was known to have stopped attending the meetings of any sect or having any set prayers for his household, and evidently did rather despise the general reader. The idea was only refuted by the discovery among State papers, where it had been hushed up, of Milton's *De Doctrina Christiana*; which happened in 1823, the year after Shelley was drowned. This made clear that in later life Milton was an Arian, disbelieving the identity of the Son with the Father, and held some other rather technically heretical opinions; but that he would very much expect a reader of his epic to take its argument seriously. The document is a summary in Latin of Milton's theological views with the Bible texts for defending them, evidently kept up to date for many years by minor alterations and additions; but he had parts of it copied tidily, so there we have only the near-final version. A splendid piece of detective work on this object was done by Professor Sewell (*A Study in Milton's Christian Doctrine*, 1939). With most authors one cannot date the entries in a slowly accumulated notebook, but a blind man has to use a secretary, whose handwriting and dates of work can sometimes be ascertained. Sewell's results I understand are generally accepted, and they show that Milton was actually puzzling his head about revising his theology while he was writing his epic. He probably became an Arian in the course of composition, and the reason why there is hardly anything about Satan in an otherwise complete theological survey is presumably that he cancelled that part after writing the poetry for Satan. Incidentally, when you consider the difficulties for a blind man of keeping this long document up to date, you are not inclined to say that he lacked "the kind of energy of mind needed for sustained analytic and discursive thinking". However, these deductions from the manuscript are quite recent. The immediate effect of publishing the curiosity (the young Macaulay wrote his essay on Milton under pretence of reviewing it) was to make people feel that Shelley was broadly right, and probably this was an important factor in making Shelley's attitude to the poem part of our accepted critical tradition. Most Victorian literary men would prefer to decide that Milton's picture of God was harsh and eccentric; well, Shelley had happened to be correct there, because Milton had turned out not to be a Christian anyhow, so there was no more bother. Such a man also had a helpful kind of aesthetic attitude in that he did not require a poem to be a source of doctrine; he would not be at all shocked by my slogan 'Back to Shelley'. It is only the more than Victorian seriousness of our own age, much to our credit as I don't deny, which makes us find the poem so painful.

On the other hand, before we began to worry about Milton's God being wicked, we had a long period of suspecting that his Satan was in some romantic way good. This was encouraged by discovering Blake, who of course had remarked in *The Marriage of Heaven and Hell* that Milton like all true poets was of the Devil's party without knowing it. It seems bad luck if Shelley never heard of Blake, but he may have come across this epigram and disliked it. Recent studies have made clear that Blake meant the whole thing by such utterances, not merely that Milton's Satan was good but also that his God was bad; but the Victorians took him to mean that Satan had a sort of double-talk virtue, as an artist or something. This made Blake rather confusing while he was being discovered, whereas the sheer goodness of Shelley's position, however dangerous his practical deductions might be thought, always shone out clearly. I had perhaps better demonstrate that Shelley is not a Satanist. His own hero Prometheus, he remarks in the preface, is

> susceptible of being described as free from the taints of ambition, envy, revenge, and a desire for personal aggrandisement, which, in the hero of *Paradise Lost*, interfere with the interest. The character of Satan engenders in the mind a pernicious casuistry, which leads us to weigh his faults with his wrongs, and excuse the former because the latter exceed all measure. In the minds of those who consider that magnificent fiction with a religious feeling they engender something worse.

Whether Prometheus has renounced force absolutely, and how he conquers an evil God without it, have been found subtle questions by careful readers of the poem; probably Shelley meant to admit that he had had to struggle over the treatment by the phrase 'susceptible of being described'. To take for granted that 'the interest' of *Paradise Lost* can only be resistance to tyranny is charmingly cool, and C. S. Lewis uttered a snort at the idea that Satan's wrongs are infinite; I must come back to that later. But it is merely wrong to assume as C. S. Lewis does, and as so many people would nowadays, that Shelley preached immorality and anarchy. In defending Milton's treatment of the Fall Lewis says:

> The truth and passion of the account are unassailable. They were never, in essence, assailed till pride and rebellion came, in the romantic age, to be admired for their own sake.

Shelley was not doing this; he was accepting as heroic any apparently hopeless resistance to something a man's own conscience tells him to be wrong, and I think people like C. S. Lewis are very unwise to talk as if this moral attitude was invented by the Romantics. No doubt Romantic authors did present it as a frequently needed virtue, because of the political situation around them; but Shelley especially, though without seeming at all unusual there, based his main moral argument on the Gospels.

His basic objection to the Christian God is that God considers punishment inevitable if Adam eats the apple, as is prominent when Milton makes God say "Die he or Justice must" (III. 210). This superstition is no part of English justice, because the prerogative of mercy has long been a fundamental power of the Crown. Oddly enough the phrase is a metaphysical conceit, in the fashion that Milton usually avoided; and the English language seems designed to make it sound fatuous, rather as the translation turns round and bites the man in Chekhov who says he is 'above love'. There is an assumption here, as Shelley points out in his incomplete *Essay on Christianity*, that punishment is 'just' apart from any intention either to improve the criminal or to deter his fellows from imitating him:

> My neighbour, or my servant, or my child, has done me an injury, and it is just that he should suffer an

> injury in return. Such is the doctrine which Jesus Christ summoned his whole resources of persuasion to oppose. 'Love your enemy, bless them that curse you'; such, he says, is the practice of God, and such must ye imitate if ye would be the children of God.

The pronouns are worth attention here. Shelley does not speak as an Underdog or Outsider, tormented to hysteria by his wrongs, but as the heir to an estate who may expect to do a good deal of administration himself; he takes for granted that he ought to learn to be a good judge, not that he is a victim. It would be interesting to hear some of our recent defenders of Milton try to defend the Gospels, and prove that they do not merely report the sayings of a sentimental liberal.

The main statement of Shelley about the poem is in the *Defence of Poetry*; it may seem wilful if you have not already in mind the argument from the Gospels, but I see no answer to it if you have:

> Nothing can exceed the energy and magnificence of the character of Satan as expressed in *Paradise Lost*. It is a mistake to suppose that he could ever have been intended for the popular personification of evil. Implacable hate, patient cunning, and a sleepless refinement of device to inflict the extremest anguish on an enemy, these things are evil; and, although venial in a slave, are not to be forgiven in a tyrant; although redeemed by much that ennobles his defeat in one subdued, are marked by all that dishonours his conquest in the victor. Milton's Devil as a moral being is as far superior to his God, as one who perseveres in some purpose which he has conceived to be excellent, in spite of adversity and torture, is to one

> who in the cold security of undoubted triumph inflicts the most horrible revenge upon his enemy, not from any mistaken notion of inducing him to repent of a perseverance in enmity, but with the alleged design of exasperating him to new torments. Milton has so far violated the popular creed (if this shall be judged a violation) . . .

and so on, as already quoted from the Preface to *Prometheus*. The whole passage is clearly one he was trying to get into final form, whether he copied it out or knew it by heart; he repeats it again in an essay *On the Devil, and Devils*, with minor improvements and the addition:

> This much is certain; that Milton gives the Devil all imaginable advantage; and the arguments with which he exposes the injustice and impotent weakness of his adversary are such as, had they been printed distinct from the shelter of any dramatic order, would have been answered by the most conclusive of syllogisms —persecution.

Shelley cannot have meant that Milton's God was 'impotent' to persecute Satan, but I expect he would have denied meaning only that this God could not have defended his conduct by rational argument. Shelley was accustomed to think of moral strength as politically active, and would mean that this God could not have developed any good state of affairs from the one which he had already caused.

I know of no critic who has settled down to answer Shelley here except the American J. S. Diekhoff (*Milton's Paradise Lost*, 1946), which is much to his credit of course, and he is impressive in his confidence. For too long the argument of his book is merely that, since we know God is infinitely good, we would only delude ourselves by giving attention to bits of the poem showing him as bad; and that, if he is perfectly good, Satan must be in the wrong. But on p. 52 he placidly remarks, "Here, of course, Milton's argument is circular", adding that this is "an important rhetorical means of persuasion", and his own argument gets a bit more interesting:

> There is logical proof of the point too, but this is also burdened by a question-begging device of which we must take notice. On the narrative principle affirmed by Milton himself that in a story the false speak false, we have carefully discounted the evidence of Satan. Neither his defence of himself nor his arraignment of God as a tyrant may be accepted. On the same principle, what God says must be taken to be true, and what his followers say of him. Yet it is God Milton seeks to justify. The one on trial, as it were, becomes the most trustworthy of witnesses.

Milton's 'affirmation' turns out to be a remark in the *First Defence* that the persons of a play should speak "what is most fitting to each character"; but we need no such reference to be sure that Milton would think this a platitude which even the worst dramatist could trot out. The principle, Mr Diekhoff admits, "somewhat weakens the force of the argument", but we must also judge God by his deeds.

> We shall find that we have done so in the end. For the moment it is enough to affirm that it is because of goodness yet to be demonstrated that God rules.

From now on, with firm honesty, every time the poem offers an excuse for an outrageous act of God we are told that the argument does not yet quite satisfy us; until we suddenly end a chapter with complete satisfaction at God's mercy (p. 131). This is bound to seem odd, because the doctrine of the Fortunate Fall which was to make the triumphant end of the poem has just been admitted to be confusing, for Milton himself probably as well as for us:

> Apparently he had not made up his mind, and perhaps did not regard the question as important to his main argument. He had demonstrated that the disobedience was itself bad and justly to be punished; he had shown that the whole sequel of evil events stemming from Satan's pride and the various human weaknesses of Adam and Eve were turned through God's power and mercy to a good end. To assert eternal providence and justify the ways of God to men, he need prove nothing further.

Thus the argument turns on the mercy of God; 'we' (the race of man, perhaps) are not convinced of his goodness, very intelligibly, till we learn that he will do better than what he calls justice to ourselves. But Mr Diekhoff firmly goes on to point out that there is a problem, if not about Satan, at least about the inferior angels: "for them God does not make merciful concessions; the Son does not offer to sacrifice himself for them"—whom he knew personally, as he did not yet know Man. God is now said to be good even when he isn't merciful:

> The strict enforcement of the law as laid down in the beginning is all that abstract justice requires. If God deals mercifully with men, giving them more than justice, it does not follow that he must give more than justice to the fallen angels (99).

Yet in our own case the derogatory term 'legalistic' may be freely used; *our* consciences would not let us call him good if he dealt so with us. However, this typical piece of double-talk is not the end of the matter; Mr Diekhoff points out that the minor angels choose freely, though they seem merely to obey Satan's orders, because when Abdiel differs "he is not compelled, nor is any special effort made to seduce him". This does indeed show a certain nobility in Satan and his associates; we do not find Milton's God being content to differ from someone who contradicts him. Also, says Mr Diekhoff, the motives of the bad angels are very different from those of Adam and Eve, who only try to get to Heaven in a mistaken way; the bad angels accept with acclamation the view of Satan that "a return to Heaven except as conquerors would be intolerable". This is a real argument; but, after all, the devils have been there, whereas we, like Adam and Eve, have not; the passionate loathing for God of this great multitude, their determination to escape from him at all cost, is one of the chief pieces of evidence the poem gives us about his character.

On the question why it was right to punish all the descendants of Adam and Eve, Mr Diekhoff explains that Adam had entered into a contract to that effect (p. 106). "Adam, when the prohibition is pronounced, accepts it, even though his acceptance is only tacit as presented to us." This would in any case be an exceedingly wicked bargain, which silence would best befit; I agree that it would be trivial to raise a legal objection about the means through which connivance was expressed, a leer perhaps. The broad answer is that Adam is given no official warning about his children, therefore can strike no such bargain, either in Milton or in Genesis. Mr Diekhoff seems to be an honest man, and it is rather painful to watch him at the very corrupting work of trying to defend the myth.

After considering this attempt to handle the fundamental difficulties, one can look back with more respect at the major essay by Mr Eliot attacking Milton (1936), which other critics followed up in ways that he had not intended. He had previously let drop a number of remarks that Milton's style was a bad influence on modern poets, and now this speech would put his cards on the table, or give definite examples to discuss; it was nearly all about style. He did express towards the end a firm distaste for Milton's God, but he presented that as merely his own prejudice which perhaps ought to be discounted. As to the meaning of the poem, he said:

> So far as I perceive anything, it is a glimpse of a theology that I find in large part repellent, expressed through a mythology which would better have been left in the Book of Genesis, upon which Milton has not improved.

The essay is very candid; you are shown T. S. Eliot's mind in depth, that is, both the points about style which he has in focus and the feelings about the poem which he has not yet pursued to their logical consequences. His feelings seem to me evidently right; indeed the poem, if read with understanding, must be read with growing horror unless you decide to reject its God. But it seems to me that C. S. Lewis was also right when he protested that this is merely the traditional Christian God. T. S. Eliot presumably felt, as many modern Christians do, that he wished people wouldn't mention these nasty old myths, and that they wouldn't if they were more civilized Christians. But such an evasive attitude can become very unpleasant; when leading Christians make these tacit rejections, the simpler brethren are likely to be deceived into thinking that some wrong belief is still accepted, so that they continue to act on it, with very bad effects perhaps; yet more, once the leader has started on the horrible process of connivance, he is liable to act much worse than the simpler brethren would have done. But this does not apply to Mr Eliot; a discussion about an aesthetic preference is eminently the place where the mysterious processes of accommodation should first be tried out, and he decided later, when the controversy had become plainly theological, that he was committed to accepting Milton as a Christian poet. He did this in 1947, and it would be interesting to know whether he had already seen A. J. A. Waldock's *Paradise Lost and Its Critics*, published the same year; but he would not need to have done; a movement of opinion of this kind is very independent of the printed books which sum it up. Rather in the same way, the eminence of Mr Eliot tempts one to blame him for the whole neo-Christian movement, which I think has been harmful to literary criticism, but on the issue of Milton he is very unsmirched.

His chief argument in 1936 was the stylistic one which made Keats rewrite *Hyperion*; that the style of Milton is so mannered or learned as to cut out the natural energy and up-to-dateness of the spoken language. Milton certainly has often been a bad influence on minor poets, but speaking as one myself I do not think that nursemaiding us on such matters does much good. In his attack on Milton's own style, Mr Eliot took an example which refutes his argument. It is the speech of Satan to his assembled troops, breaking the news that he will lead them against God, which all but Abdiel greet with acclamation (v. 770-800). Mr Eliot said that the 'involved syntax' is not 'aimed at precision'; he quoted in comparison a particularly tiresome sentence by Henry James, commenting on his characters in the middle of a novel, and said that its convolutions are "due to a determination not to simplify". It seems to me that Mr Eliot does not know when Milton is good, and I certainly do not know when Henry James is good; I always feel sure he is jabbering like that only to make the reader as hopelessly confused about the rights and wrongs of the case as he is himself. You may answer that that is precisely what Satan is doing in the passage quoted, but Satan has better reason for it than Henry James, who was not at the moment risking his all on a brief speech to a multitude. Clearly Satan needs to have a command of the spoken language here, so that Milton would be particularly wrong not to give it to him, but we need not quite require his style to be 'aimed at precision'. Mr Eliot says that Satan

> is not *thinking* or conversing, but making a speech carefully prepared for him, and the arrangement is for the sake of musical value, not for significance.

It is odd to reflect that this was written while the spellbinder Lloyd George was still a power in the country. A speaker can at times feel so much in contact with the minds of a large audience that, instead of doing any of these three things, he invents at the moment what will swing them decisively on to his side; and here Satan is made to do it at the electric speed of thirty lines. It is so thrillingly 'spoken' that one is driven to inquire why so good a critic could not understand how it is meant to be read. To be sure, Mr Eliot would have hated listening to Lloyd George too, but he would not have imagined that those speeches had been cooked up by a secretary. The reason why Satan can win over his army so quickly is that they already hate God, or hate the recent ukase of God, so much that they do not require completed arguments; various points have to be cleared, but Satan can drop one sentence or argument and start another as soon as they are confident that he is taking the right line. The mind of Mr Eliot, I submit, totally jibbed at imagining angels who hated God as much as that, whereas Milton thought it only to be expected; so Mr Eliot fell back on some theory of Mr Ezra Pound that the words are 'only musical'. I agree that the scene is a surprising one, and must examine its politics later on. But, to start with, if one view makes a bit of poetry very good, and another makes it very bad, the author's intention is inherently likely to be the one that makes it good; especially if we know that he writes well sometimes. We could not use language as we do, and above all we could not learn it when babies, unless we were always floating in a general willingness to make sense of it; all the more, then, to try to make a printed page mean something good is only fair. There is a question for a critic at what point this generous and agreeable effort of mind ought to stop, and with an old text (the *Hamlet* of Shakespeare for example) it is no use to impute a meaning which the intended readers or audience could not have had in mind, either consciously or unconsciously. At bottom, you are trying to imagine the mind of the author at the moment of composition, but this may be too hard taken alone, so you need to remember that he was intensely concerned at that moment with whether the words he had found 'expressed' what he was trying to say, that is, whether they would have the effect he wanted upon the audience he was imagining. Sometimes the audience would get the effect without understanding how it was done, so that their 'unconsciousness' needs to be put into the definition; but as a rule this only concerns matters which they could understand if they switched their attention. I have put in this tiny bit of theorizing for fear that a reader may suspect I am working on some much wilder theory.

Mr Eliot's later essay on Milton was also first given as a speech to a learned Society, and strikes a reader even more as handling a social occasion, but this too is candid because he chiefly wanted to say that his earlier remarks had been misunderstood. Fashions having changed, he said, he no longer thought the style of Milton a bad influence, though he still thought that it had been when he said it was. He still found Milton not to his personal taste, perhaps chiefly from being musical rather than imagist; but such powers of imagery as Milton had, powers for example to suggest vast space, were given their best possible scope in the epic. This might seem to settle the question, but he then gave the example of the chains:

> To complain, because we first find the arch-fiend 'chain'd on the burning lake', and in a minute or two see him making his way to the shore, is to expect a kind of consistency which the world to which Milton has introduced us does not require.

Imagism seems to me such nonsense that I cannot guess what may be decided by its rules, but Milton tells us at once that God deliberately released Satan from his chains. The first words of God in the poem, however, which come in Book III, imply that he didn't; and the only way to explain this later passage is to regard it as one of God's blood-curdling jokes. Mr Eliot would naturally not be inclined to suppose so, and this I think (to do him justice) was what had become fixed in his head, as a theological contradiction, though he only remembered it in terms of imagery. He then praised Milton, with graceful charity, precisely because of the visual weakness of his descriptions of Paradise, where "a more vivid picture . . . would have been less paradisiacal". One might puzzle about this a great deal, but surely Mr Eliot was only escaping from his position of 1936, when he had said:

> The eye is not shocked in his twilit Hell as it is in the Garden of Eden, where I for one can get pleasure from the verse only by the deliberate effort not to visualize Adam and Eve and their surroundings.

That, you see, had made nonsense of the complaint about lack of imagery, because the images excited by Milton's Paradise would have to be fairly vivid before this struggle could impose itself. So long as you gave Mr Eliot images of someone being tortured his nerves were at peace, but if you gave him an image of two people making each other happy he screamed. Now, making vague boasts almost to this effect was part of the entertaining moral paradox of his whole critical challenge—we should remember that he was young in the great days of Oscar Wilde; but my eye does not rest with conviction on this Image of the mind of Mr Eliot, and I suspect he got into both confusions out of a sustained loyalty to Mr Ezra Pound. Even so, by 1947, the question of imagery appeared as a comfortable distraction from the critics who had argued that Milton's God was wicked. The naked figures in Paradise, by the way, strike me as of the Venetian school.

I had better give an example of the pro-Christian polemic in rebuttal of these attacks; naturally it is in a very different tone from the writing of Mr Eliot. Learned discussions frequently refer us in a footnote to an article in the *Review of English Studies* for October 1945 by S. Musgrove, called "Is the Devil An Ass?" In order to refute anyone who thinks that Milton imputed any merit to Satan, this article combs through the text for insinuations against him, and the effect is very like the wartime propaganda then current.

> Significantly, after his very first speech, Satan is described as 'rack't with deep despare' (126)—and despair is the unforgiveable sin.

A commander who is not afraid to weep before his troops at having led them into a defeat so total as to prove they have no hope from direct attack may well feel despair even when he talks bravely about evasive action. To be sure, medieval theory defined a special kind of despair as the sin against the Holy Ghost, but this would not be immediately obvious to readers way back in early times under Charles II. It is like the priests in *St Joan* who obstruct her trial for heresy by accusing her of stealing a bishop's horse. Similarly, when Satan praises Adam and Eve:

> *whom my thoughts pursue*
> *With wonder, and could love, so lively shines*
> *In them divine resemblance* (IV. 365)

"He *could* love them *because* of their resemblance to the divine. . . . That is, the memory of God and Heaven is still working in him." But all the rebel angels take for granted throughout their speeches that they too are divine, and Satan need only mean that the earthly creatures are fit companions for himself. Mr Musgrove shows himself well aware, later on, that nobody could love anybody for being like Milton's God. When Satan is discovering arguments to use to Adam and Eve, we are told that "he is beginning, not merely to tell lies, but to tell lies to himself" . . . "beginning to believe his own propaganda":

> *Hence I will excite their minds*
> *With more desire to know, and to reject*
> *Envious commands, invented with design*
> *To keep them low whom knowledge might exalt*
> *Equal with Gods . . .* (IV. 525)

> Now Satan knows (or knew) well enough that envy and a positive desire for suppression are not and cannot be parts of God's nature, which is wholly good . . .

—and yet the grammar shows that he half believes what he is inventing. But Satan always did say, from the start of his revolt, that God had such motives; and I do not see how a candid reader of the poem could disagree with him. Like most such characters, he could not have won his followers if he had not believed his own propaganda; probably he is beginning to doubt it here, but he can still feel genuinely indignant at the behaviour of God. Arguments from what Satan must have known merely presume that we should ignore the text to improve its theology. Then again, when captured in Paradise, Satan demands legal proof that he was harming Eve by whispering in her ear what he believed to be true. Mr Musgrove rebukes him for telling a lie; surely this implies a quaint innocence about what heroes on our own side might think proper when in enemy hands. And so forward; the steady flow of such arguments is enough to turn any fair-minded man into a Satanist.

What is peculiar about Mr Musgrove's position comes out when he proceeds to argue that "Satan's earlier biography, as given in V and VI, tells against the romantic view". His reason is that

> . . . the imaginative atmosphere which clings about Satan in Heaven is exactly that which clings about

> the other angels, fallen or unfallen, as about the Deity himself; chilly and somehow unconvincing. Satan even shares God's heavy sarcasm.

As I understand Mr Musgrove, he praises Milton for showing in this way that Satan is not impressive "in the context of Heaven, in the light of truth". But what can these metaphors mean if God is just as bad as Satan?

> There is no more enkindling warmth about one than the other; the only difference being that Satan is hopelessly wrong in his intellectual position.

The basic intellectual position of Satan is simply to deny the moral superiority of God; plainly, if what Mr Musgrove says is true, Satan was in the right. There is plenty more; Mr Musgrove has yet to triumph over the nerve-racking admissions of Satan upon Niphates' top; but all that gets proved, it seems to me, is that Satan has a better sense of honour than his critic. However, I may well be wronging Mr Musgrove, whose position is hard to grasp from the brief fighting essay. Clearly he feels that his essential duty is to rebut 'romanticism', and the term seems to include any generous sentiment or even any satisfaction at reaching a large general truth; he appears content to despise God no less than Satan. And yet one might deduce from the bit just quoted that some kind of 'enkindling warmth' would seem to him all right. It only strikes me as peculiar to find the reference regularly listed as one of the well-known Christian victories.

Another way of reading the poem is, as we may be thankful, the aesthetic one; but European critics find it rather hard to be purely aesthetic about an exposition of Christianity, and I thought an Indian did it best. However, I do not mean what the grand reigning American tradition calls aesthetic; under that, as I understand, a student who literally obeys Teacher can get no direct experience from an art-work at all. He must enter an alien world called 'historical' from which his own conscience and knowledge of life are excluded. This was already hard enough, for the seventeenth century, before Miss Rosamund Tuve added that its authors are medieval, and only to be understood by a knowledge of medieval liturgies rivalling her own; many English critics, I gather, have been so hypnotized by the difficulty of her own prose style that they regard all authors of the period as having a sensibility unnervingly unlike a modern one, and prepare for reading them as for an anthropological expedition. Naturally, this is almost the opposite of what used to be called an aesthetic approach; for example (rather in spite of its title) Mr B. Rajan's *Paradise Lost and the Seventeenth Century Reader* (1947). "Sublimity is the virtue celebrated by Milton's style," he said; and I think that if you hang on to this basic truth you can make sense of the narrative again and again. Unfortunately he went on to argue that the poem "could not be dramatic and should not be expected to be", which throws away most of the merit of his position; and I do not like his agreeing that it was 'trivial' of Adam to choose to die beside his wife. Then, in dealing with the problem whether the Devil is an Ass, ridiculous because he chooses to fight omnipotence, Mr Rajan swings round and explains the effect as a 'dramatic' one. "Though conscious we are not always or inescapably conscious" that God is omnipotent. "The conflict then is neither Promethean nor farcical. It is dramatically real in proportion as you assent to the illusion of equality which the poem communicates" (p. 96). This is quite true except that he does not seem to realize what it means. How could the illusion be any more real than it is, in a poem? What other convincing process was open to the poem beyond convincing our imagination? Christians who read the poem as Mr Rajan does, I should fancy, are in greater spiritual danger than they suppose from their aesthetic play; "in proportion as you assent to the illusion of equality" you secretly accept the righteousness of Satan's basic claim. Milton himself, I should have thought, was a particularly unlikely kind of man to have toyed with the Devil in this way, but in any case, if he did, he was doing what Shelley praised him for. Indeed I think that critics like this, though admirable in the large admissions which their technique makes them feel free to make, are just accepting the position of Shelley while inventing means to evade his conclusions. The main reason why this leaves the mind unsatisfied, I think, is that one becomes so baffled in trying to imagine how Milton came to write as he did.

Chapter 2

SATAN

It seemed best to begin by recalling some of the recent bones of contention, but now I must follow the story of the epic, more or less in its own order, and try to recapture the way it was meant to strike a fit reader. The chief thing to get clear, I think, is that Milton regularly presents a fall as due to an intellectually interesting temptation, such that a cool judge may feel actual doubt whether the fall was not the best thing to do in the circumstances. Milton could not otherwise become seriously interested in the case, or feel that it was worthy of his powers; and the effect is that he would see more point in the views of Blake and Shelley than a modern 'historical-minded' critic feels permitted to suppose. The case of Satan comes first in the epic, and has long been thought the most interesting, but we know least about it; his period of decision is presented indirectly, if at all, and its background is hard for us to envisage. We need therefore to make deductions from what the supernatural characters let drop about what happened earlier, much as we would in a play by Ibsen; whereas most critics just assume that Milton regarded the story as obvious, and made the devils tell lies. I should think that, having written both history and propaganda, he would feel himself fairly well equipped to estimate what kind of truth lay behind the traditional propaganda of the devils.

A reader may shrink from the prospect of ingenious misinterpretation thus opened before him, but I can claim to start by removing an unnecessary 'problem' which has been much bothered over. Sir Walter Raleigh, in a fine sentence, remarked that Satan's "very situation as the fearless antagonist of Omnipotence makes him either a fool or a hero, and Milton is far indeed from permitting us to think him a fool". This has led to discussion on the basis "Hero or Fool?" (the title of an essay by Sir Rostrevor Hamilton which makes a number of good points); but until Satan is in sight of Paradise he is convinced that God is *not* omnipotent. Then, very dramatically, "horror and doubt distract / His troubled thoughts" (IV. 20). I maintain that he does not doubt the thesis he keeps asserting till the poem tells us he does; surely this is not an over-subtle theory. Raleigh's remark was sympathetic, because Milton does want to make Satan a very high-flying character, and sometimes uses ambiguous language to heighten the drama. The great line

Who durst defy th'Omnipotent to Arms (I. 50)

is not ascribed to one of the characters; for consistency it has to mean that, though Milton believes God to be omnipotent, Satan dared to hope he could be defeated. Not all the rebel angels are heroic, and they all think as Satan does; we first meet them in Book I astonished to find God able to send them to Hell, and even yet doubting his omnipotence. Satan no more set out to attack omnipotence than Belial did, and if he had done Belial would not have followed him.

We are told at the start that Satan "trusted to have equal'd the Most High" (40), and he says in his first words, by way of excusing the defeat of the rebels,

till then who knew
The force of those dire Arms? (95)

They knew, of course, as rebels usually do, that they

might be defeated and were risking severe reprisals; thus Beelzebub in his reply says that Satan

> *Fearless, endanger'd Heav'ns perpetual King;*
> *And put to proof his high Supremacy,*
> *Whether upheld by Strength, or Chance, or Fate* (130)

If he *endangered* God, the rule of God is not inherently *perpetual*; Milton would intend the words as a slight contradiction which the speaker does not know how to resolve. In the same way, the rebels often call God 'Almighty', but I need only show that they give an ordinary meaning to the English word; Milton might intend to write 'on two levels' about such matters, if only to reassure his simpler readers, but even if he didn't the language would make it hard to avoid. Among men, it would be correct to call an opponent 'all-powerful' meaning 'able to defeat any opposing combination in battle' though he were not a magician; and such is all Beelzebub can mean by saying he is now sure God is Almighty, since he has beaten 'such a force as ours' (145); he adds at once that God can't kill the rebels, who are 'Gods and Heavenly Essences' like himself. They do not much deny the goodness of God, as the idea hardly occurs to them; Beelzebub goes on to suspect, what Milton tells us to be true, that God has allowed them to recover consciousness merely to give them further torture. What they do not yet realize is that his infinite malice cannot be outwitted. The analytic mind of Satan, however, in his answering speech, does consider the question of God's goodness; he says that his side, however impotent otherwise, will from now on do ill to oppose the good works of God (160). This may seem embarrassing for his defenders; it is hard to regard him as ironical here, and Shelley would perhaps have said that Milton was pandering to his audience for a moment. 'Good' was evidently one of the titles assumed by God, like 'Almighty'; during the war, Satan says 'him named Almighty' (VI. 295), and later 'he Almighty styled' (IX. 135), while jeering at God for having taken a week to create the world. Thus one may regard this act of verbal defiance as pathetically innocent, though terrible, because Satan when he makes it does not know what doing ill feels like, though God will make him learn. He was technically not ignorant of good and evil before his fall, as Adam and Eve were (XI. 85), but comparatively ignorant one would expect. There is at any rate a heavy dramatic irony in the next lines, when Satan hopes that this procedure

perhaps
Shall grieve him, if I fail not, and disturb
His inmost counsels from their destin'd aim. (I. 165)

Milton steadily drives home that the inmost counsel of God was the Fortunate Fall of man; however wicked Satan's plan may be, it is God's plan too.

On reaching land and observing Hell Satan makes a third grand speech, still only to his intimate Beelzebub, so that it is not merely propaganda for his troops. He welcomes any privation rather than endure the presence of God,

Whom reason hath equall'd, force hath made supreme
Above his equals. (250)

It has been clear from the start that some kind of metaphysical claim against God is the basis of Satan's actions, but here we get the first of a number of hints, cumulatively strong, that he had held an actual debate on the rights of God, for senior angels only, before the crisis which made him call them out for immediate military action. One can suppose instead that he is forcing his case here, and means only that his army accepted the arguments which he gave them in the brief speech after mobilization; and I agree that he is prone to mis-statement after reaching Niphates' top; but these early phrases fit together more naturally if God's 'equals' have exercised their reason together, as Parliament did against Charles I.

Satan too calls God 'Almighty' here, but Milton expects the reader to impute a tone of irony, because Satan is retorting upon God a familiar accusation against himself; he may also mean to express doubt whether God created Hell, but in any case he sneers at the metaphysical meaning of 'Almighty' while accepting the common one:

th' Almighty hath not built
Here for his envy, will not drive us hence: (260)

I am not denying, what Milton regularly asserts, that Satan fell out of pride and envy; but as Satan believes God to be a usurper he genuinely does believe him to be envious. As soon as we waive our metaphysical presumptions, we easily recognize that the motivation will be complex as in human affairs. In another case, resisting Charles I for example, the emotional forces actuating Satan could have made him work for the public good with increasingly public-spirited sentiments. As has often been pointed out, he is in the wrong solely because of an intellectual error; and we are ill-equipped to feel certain that we ourselves, in his place, would have decided rightly from the right motives.

His next act is to rouse the other rebels from the lake (320), and his scolding presumes a military situation in which they should be ready to defend themselves, hence that their foe is not all-powerful. In addressing them when risen (625) he at once calls God 'Almighty'; but he cannot intend the metaphysical sense of the word, because he congratulates them on having stood against him for a time. I grant indeed that the effect is quieter than before; after getting them to rise with the bark of a sergeant-major, he has now to coax and comfort them; and the assurance that he won't lead them to another direct assault upon God is necessary to give them enough courage for other activities. (We do not much notice the change of tone because the splendid description of pagan gods comes in between.) But part of their comfort is that they can be proud of the War in Heaven; "that strife / Was not inglorious, though the event was dire".[1] We find later that Satan is gently recalling here what he had pressed strongly during the war in Heaven; indeed it is the most definite theoretical argument of the rebels against the claims of God (VI. 425). If they can fight against him for three days, that is enough to prove that he has not got absolute or metaphysical power; he is not the God of Aquinas; therefore he has been cheating them, and, however powerful he may be, to submit to him would be dishonourable. Milton does not treat this argument as absurd; his story indeed rebuts it, but at the cost

[1] Mr John Peter (*A Critique of Paradise Lost*, 1960) deduces that God only allows half of the good angels to fight, from his words when telling Michael to drive out the rebels:

> *lead forth to Battle these my Sons/Invincible . . .*
> *Equal in number to that Godless crew.* (VI. 50)

I am much in sympathy with his book, but there is no need for his deductions from the one phrase *equal in number*. It is often used to mean 'not less than', and here the logic is 'Be fearless, because . . .'. God encourages his troops and implies that they ought to be able to win, but avoids insisting that they are double in number.

of implying that God intentionally deluded Satan. The Father tells the Son that he has delayed his victory to prove to the loyal angels the unique powers of the Son (VI. 700); however, as God knows all consequences, he must also have known that these tactics would make Satan argue as he does.

We may now consider the chains, which Mr Eliot could not make a picture of. I agree that they are probably a metaphor for some other means of immobilization; probably material chains could not even now hold Satan, who can still make himself any size he likes, though God has imposed some grave change on the half-gaseous nature of the rebels. Whatever the chains are, we are left in no doubt what happens to them; they hold for nine days, including the seven of Creation (but not the following day, when Adam woke up in Paradise, VIII. 245), and then God deliberately removes them:

So stretched out huge in length the Arch-fiend lay
Chain'd on the burning lake; nor ever thence
Had risen nor heav'd his head, but that the will
And high fore-knowledge of all-ruling Heav'n
Left him at large to his own dark designs
That with reiterated crimes he might
Heap on himself damnation, while he sought
Evil to others, and enrag'd might see
How all his malice serv'd but to bring forth
Infinite goodness, grace and mercy shown
On man by him seduc'd, but on himself
Treble confusion, wrath and vengeance pour'd. (I. 210)

Here we are specifically told that God's actions towards Satan were intended to lead him into greater evil; thus we have no reason to doubt that God had previously intended to give Satan a wrong metaphysical argument when he made the War in Heaven last three days. It may still be thought that there is a confusion about the chains when Satan decides to rise from the flood:

> *But see the angry Victor hath recall'd*
> *His Ministers of vengeance and pursuit . . .* (170)

Satan remembers for ten lines what happened while they were falling from Heaven, and ignores the chains altogether. But he imagines that the pursuing troops have only just been recalled; the rebels are as if emerging from a drug, and remember nothing of the intervening period. Indeed Moloch, after more time for reflection, specifically says they were under a drug:

> *Let such bethink them, if the sleepy drench*
> *Of that forgetful Lake benumb not still . . .* (II. 75)

Already when Satan and Beelzebub rise Milton explains to us that they are both in a delusion:

> *Both glorying to have scapt the Stygian Flood*
> *As Gods, and by their own recover'd strength*
> *Not by the sufferance of supernal power.* (I. 240)

Henry James himself (a very unvisual author, I should have thought) would have told Mr Eliot that the scene ought to be presented from the point of view of the devils, so that he had no grounds for grumbling that he could not make a picture of the chains; indeed, Milton does more explaining than Henry James would have allowed. But it is understandable that the long sentence just quoted, which explains for us the overall intention of God, might seem best interpreted as 'only music'. God's infinite mercy to Man pokes up in one line merely so that Milton can swoop to the kill at the end of the sentence; he patently does not feel the doctrine just then as anything but one more boast about God's triumph over Satan. (I am not denying that Milton felt a personal dislike for Satan.) Modern Christians, very properly, tend to dislike reading the line as a shrill high war-whoop before launching the tomahawk, so they feel that the only decent way to read it must be 'dead-pan'.

A reader may be feeling it unpoetical of me to nag away at the theological argument without a word for the sheer splendour of the first utterance of Satan. I have delayed considering it because I do not believe it can be read aloud properly unless you realize what it means. The belief that he has proved God not to be omnipotent is so rooted in his mind that, as soon as he emerges from the drug, we find it already permeating almost every clause of his defiance; and this is what decides the emphases, so that you are not even getting the sound of the poetry if you refuse to see the point of it:

that fixt mind
And high disdain, from sense of injur'd merit,
That with the mightiest rais'd me to contend,
And to the fierce contention brought along
Innumerable force of spirits arm'd
That durst dislike his reign, and me preferring,
His utmost *power with* adverse *power* oppos'd
In dubious battle *on the* plains *of Heav'n,*
And shook *his throne. What though the field be lost?*

—that is unimportant beside winning the proof that Satan's cause is just. Opponents in this controversy have often jeered at my side for being so romantic as to believe the Father of Lies; but the idea which first appears in his mind as he recovers consciousness is also the first that he presents in his formal address to his troops, an impressive degree of sincerity, in a politician. Surely it is the modern orthodox here, and not my faction, who are unnecessarily puzzling their heads and thereby spoiling the poem.

However, I must not fall into arguing that, unless you accept my theory, you cannot appreciate the speech; that would be absurd because it has such a powerful direct impact. While I was refugeeing with the combined North-East China Universities in 1938 or 1939 I was kindly asked to do my bit at a sing-song, as the only Englishman present though not quite the only European, and found I remembered enough of this passage. It was received with fierce enthusiasm, but also with a mild groan from some of the older hands, who felt they had been having enough propaganda already. I am not sure how familiar it would be with that audience, but I know at least that it goes over as a direct political speech, which is what Mr Eliot said the style of Milton could not do. The audience, you understand, really did mean to resist to the end however powerless, exactly like Satan and with the same pride in it; also, not being Christian, they would not require a separate theological argument before they could sympathize with him. To follow the story as a whole, one needs to realize that Satan's argument would be correct if God had not given him a false premise; but a normal reader of the speech does not need this idea, because he vaguely invents enough background to justify the emphases which the rhetoric and the music require. I only maintain that our recent pious critics, eager to catch Satan out on a technicality all the time, must be unable to read his speeches aloud.

There is something so confidently low-minded about their position that I had better insert a reflection on the Gamble of Pascal. He argued, while more or less inventing the mathematics of Probability, that, since the penalties for disbelief in Christianity are infinitely horrible and enduring, therefore, if there is any probability however tiny (but finite) that the assertions of the religion are true, a reasonable man will endure any degree of pain and shame on earth (since this is known beforehand to be finite) on the mere chance that the assertions are true. The answer is political, not mathematical; this argument makes Pascal the slave of any person, professing any doctrine, who has the impudence to tell him a sufficiently extravagant lie. A man ought therefore to be prepared to reject such a calculation; and I feel there has been a strange and unpleasant moral collapse during my own lifetime, because so many of our present literary mentors not only accept it but talk as if that was a moral thing to do. Clearly, if you have reduced your morality to keeping the taboos imposed by an infinite malignity, you can have no sense either of personal honour or of the public good; but one finds this same neo-Christian tone complacently adopted even by writers who do not pretend to believe in the religion—they regard it simply as a general moral truth that one ought to tell lies in favour of the side which is sure to win. But Milton's devils do not; the sources and extent of God's rights and power are for them a matter still under debate, so that they are exactly in the position Pascal envisaged; and they assume that to obey God merely out of cowardice, while his rule becomes increasingly harsh, certain that his demands are unreasonable but not that he could carry out his threats, would be gross dishonour. Their position is thus identical with that of persons such as Milton who had dared to deny that Charles I had Divine Right; identical morally, though Milton believes that God actually had it and Charles hadn't. Whether the rebels deserve blame for their initial doubt of God's credentials, before God had supplied false evidence to encourage the doubt, is hard for us to tell;

but once they have arrived at a conviction they are not to be blamed for having the courage to act upon it. I hope I will not be told that this moral doctrine is sentimental because it was invented by Shelley; it has been an essential bit of equipment since the human mind was first evolved.

Such then is the basic situation as the poem opens, and we gradually learn more about how this problem for the rebels arose. The intended reader is sure already that Satan fell, but is prepared to learn more about how and why he fell, since that is not a matter of doctrine; thus the poem begins at the right point, not only by epic formula. Satan in his address to his troops says that God

Sat on his Throne, upheld by old repute
Consent or custom, and his regal State
Put forth at full, but still his strength conceal'd
Which tempted our attempt, and wrought our fall. (I. 640)

A reader who has completed the poem can hardly deny that this is true; and presumably the comfort of the reflection, though Satan is mainly concerned to win their hearts with the pathos of the thing, is that such tricky behaviour is not what one would expect of total Omnipotence; so that there is probably yet hope of circumventing God by trickery, as is being proposed. Then comes a rather baffling detail, which Milton seems to have invented to explain how Satan can plan as he does:

Space may produce new Worlds; whereof so rife
There went a fame in Heav'n that he ere long
Intended to create, and therein plant
A generation, whom his choice regard
Should favour equal to the Sons of Heaven; (650)

and Satan already proposes that 'we' should go there, before the debate in Book II. The phrase 'Space may produce new worlds' might be used by Professor Hoyle, and acts as the first hint to the reader (not of course to the rebels) of Satan's doubt whether God can really create anything. By the way, Raphael in v. 495 half expects 'time' to turn men into angels, so that ideas of a quasi-automatic progress seem to have been widespread in Heaven. We gather that the angels regarded this rumour as a threat to their status in the hierarchy, just as they did the promotion which actually caused the revolt. The source of a rumour in such a hierarchy on earth (a battle-ship, for example) is usually mysterious; but in Heaven it is hard to see who could be the ultimate source but God himself, as part of a war of nerves.

In Book II we have the debate of the rebel leaders, and can learn their general state of opinion. Satan's introductory address claims leadership under 'the fixt laws of Heav'n' but also from their free choice of his merit, and prophesies that, having learned in adversity

firm accord
More than can be in Heav'n, we now return
To claim our just inheritance of old (35)

Some critics have argued that Milton intended this boast as an evidently farcical one, because it confesses that the devils would quarrel as soon as they began to succeed, so that their moral corruption makes all planning inherently hopeless for them; other critics have answered that it is a passable sophistry from a defeated commander, and though nonsense would not entail loss of epic dignity. I think all this greatly underrates our general human readiness to interpret paradoxes if we want to, let alone the Renaissance concentration upon paradoxes. Satan is talking in a high Roman manner. Consider the good Duke in *As You Like It*, who is greatly admired for praising the benefits of exile; nobody is surprised at his returning to his dukedom as soon as possible, because he was always considered to be expressing a noble paradox. After the conference, the rebels praise with free reverence the virtue of Satan; they 'extol him equal to the highest in Heaven', thus denying the unique goodness of the Father, because 'for the general safety he despised / His own' (480); and well they may, as Milton has made this scene of choice a detailed parallel to the self-sacrifice of the Son in the next Book. Not content with structure, he drives the point home by a personal comment, no doubt intending blame to the leaders of the Commonwealth:

> *O shame to men! Devil with devil damn'd*
> *Firm concord holds, men only disagree*
> *Of creatures rational . . .* (495)

The force and music of the poetry here prove that he had been feeling this pent-up comment deeply. As a matter of theory, he says that they have not yet lost all the effulgence of God's presence (or not yet been corrupted by God's plans for them); but also he does not feel that they are as yet at all contemptible. However, there is a more general puzzle about the debate. Satan never claims that they remember a time before God usurped, though his argument seems to require it; indeed, we know they do not, from his reply to Abdiel in v. 855—"We know no time when we were not as now." It merely seems to them reasonable to claim that order and justice are older than any individual ruler. The first readers would look at the text very politically, seeing parallels to recent English history; no doubt they would think of the rebels as like historians under Charles I praising our freedom under the Anglo-Saxon monarchy. However, this weakness in Satan's argument need not make him look absurd; how

God managed to usurp we never hear the rebels discuss, but we are encouraged to think that they have already done so. Milton could hardly be expected to give a fuller account. As for his own attitude, he would probably feel that he was free to suggest what he could imagine but ought not to make positive assertions, in large matters, beyond what he could claim to deduce from Holy Writ; hence we may expect some hints which we are to work out for ourselves.

Moloch then argues that they had better fight God with 'his own invented torments',

> *Turning our Tortures into horrid Arms*
> *Against the Torturer* (65)

because *either* this will force God to destroy them, so that he can no longer torture them, *or*, "if our substance be indeed divine" so that the *soi-disant* God can't destroy them, then

> *we are at worst*
> *On this side nothing;* (100)

and to continue to 'disturb' and 'alarm' him "if not Victory is yet Revenge". This has been called merely savage, but it is not if you add the usual metaphysical assumptions of the rebels, which Moloch as a plain soldier leaves to his audience. If the rebels prove that they are not nothing in comparison to God, then they have disproved God's absolute claims, and to remind him for ever that he is known to be false would be a moral victory. Moloch can fairly be supposed to mean this because he is clear about the theoretical alternative under discussion; either the rebels have a similar status to God, or they have been wrong in deciding so, and had best seek death.

Belial then counsels prudence; he admits that God is

'incorruptible' against attack, which might seem to give up the whole case, but we soon find him using the same chemical metaphors ('our purer essence' etc., 215) about the rebels themselves; this makes clear that he merely thinks the two equal groups should arrange co-existence. In between these passages he has made what might seem a deeper admission:

To suffer, as to do,
Our strength is equal, nor the Law unjust
That so ordains: this was at first resolv'd,
If we were wise, against so great a foe
Contending, and so doubtful what might fall. (200)

But this does not entail that he yields on the essential point; he need not mean that this just law is God's law, so that justice is inherently on God's side. Drawing as usual upon the classics for the thoughts of devils, Milton has him say that they have been defeated by 'fate inevitable', some kind of law of Nature which may be prior to God, though it happens to endorse 'the Victor's will'; indeed this basic law of the universe is perhaps merely *vae victis*. I do not know what he thinks their strength is able to do, and perhaps Lawyer Belial is merely appeasing the pride of General Moloch in this turn of language; but a human reader is bound to be interested when he points out that fallen angels have "a strength equal to suffer" Hell, or can go on arguing there at any rate, because we gather that mankind have not. *If we were wise* has a curious effect; the lawyer, as so often among men, doubts whether the other members of the committee understood the position sufficiently clearly when they 'first resolved', and this I think makes almost certain that they have held a previous debate while yet in Heaven. Belial now believes that God's eye is all-seeing (190), though he hardly can have believed it when he attended the earlier conference; probably he then thought it merely part of God's propaganda, and has become convinced of it by subsequent events. Even so, it says a good deal for the strength of the anti-God party in Heaven that a sober lawyer like Belial was prepared to join. Milton emphasizes his beauty with an air of personal dislike (110) and finds it noteworthy that he failed to guess the winning side. Belial gives as a reason for passivity that, if they are going to live for ever, God may get bored with torturing them, or (as his last hint) something else may turn up; this I think shows how much Milton was thinking of Uranus and all that lot, supreme gods for a time but eventually eaten by their sons. Indeed, as Milton claimed that these devils eventually became known to men as the pagan gods, he would think it correct to draw on pagan legend as evidence for what devils thought about the cosmos.

Mammon comes next, and seems to me only to remove a false glimmer of hope by saying that Fate is 'everlasting'. As a matter of the effect on the reader, he makes rather clearer that Fate is conceived as distinct from the Will of God, but this does not prove that Belial had meant otherwise. Professor C. S. Lewis wrote a splendid chapter on the whole debate, challenging you to invent four speeches each more morally insane than the last, so he argued that Mammon is worse than Belial; but all this presumes that the rebels know they are in the wrong. I think Milton just wanted two reasonable-sounding speeches in favour of peace, before the dramatic shock of Satan's plan for secret war. The moral interest of Mammon's speech, which the lawyer Belial could not provide, comes from saying that God is personally so disgusting that the rebels could not endure to return to 'splendid vassalage' under him, even if allowed to (250). Mammon I take it is a tycoon or industrialist; he is convinced he can make Hell as good as Heaven, and points out that they already greatly resemble one another. Take darkness; God for his plots frequently wraps himself in darkness, whereas we scientists in Hell already sit brilliantly illuminated. We have

Magnificence; and what can Heav'n show more? (270)

A piercing query, because Milton's Heaven evidently does show hardly anything more; and when Mammon goes straight on to remark that their 'torments' are bound to become gradually less he at least shows a staggering amount of cool courage. C. S. Lewis treats him as a sensualist fighting down his pangs of shame—"Honour? Love? Everybody I meet salutes me, and there is an excellent brothel round the corner." But Milton tells us that one of the chief pains of Hell, as in human prisons, was deprivation of sex, if it may be so called (IV. 510); God had made their substance thicken just enough to keep them from their pleasure of total interpenetration. To be sure, the rebels could not have foreseen this, but there is no suggestion that they chose revolt to gain pleasure; they did it on a point of honour or, if we need a derogatory term, out of pride. It is true that they are being driven into moral absurdity, calculated to make their characters rot; and I think that this turns the grand sermon of C. S. Lewis into a denunciation of Milton's God. But a reader does not need to agree with the devils in order to understand what they say; surely there is no critical merit in belittling the whole story, though it was intended to be very sublime, by refusing to envisage the situation of angels who have become convinced that their God is bad.

It is convenient to deal here with the Sixth Book, recounting the War in Heaven, which bears out this argument but is otherwise tiresomely absurd. God invents pain, for bad angels only, and it cannot subdue them; they are impressively superior to the good ones. What can war have meant before, with no death, and bodies which can leak out of any hold? Both sides wear armour though they can turn themselves into gas (350); this must be unusually stupid Science Fiction. Several critics have argued that Milton thought it funny, a satire on the military swagger and false heroics of Satan, because Milton thought war an inferior subject for epic compared to patience and martyrdom (IX. 30). No doubt he would think that his own patience as a scholar and coolness in waiting for martyrdom at the Restoration was up to anything a soldier could boast, but he was not a pacifist (we hear he was a good fencer when young); and the scorn of Satan when the good angels capture him feels to me hard to explain away as something the author intended us to despise:

> *to try once more*
> *What thou and thy gay Legions dare against;*
> *Whose easier business were to serve their Lord*
> *High up in Heav'n, with songs to hymn his Throne,*
> *And practis'd distances to cringe, not fight.* (IV. 940)

We should also notice that "Then Satan first knew pain" (VI. 325) does not fit, because Sin tells him that "all of a sudden miserable pain / Surpris'd thee" (II. 750) when she was born from his head, and on any view this must have happened earlier. The slip might be called evidence that the narrative of Sin is only an 'allegory' in the sense 'not really part of the story'; but I should think it means that Milton was rather casual about the War in Heaven. The recent objections to the style of *Paradise Lost* seem to me wrong-headed when Milton is using it to say something real, but they do apply to the Sixth Book. All the same, we get a consistent account of the rebel theory. After the first day of fighting, Satan argues to his troops that they have already disproved the metaphysical claims of God, in that he has not defeated them at once;

> *then fallible, it seems*
> *Of future we may deem him, though till now*
> *Omniscient thought* (VI. 430)

The obvious deduction is that God is not omnipotent ("if one day, why not Eternal days?"), but Satan throws in a claim that his infinite foreknowledge has also been disproved, which tells us that the rebels have at least heard of it. Nisroc, a rather difficult General, then says that he won't put up with God's invention of pain unless Satan invents something back, which turns out to be gunpowder; but he addresses Satan as

> *Delivrer from new Lords, leader to free*
> *Enjoyment of our rights as Gods* (450)

so that even this rather untheoretical type accepts the basic claim of Satan's faction, that God has been cheating the angels out of their equal status with him. We tend to think of Satan as a djinn emerging from a bottle, but when put back into the society which voted for him he makes a different impression. He thinks of more arguments than the other malcontents do, but along the lines they want; so that he need not be considered to fall through a unique craving to gratify his own vanity.

Returning to the debate in Pandemonium, Beelzebub rounds off the discussion by a speech arranged with Satan beforehand to swing the council into voting that Satan shall go to Eden alone. Some eager critics have called this dirty of Satan, but a reader accustomed to committee-work would recognize that he had been too proud to lobby, and that his moral standing turned out strong enough for him to get his way without it. To arrange with his known friend to propose his plan, and then speak for it himself at once, is not underhand behaviour. The chief interest for the reader in the speech of Beelzebub, who accepts the majority opinion that God will keep his unjust power for ever, is that he gives an entirely different account of the decision to create man:

There is a place
(If ancient and prophetic fame in Heav'n
Err not) another World, the happy seat
Of some new race call'd Man, about this time
To be created like to us, though less
In power and excellence, but favour'd more
Of him who rules above; as was his will
Pronounc'd among the Gods, and by an Oath,
That shook Heav'ns whole circumference, confirm'd. (II. 345)

This is an odd story, and one might doubt whether Milton is bothering to be consistent; God sounds particularly like Zeus in this devil's account, whereas Raphael reports him later in the poem as saying he is going to create us to spite the devils (VII. 150). But his foreknowledge prevents the two stories from being inconsistent; he would have known throughout all past time that he was going to want to spite them. Milton has often been found more consistent than had been supposed, and the indications of time here leave room for both accounts; the announcement by God, which shook all Heaven, is already *ancient*, but the rumour that the promise was to be implemented *ere long* is recent; and it was a likely thing for the conspiring angels to invent, while they puzzled over what the summons was for and recalled the prophecy. The words have to imply that the rumour was current before God promoted the Son, which turned out to be the purpose of the summons, because everything after that happened with decisive speed, leaving no time for rumours. Another account is given by Satan when persuading Sin; he says he is looking for

> *a place foretold*
> *Should be, and, by concurring signs, ere now*
> *Created* . . . (II. 830)

Perhaps he is merely trying to impress her, while Milton reminds his readers of augurs inspecting livers and so forth; but we do find God giving 'signs' at IV. 1000, XI. 195, XII. 230 and 300. Or again, God might simply have put the knowledge into Satan's head while he was drugged in the lake, but that would leave unexplained the narrative of Sin. It is a more Miltonic or statesmanlike view that the angels began buzzing with rumours, and interpreting 'signs', as soon as God named the date for the grand Summons. Presumably he wanted to drive into the open the insubordinate angels, at the first stage of his programme.

Thus, as we read on, our next problem is to fit the narrative of Sin into what had happened. Most critics have dismissed it as 'allegorical', but Dante considered that an allegorical narrative had to be properly dovetailed, and indeed that the Bible was both historical and allegorical too. Milton would not believe that an epic can include an allegorical bit making assertions about previous events which can be ignored; at least, I have never read an argument for this assumption. He expects the reader to be interested in the previous history of Satan, after beginning his epic at a crisis for Satan; I expect you would have found him very irritable if you said 'Of course, the narrative of Sin may be ignored.' Once you accept it, there can be no doubt that Satan called a council about the claims of God before he revolted; the merit of trying to approach the question in the order set by the poem, I submit, is that you realize how many hints have already been dropped so as to make the narrative of Sin credible though dramatically surprising when first reached. This is after all a standard technique in novels to make a character seem real. In the same way, the first audiences of *Macbeth* were meant to be astonished when Lady Macbeth accused her husband of having proposed the murder of Duncan to her before the play opened; but they were expected to recover their theology, after being frightened by the witches, and think: 'Of course, yes; they couldn't really corrupt him, any more than they could Banquo, unless he had already prepared his will to yield.' The surprise was meant to be one they could get over, with a certain pride, after a few moments' reflection. In the unfamiliar world of the epic our reactions are less firm, but Milton too would want to say that the real fall of Satan had happened before he decided to order his army north.

Granting then that we can believe Sin, she was born from Satan's head at an assembly of Seraphim for conspiracy against God (II. 750). One might vaguely suppose that, because Satan had not fallen till he ordered the revolt, this must be the meeting where Satan's brief remarks were acclaimed by all except Abdiel. Abdiel would be likely to mention so bizarre an occurrence, but it might have happened after he had been given a free pass to the other camp. This does not give enough time for what she describes. When she first emerged from Satan's head, she recalls, the conspirators were afraid of the portent, but 'when familiar grown' she became a general pet; she was faithful to her father, who, she says,

> *full oft*
> *Thyself in me thy perfect image viewing*
> *Becam'st enamour'd, and such joy thou took'st*
> *With me in secret, that my womb conceiv'd*
> *A growing burden. Meanwhile War arose . . .* (765)

Thus the war arose late in her pregnancy, and after a general change of sentiment; but war arose the morning after the meeting where Abdiel stood out. I agree that the episode of Sin is bad allegory, because it makes the biology of the angels too hard to get clear; but it shows that Milton regarded this previous conference of the rebel leaders as an actual event in the story he was imagining. The idea may have grown upon him as he went along, but even so it is presented as settled doctrine halfway through Book II. This seems an important point, because it lets us recognize their theological opinions as rationally considered, and the leadership of Satan as one which our minds can understand.

In Book III, after reaching the sun, Satan disguises himself as a 'stripling' cherub to inquire the way to Paradise from Uriel.

> *Not of the prime, yet such as in his face*
> *Youth smil'd celestial . . .* (635)

This makes another puzzle about the biology of the angels, and a much worse one; because we can accept a unique birth of Sin followed by incestuous Death, arranged by God, but we can't imagine all these angels without a picture of their habitual mode of life. Satan can assert without fear of contradiction, as an essential part of his argument (V. 860), that no angel has seen God create an angel, and he goes on to presume that angels are in an argumentative sense 'self-begot':

> *self-rais'd*
> *By our own quick'ning power, when fatal course*
> *Had circled his full Orb, the birth mature*
> *Of this our native Heav'n, ethereal Sons.*

A human reader feels certain that these puzzled creatures do not produce young. The contradiction within the poem of course is what feels bad, not a disagreement with accepted opinion about the mode of production of angels. However, one can say why the detail feels natural enough, and this is probably why it felt so to Milton. The cherub counts as young because he has recently been promoted to the position, from the vast dim class of proletarian angels who are needed so that angels with titles may issue orders. The defection of a sheer third of the angels, many of them evidently superior ones, would seem to give a unique opportunity for promotion. I have to admit that, if Satan merely removed his entire command as it stood, the other commands would be likely to stand pat; but Raphael's account may well be cursory there. Soon afterwards we meet a real 'young' cherb, Zephon (IV. 845); this is when Satan is discovered at the ear of Eve, and Satan treats him with withering social contempt. Some critics have found an inconsistency here, because he accepts arrest by two angels and then threatens to fight the whole troop to which they lead him; but it is a point of honour to refuse to fight except with his equals. This is the reason he gives, and Milton does not contradict it while adding that his feelings were more complex. He would be embarrassed at being caught as a toad, and he "felt how awful goodness is" when confronted with the severe youthful beauty of the cherub. Milton of course is thinking of human youth, but there is no inconsistency in regarding Zephon as recently made a cherub; he has been fitted out with a new appearance, and is much keener than the old hands. The scene may be from an earlier play, as has been deduced from the words of Gabriel (870), and this might explain a confusion; but drama is needed here (Satan is relieved of his shame by the prospect of a fight), and no confusion need be found. Earlier, in the sun, the reason why Satan disguised himself as one of these 'youths' (III. 635) was to avoid suspicion; Uriel is surprised that any of the good angels can be bothered to come and look at the new creation—they are resentful about it, because afraid of having some further promotion made over their heads. But Uriel finds it natural for a promoted proletarian to be a busybody, trying to curry favour no doubt; and this explains the touch of patronage which can be felt in his remarks, even though he genuinely feels that this angel deserves praise. Such a tone cannot be distinguished from treating him as literally a young one.

Satan does this chiefly to learn about the creation, and the truth comes as a great blow to him. Uriel says:

> *I saw when at his word the formless Mass,*
> *This world's material mould, came to a heap;*
> *Confusion heard his voice, and wild uproar*
> *Stood rul'd, stood vast infinitude confin'd;*
> *Till at his second bidding darkness fled . . .* (III. 710)

So God did create the world (one can no longer anticipate the theory of spontaneous creation by space), and this makes it more probable that he created Satan too. Such is the end of Book III, and Book IV begins with Satan in despair. In the first words, by the way, "O for that warning voice" etc., Milton wishes very lyrically that Adam and Eve could have been warned by himself, "and scap'd /

Haply so scap'd his mortal snare"; this shows he felt there was something inadequate about the warning of Raphael, though he avoids directly claiming that he himself would have done better. We next have a convincing description of the horror, so far from rejoicing or triumph, which overcame Satan as he approached the scene where he must perform his first really wicked, that is, unkind action. He is also said to doubt, as is necessary; because, unless he now doubted his theological position, he would not think it wicked at all to release our parents from their tyrant. You might argue that, when the test comes, his unconscious knowledge that he is wrong boils up, but this is hardly more than repeating that his judgement swings round in an unexplained manner. He is a very argufying character, but here he leaves a logical gap; Uriel has convinced him that God created the world, but he has also become convinced, if only for the time, that God created Satan too. He has thus lost his tremendous bet; the metaphysical claims of God were somehow justified after all, and only harm can follow from the success of his heroic effort.

I think that what convinces him is just the overwhelming beauty of the newly created world. This fills the gap, and the best reason for believing it is the principle of Mr Rajan, that the virtue celebrated by the poem is sublimity. The scenery of the interior of the sun, a wonderful piece of invention as C. S. Lewis remarked, had been affecting him while he heard the bad news from Uriel, and now he is in sight of Paradise:

Sometimes towards Eden which now in his view
Lay pleasant, his griev'd look he fixes sad,
Sometimes towards Heav'n and the full-blazing sun. (IV. 30)

Later, after he has toured the earth including both poles, Milton makes him say:

O Earth, how like to Heav'n, if not preferr'd
More justly, Seat worthier of Gods, as built
With second thoughts, reforming what was old:
For what God after better worse would build? (IX.100)

I am not sure whether Milton or Satan is the stronger authority here, and hardly know which of them is speaking; the blind man, though expecting Heaven, thought we should not allow ourselves to fancy that anything could be more beautiful than the scenery of this world. I have to confess that, on Niphates' top, Milton only lets Satan say that he hates the sun, but that is an intelligible way to express his feelings. One should remember that, apart from the development of English nature-poetry, this was the age of the first European landscape-paintings, and Milton was proud of his universal culture and his trip to Italy; he lavished all his power on his descriptions of the newly created world, and such an attitude to Nature was usually regarded as a kind of submerged proof that God had created it. Thus a fit reader might expect Satan to change his mind on this ground; and the idea, as well as making him consistent, keeps us from spoiling his poetry by thinking him insincere beforehand.

A nephew of Milton reports that the Niphates speech, addressing the sun by name rather theatrically, had been written some time earlier for a play; this may be why Satan fails to explain his change of mind, but I dare say he would not have done that in any case. He takes his new opinion as settled, and is fully occupied in considering what can be done about his situation as now viewed. Indeed he does not discuss his previous opinion either; he fell, he says, because he felt God to be a usurer—the gift God made in creating him had appeared to him, perhaps wrongly, as only an initial lump sum, whereas a more generous nature would have accepted endless repayment. No doubt this is true, though expressed with pathetic moderation, of his frame of mind when he first thought of revolt. But he is still certain that it would be useless to submit; he would later recant, he knows, though he does not examine the reason:

For never can true reconcilement grow
Where wounds of deadly hate have pierced so deep: (IV. 100)

indeed, "this knows my punisher"; such is the only point at which he still sounds like accusing God. He again concludes that he will do Evil to spite God's intention of Good, and this time appears to have some inkling of the meaning of the form of words:

Evil be thou my Good; by thee at least
Divided Empire with Heav'ns King I hold
By thee, and more than half perhaps will reign;
As Man ere long, and this new World shall know. (110)

The sequence is a dreadful one, but his verbal opposition to a titular claim of God cannot decide whether the claim of God is false, which was the point originally at issue. He merely finds himself forced to take his phrase seriously. Many critics have thought that this speech cannot be reconciled at all with his previous ones; he has become an entirely new character, they say, as if Milton had become alarmed at realizing he had made Satan too good. Surely it is only fair to the author to interpret the words so as to make the character consistent, when this is found to be quite possible. The sharpness of the jolt does rather suggest that Milton was fitting in some old material; but he might have judged that the sudden change in Satan's beliefs needed to be expressed by a jolt.

On the other hand, it is often confidently asserted that

this speech admits his previous speeches to have been all lies; a view which makes the character consistent by making him ridiculous, though I think some critics combine it with complaining that he has become a quite different character. We have not had Satan alone before—he has always been either negotiating with rival powers or encouraging his followers, so this is the first time he could have told us that he regards lying to his followers as a painful duty. I think Milton would realize that the words could be taken like that, but would regard it as a crude interpretation. It is quite usual in the theatre to have a crude interpretation available so that no one in the audience frets; thus Angelo in *Measure for Measure* is genuinely astonished by his craving for a nun, a fetishism as it would be called now, but if you find this abstruse you can take him as a simple hypocrite. The device is hardly worth calling an ambiguity, and I think it is all that need be imputed in the case of Satan.

Always an extremist, Satan now admits all the claims of God, even his claim to goodness, because a generous mind would feel no burden in paying a usurer incessantly. But 'submission', he goes on,

> Disdain *forbids me, and my dread of shame*
> *Among the spirits beneath, whom I seduc'd*
> *With other promises and other vaunts*
> *Than to submit, boasting I could subdue*
> *Th'Omnipotent. Ay me, they little know*
> *Under what torments inwardly I groan:*
> *While they adore me on the Throne of Hell,*
> *With Diadem and Sceptre high advancd*
> *The lower still I fall, only supreme*
> *In misery; such joy Ambition finds.* (85)

No doubt this is theatrical, but when C. S. Lewis blames

Satan for always talking about himself it is fair to remember that is what his readers always want him to talk about. That he boasted he could defeat God in battle, and found he couldn't, is no confession because it has been plain to all since the beginning of the epic. That the commander after defeat thought it his duty to express confidence in evasive action, hiding his anxiety, is no confession either; indeed, as he wept in the presence of his troops, we might reflect that he was less stoical than he now claims. In his present mood, we must suppose, he feels that his duty has tarnished his honesty; this gives a close enough connection of thought with the next sentence, after the colon. There he recognizes that his situation, as the opponent of a genuine God, is driving him morally lower and lower; but he does not say that he had already realized it while being adored on the throne of Hell. This may put too much weight on the blind man's use of a colon, though he was firm enough about his text to print some very fussy corrections; but anyhow the two main verbs make two sentences, whatever the punctuation. I do not deny that my opponent's interpretation is the easier; it seems likely that Milton was ready to avoid disturbing the simple-minded reader, though he would aim more at the fit one, who could appreciate his sustained analysis of Satan's character. What Milton had to say was so grim that he might reasonably use some of the tact which modern critics find him so lacking in.

Satan then jumps over the wall into Paradise, already watched by Uriel because the passion of his soliloquy has betrayed him. Evidence of confusion has been found in "Uriel once warned" (IV. 125); but it only means that Uriel after being asked the way by this character felt enough curiosity to follow his later movements. The idea of a soliloquy being observed has been found absurdly theatrical or literary, so I make bold to remark that it once happened to me. I had landed at Los Angeles on my way from China to England, and there is a park in that city which rises to a fairly bluff summit. I went to the top of it and screamed; this was in 1939, so my feelings need not all be blamed upon Los Angeles. After I had been screaming for a bit I found I was being shot at by boys with air-guns; this satisfied me in some way; I came down the hill, and took the train to San Francisco. The incident on Niphates' top, strikes me as a rather life-like thing to have happened to Satan.

He next soliloquizes while perched on the Tree of Life disguised as a cormorant; it is his first view of Adam and Eve, who are romping with an elephant and other beasts at the time, and he makes the eerie offer to them of all he has:

> *Hell shall unfold*
> *To entertain you two, her widest Gates,*
> *And send forth all her Kings.* (IV. 380)

I would still deny, as I did in my book *Pastoral*, that this is meant only as the leering irony of the stage villain. It may seem absurd to suppose that he could have any good intentions towards them, but the text seems designed to leave the point open. They are pawns in his game, but he may prefer to have them do comfortably once they are on his side. He does not express ill-will towards mankind in his speeches around I. 650 and II. 400, whereas Beelzebub talks very spitefully about us, thinking we may become favourites of God with an unjust position in the hierarchy like the Son (II. 370). Satan does allow Sin, Death and Chaos to suppose he intends us harm, vaguely expressed (II. 840, 985), but he would see that as the only way to make them let him pass. God says in III. 90 that Satan will try to destroy or pervert Adam and Eve, "And shall pervert; For man will hearken to his glozing lies"; but Satan may believe in his offers up to the very moment when he makes them. The speech on Niphates' top has no reference to mankind, except to say in the last line that they will soon know his power. His next speech is the one now in question, so we do not reach it with much evidence that his intentions towards us are bad. He knows indeed that we will suffer bodily pain in Hell, as he and the other rebel angels do; but they can carry on life in a high manner, whereas Milton seems to accept the usual view that we can only remain in passive agony (II. 600). Satan evidently does not know this, and so far the irony of his offer belongs only to the God who made Hell. Satan may well think that it is worth enduring a period of suffering to be on the honest side, as Milton himself would. In his next soliloquy, around IV. 530, he expresses a rather self-indulgent pity for them and says he must bring upon them 'death' and 'long woes'; but in Milton's world death is a very subtle or almost meaningless term, and they might gain honour in the end as a reward for their long woes. By the way, C. S. Lewis need not have called Satan "a thing which peers in through bathroom windows" because he feels jealous here of the sexual pleasures of Adam and Eve; God has recently cut him off from his own corresponding pleasures, and he is straightforward enough about it. But I agree that his temper has begun to spoil, so that he eyes them "with leer malign"; indeed, his character rots away so fast now that his speech on first view of them is his only really puzzling one. Going by the sound-effects, as one should, the offer of high honour in Hell feels very sincere; we are to observe that Satan genuinely did find our parents less beneath his own angelic class than he had expected, so that he was gratified at least for a moment by sentiments of romantic generosity. But other lines of the speech are insinuatingly horrible.

I argued in my book *Pastoral* that Satan is not a consistent character, being something more basically dramatic instead; and I now think this wrong. There was a fashion for attacking 'character-analysis', especially in Shakespeare, which I have taken some time to get out of; maybe it has a kind of truth, but it is dangerously liable to make us miss points of character. I would still say, indeed, that there is an unnerving strain here between the two ways of reading the passage; you can either shudder at Satan's villainy or take the offer as sincere, and feel the agony of his ruined greatness. But both are within him; what I had not realized is that he has only just begun to doubt whether he has anything to offer them. He is still partly thinking of himself as a patron of Adam and Eve, who can save them from their wicked master; thus he seems genuinely indignant (520) at hearing the conditions of ignorance which God has imposed upon them. We could not expect him to stay in the mood of self-abasement reached on Niphates' top, accepting all God's claims, especially as even then he still found God intolerable. Thus his reasoning mind may probably be sincere when he offers high honour in Hell; but even as he speaks his lips are twisted by the new suspicion that God is only waiting to turn all he does to torture. I readily agree that from then on he is rotting away; but also, he rightly suspects that God is plotting to make him rot away; his story is more like the Orwell *1984* than anything else. The poetry of the offer is so haunting that I have long felt it must have meant something important to Milton, though I could not understand what; so I feel confident of this explanation now.

It seems best to consider the later details about Satan at once, which may be done briefly. The final soliloquy is in Book IX, before the Temptation, after going seven times round the world to hide in darkness for a week. His praise of the beauty of the world, though evidence of Milton's intention I think, is used by Satan merely to argue that the world ought not to have been made for such inferior persons; it is great indignity even for conformist angels to have to wait on them, and still more for himself to have to turn into a snake. His self-pity has reached the point of saying "Only in destroying find I ease", and he thinks it will be 'glorious' to mar the creation. We find him again uncertain whether God created the angels (God is evidently not still creating 'young' ones), but the doubt no longer gives him any moral support:

he to be aveng'd
And to repair his numbers thus impair'd,
Whether such virtue spent of old now fail'd
More Angels to create, if they at least
Are his Created or to spite us more
Determin'd to advance into our room
A Creature form'd of Earth, and him endow . . . (145)

I fully agree with the disgust felt by C. S. Lewis for Satan's character as it has now become, and could even agree that his doubts about God are now merely a means of deceiving himself. But surely one must also feel horror at the God who has deliberately reduced him to such a condition. Even now, he is still capable of being struck 'stupidly good' when first confronted with Eve alone (IX. 465). He is a less painful sight after the Fall, because totally corrupt and merely the Devil; as when he meets Sin and Death, on his way back to Hell, and urges them forward to enslave and destroy mankind (X. 400). His boastful speech on his return admits that God created the world, though still not that he created the angels. God then turns all the rebels into snakes, thus proving to them that he was only playing cat and mouse all the time; and then of course turns them back, so that they may continue to work upon mankind.

Most critics are now agreed that there is a gradual calculated degradation of Satan, but this bit of understanding gets obscured by a hunger to argue that he is very bad from the start. The chief merit of the shape of the poem, I think, which has often been called magnificent architecture, is that it presents the change in Satan with such force. We first meet him certain of the righteousness of his cause though defeated, follow him into doubt and despair, switch back in the narrative of Raphael to find him confident that his cause will be victorious as well as just, then return to the story and find his character rapidly rotting away. As there is no slip-up anywhere in this involved programme, we can at least be sure that it was intended.

Raphael warns Adam and Eve that he is doubtful what it is lawful to tell and what he is capable of expressing to them, then begins abruptly with the summons of all angels before the throne of God to hear the formal appointment of the Son as an absolute ruler; to be obeyed on pain of eternal expulsion into outer darkness. That night, Satan wakes his next subordinate and says

Sleepst thou Companion dear . . .
Thou to me thy thoughts
Wast wont, I mine to thee wast wont to impart . . .
New Laws from him who reigns, new minds may raise
In us who serve, new Counsels, to debate
What doubtful may ensue, more in this place
To utter is not safe. (v. 670)

Clearly, private discussion about the claims of God between these two has gone on before, but 'new Counsels, to debate', with a capital letter, also implies a wider and more formal conference. Then Satan orders all his troops to fly during the hours of darkness to his northern palace; presumably all of them except Abdiel became devils, and an angel of, say, the Southern Command did not have the option. But the generals must not feel afterwards that they have had no option, as both Milton and Satan well understand. They must be told privately that this is an order from God, intended to prepare for a reception of the Son, who will make a royal tour 'and give laws' (they never discover, we gather, that this was a lie); indeed, Satan's 'next subordinate' has a good deal more to do during the night:

> *he together calls*
> *Or several one by one, the Regent Powers . . .*
> *Tells the suggested cause, and casts between*
> *Ambiguous words, and jealousies, to sound*
> *Or taint integrity, but all obeyed . . .* (700)

Presumably they had agreed to revolt after the Summons if God announced the creation of mankind and gave us too high a status; but God instead exalted the Christ, and after this surprise they had to reach a hurried decision. Without a previous council, the patter from a messenger could hardly be sufficient. Naturally the political mind of Milton understands what had happened better than Raphael does. As to Satan's lie, it may be regarded as an ordinary wartime propaganda operation, designed to anticipate what the enemy is certainly going to do.

On reaching his own palace Satan addressed "all his Train" (765), "an infinite Host" (870), which must mean all troops; Abdiel is described as a seraph, but Milton seems to use these terms with deliberate casualness; we gather that though an officer he was not senior enough to have gone to the staff meeting. I must quote the whole speech because it has rightly been found politically confusing, as well as seeming to Mr Eliot a typical example of the corruptness of Milton's style. What is hard to follow about it is that, both for Milton and Satan, it is partly sophistry and partly truth; and we are not to assume that Milton thought the verbal paradoxes in it inherently dreadful, because he ascribed some of them to God as well.

Thrones, Dominations, Princedoms, Virtues, Powers,
If these magnific Titles yet remain
Not merely titular, since by Decree
Another now hath to himself ingross't
All Power, and us eclipst under the name
Of King anointed, for whom all this haste
Of midnight march, and hurried meeting here,
This only to consult how we may best
With what may be devised of honours new
Receive him coming to receive from us
Knee-tribute yet unpaid, prostration vile,
Too much to one, but double how endur'd,
To one and to his image now proclaim'd?
But what if better counsels might erect
Our minds and teach us to cast off this Yoke?
Will ye submit your necks, and choose to bend
The supple knee? ye will not, if I trust
To know ye right, or if ye know yourselves
Natives and Sons of Heav'n possesst before
By none, and if not equal all, yet free
Equally free; for Orders and Degrees
Jar not with liberty, but well consist.

Who can in reason then or right assume
Monarchy over such as live by right
His equals, if in power and splendour less,
In freedom equal? or can introduce
Law and Edict on us, who without law
Err not, much less for this to be our Lord,
And look for adoration to th' abuse
Of those Imperial Titles which assert
Our being ordain'd to govern, not to serve. (V. 770)

The modern duty of catching Satan out wherever possible becomes easy here, and we are told that he is ridiculous for rejecting the supremacy of God and yet claiming the supreme position in a hierarchy for himself, whereas that can only be derived from God. Human royalty, we are reminded, is an 'image' of this truth, and Satan uses the word, as well as calling the Son an Anointed King; thus bearing involuntary witness that royalty accredited by God is the only source of honour (meaning titles and so forth). Well yes, many people have thought so, but by no means all, and Milton was prominent among those who haven't; the first readers of the poem, let alone the licensing authorities, must have been agog to know whether Milton intended satire against Charles II or against Cromwell. It is answered that Milton need be in no political inconsistency; he believed that the Stuarts had lost the mandate of Heaven but that the Queen of Sweden, whom he adulates in the *Second Defence*, hadn't, so he may well have thought that the Son of God hadn't. But the whole political position of Satan rests on a denial that God is the source of all goodness, and *a fortiori* of all titles; his deductions here are merely public-spirited, though their expression is somewhat marked by the poetical double-talk so often found necessary in our human political speeches. He is talking standard republican theory, and in effect Milton presents that as inherently based, not indeed upon atheism, but on a non-authoritarian view of God as immanent. Satan cannot express it well, because the only God he knows is an authoritarian one whom he considers false; but 'Sons of Heav'n' is at least a metaphorical claim to have an immanent Parent. It is curious that modern critics discuss the speech as if they were angels, baffled by the tortuous operations of the human mind, whereas the angels think like real political men. As the views of Satan have been so much despised, I had better offer some reflections about their history.

The men who organized the first towns needed to do a heavy piece of psychological engineering, otherwise the peasants would not have continued to send the town food in bad years; the peasants had to be convinced that their own crops would fail unless they satisfied the town's god or magical king. But, in what we regard as 'historical times', rightly enough because nothing of much interest could get written before, various nomad groups had conquered towns and found that they could maintain the food supply without such intense ideological pressure. Rome after conquering the Mediterranean world found that a return to emperor-worship was the only way to handle the countries where it had been invented, but the Romans and Greeks continued to be proud of their earlier freedom, and Renaissance characters such as Milton and his first readers agreed with them (Plutarch seems to have been the strongest influence) while usually admitting that kingship was somehow needed in our present fallen world. Also the nomad tradition of the Hebrews had caused the Old Testament to present the institution of kingship as a national error or punishment (I Samuel viii-xii). These after all were the only two legs Milton and his first readers could stand on for ancient history; and the recent labours of archaeologists have shown that they were not misled. Whatever Milton's own political position had been, a man of his learning and breadth could not have intended to make Satan contemptible merely by making him express republican opinions. The argument indeed can be put the other way round; Milton does not use the parallel to make republicans absurd, but to make Satan more plausible. He does not revolt directly against God, but against God's appointment of a 'regent' described in detail as a King; and at the climax of his speech, where he leaps to a new argument so that connecting grammar is hard to invent, he claims that to submit here would be worse than submitting to a tyrant, because the Son actually demands worship, the full ancient barbarism, as if he were a Pharaoh. He is shocked by it, exactly as the Romans were by Cleopatra. "How can one of us justly become King over the rest, and give us laws though we arrange our affairs better without such an institution? And, if he could, how could this be an adequate reason" (hence the words *for this*) "for him to seek to be worshipped as a God, by misusing one of our customary terms of honour?" Surely one can feel Milton himself snort here; he is not finding Satan patently absurd, and the long-term human history behind the speech is so present and genuine that we ought not to find him so either.

I grant that Milton is conscious of the danger of tyranny from a politician who starts off like Satan. Nay more, he does such justice to the character he is imagining that he makes Satan get uneasy about it too. Satan repents on Niphates' top for having let himself be adored on the throne of Hell; at least, it is natural to read the words so, because we expect *adore* in his mouth to mean excessive abasement, only due to a transcendental God such as he has denied, so that we make him sneer when he says it; thus we make him confess that he has at times accepted for himself what he had disapproved of giving to the Son. But this would be hard to avoid, and to worry about it only proves that he is a deeply conscientious republican. We also need to realize that he is a rippingly grand aristocrat; when he withdraws his troops to his northern fastness (northern because of Isaiah xiv. 13: "I will exalt my throne above the stars of God: I will sit also upon the mount of the congregation, in the sides of the north") he is not so much a Scotsman, though that has been proposed, as a Yorkshireman, technically subject to the King in London but well known not to 'derive his honour' from there. His castle is as grand as the King's:

At length into the limits of the North
They came, and Satan to his Royal seat
High on a Hill, far blazing, as a Mount
Rais'd on a Mount, with Pyramids and Towers
From Diamond Quarries hewn and Rocks of Gold,
The Palace of great Lucifer (so call
That structure in the dialect of men
Interpreted) which, not long after, he
Affecting all equality with God . . .
The Mountain of the Congregation call'd. (v. 755)

A Norman lord in England did not entertain the modern idea of a nation; his obligations of loyalty were often complicated, and his main view of the English throne was that he would only let one of his cousins have it, and would then help the rest of the family to keep it under decent control. That of course was why the barons could make King John sign Magna Charta. The point was very clear to Milton and his first readers; after a hint that Satan was like a Norman baron, they could imagine him expressing his views on kingship at greater length. A slight break with tradition gives another hint; Satan had almost always been described as the chief of the angels, but Milton makes Raphael doubtful whether he should be called so or not (v. 655); the reason is that he was a 'peer'. As Macaulay said in his review of the *De Doctrina*, indeed considered the chief thing to say, the Divine Right of Kings was a Renaissance development, related to the improved weapons and increased wealth which gave them a standing army capable of putting down popular revolt; it was decisively important that the English, almost alone in Europe, succeeded in resisting this new absolutism. And among their needs before they could raise the nerve to cut off King Charles's head had been a good deal of historical study, including the recovery of Anglo-Saxon. Nobody would love Satan for being a Norman baron, but they could not think him farcical or nearly lunatic for expressing the opinions of one; as often happens, the old far-right-wing opinions had recently been used to support left-wing opinions. Indeed, the only man in the seventeenth century who had come near recommending the return of power to barons was Milton himself, whose desperately courageous second edition of the *Ready and Easy Way to Establish a Free Commonwealth*, printed three weeks before the Restoration, had said: "Split up the country under local rule again, by counties or city states; then the King will find he has nothing to take over." I expect he composed the speech of Satan about two years later.

Having tried to present the aristocratic side of the brief speech, I must now ask the patience of the reader while I explain its democracy. This dual arrangement may seem over-subtle nowadays, but the first readers were well accustomed to the idea that nothing is more politically dangerous than an aristocrat who can raise the mob. Instead of calling Satan ridiculous for remaining a lord when he rebels against his king, we may more plausibly call him ridiculous for treating everybody else as a lord. The speech to all troops begins and ends with their 'titles', and the last line positively asserts that they are all ruling-class characters, though there is nobody in the universe for them to rule (they are not to rule the loyalist angels, whom Satan regards as equally wronged by God). I admit that Milton knows what is wrong about this; he means to be sardonic in a later echo of it, when Satan is no longer morally conscious enough to feel the irony. He addresses the same audience on returning to Hell in triumph after procuring the Fall, and the first line is an exact repeat of the roll-call of titles (I dare say the child Milton first heard this kind of thing from the gallery when his father was at a City banquet, but he would anyhow hear it often):

> *Thrones, Dominations, Princedoms, Virtues, Powers,*
> *For in possession such, not only of right,*
> *I call ye and declare ye now, returnd*
> *Successful beyond hope, to lead ye forth . . .*
> *Now possess*
> *As Lords, a spacious World, to our native Heaven*
> *Little inferior, by my adventure hard*
> *With peril great achiev'd.* (X. 460)

He has never called them 'ye' before, and probably the effect was a kind of coarse mateyness, as when lords in Restoration comedy talk like rogues among themselves. He still does not even hint that they will ill-treat mankind, let alone order them to, but he has found them somebody to rule with their titles, anyhow. It is fair to reflect that Satan did not invent these titles for them, but God; and, as for Milton, if you feel he is rather too keen on titles, they were almost the only thing he knew about these angels, so that he had to use them to invent the speeches. He can hardly have considered making everybody a lord bad, because God makes all mankind lords when he says to Adam:

> *Not only these fair bounds, but all the Earth*
> *To thee and to thy Race I give; as Lords*
> *Possess it, and all things that therein live . . .* (VIII. 340)

To be sure, this is merely quoting Genesis i. 28, where God gives mankind dominion over all other living things; but Milton uses the word *Lord*, and had not invented the political paradox. It is especially sharp in Revelation xx, which he quotes when describing the Last Things. There we find that during the Millennium the blessed are to reign with Christ for a thousand years, but that "the rest of the dead lived not again till the thousand years were finished", so that the blessed will have nobody to rule over. Satan may well have the same meaning, and not use the royal plural about himself, or at least only use it as a half-conscious secondary meaning, when he says in Hell "Here we may reign secure" (I. 260).

The democratic side of the speech, even more than the aristocratic, would have enough relevance to current politics to make the first readers willing to interpret its paradoxes rather than judge them merely absurd. You get a certain amount of seventeenth-century complaint (as in a remark of Hamlet) that the social hierarchy is getting confused, but I do not know that any writer deplored the liberation of the serfs; and "equally free (though still at the bottom of the hierarchy)" is about all you could say when explaining his new position to a liberated serf. The change was much supported by nationalist sentiment, because that presumes any Englishman to be worthy; and the sentiment had been supported by acquiring a national dynasty, which took care to reduce the importance of Norman barons. Henry V became a national legend not so much for conquering the French as for refusing to do his French lessons, and becoming a real Englishman by hanging about the pubs with people like Falstaff; Shakespeare well understood what his audience wanted from the story, and his Henry offers to make all his band of heroes ruling-class, 'though ne'er so vile', if they get through the tight place of Agincourt. Milton was by no means above this kind of sentiment; he said that whenever God has a particularly difficult bit of work to do he gives it to his Englishmen. The word *native* acquired a rather baffling importance for this work; earlier uses of the Latin word, often simplified as *neif* and suchlike, had meant 'a serf, bound to the soil', but the later sixteenth century, with a very good bit of pedantry for once, turned it back into a boasting word, meaning just what the Queen did when she boasted under pretence of humbling herself that her ancestry was 'mere English'. Satan uses this word with great effect when he says that his troops are "Natives and sons of Heav'n"; rather barrack-storming perhaps, but very intelligible. It is true that Milton had become disillusioned with the people of England, a point well documented by M. Saurat; but still, he would not think Satan patently ludicrous for saying what he had often said himself. Our modern reactionary critics tend to assume that nobody could be such a fool as to be a democrat, way back in early times; but a certain amount of democratic sentiment is inherently part of the cost of enjoying a nationalist sentiment.

On the other hand, the way the idea gets twisted when

Satan is corrupt does seem a sardonic reflection by Milton, and might be meant to imply that Satan was wrong at the start. 'All angels are lords' merely makes them feel dedicated, a state of mind highly approved by Milton; but it turns into 'every angel deserves to have some men as his slaves'. The slave trade from Africa to America was already in progress, but perhaps this is the one place where Milton was being wiser than he knew. He had come to be anti-democratic in the sense that he thought men needed to be ruled by educated and dedicated persons such as himself, but he had also found that no ruling group came up to the standard he would set for them. Without needing to try to, he would hold the political scales sardonically even. Surely the first readers must have found this intriguing; the only good writer who had defended the regicide was ascribing to the devils the sentiments still firmly held by himself and his proscribed party. They would not find the speech particularly dull and cooked-up, as Mr Eliot did; and they would not be at all sure how far the author meant the devil's remarks to be wrong. After all, none of the scandal-mongers accused him of ratting here, and said: "We were astonished that his life was spared, until we found him meekly ascribing to Satan his own political opinions."

The speech of Abdiel in reply turns almost entirely on the argument that God had created Satan, though it also calls God a King and says he is known by experience to be good. Abdiel lets drop, about three-quarters of the way through, that God created the angels by the agency of his Son, "as by his Word", and uses this to introduce the exasperating argument that the Son condescends if he even notices Satan enough to order him about. Nobody has mentioned the doctrine in the poem before; God does not say it in his pronouncement giving power to the Son

(v. 600). It was the only argument which could have satisfied the mind of Satan, but God preferred to issue a bare challenge; indeed, we could hardly be sure that Milton believed it himself if we had not the *De Doctrina*. Satan in his reply calls it a "strange point and new" (850); and, as the answer of Abdiel merely says that God will punish Satan, this claim of the Son must at least have been an esoteric doctrine in Heaven before. No doubt Abdiel had also heard a good deal of discussion of the new appointment, from the opposing party, during that busy night. In both prose and verse Milton shows a certain amount of puzzlement about the divine Fatherhood, but the idea is at least real enough for the appointment to strike Satan as a gross piece of nepotism. He reacts with splendid intellectual energy, completely undercutting his opponent, by questioning what both sides had previously taken for granted; this is how he arrives at denying his own creation (855)—at least, such is the dramatic way to read the passage, and we are given no hint that the idea had occurred to him before. The line of thought is thus: 'Since God is obviously lying about our creation now, in this new doctrine which Abdiel has got hold of, he was probably lying about it all along.' That is, while trying to find an answer to an unexpected argument, that the Son deserves to rule over the angels because he was the instrument for creating them, Satan reflects that none of us angels know by experience how we were created, and then finds himself by mere weight of logic adding that we do not know that the Father created us either. The infinite host echo "as the sound of waters deep" (870), but we do not hear that any of them worry about this effective retort ever again. Satan however finds it increasingly important for his private self-justification, and his nerve breaks when he rejects it on reaching Paradise.

Such I think is the steel armature without which the statue of Satan could not tower so high and dangerously; I mean, many readers are impressed by his challenging intellectual dignity (and indeed loneliness) without quite realizing that this is where the impression comes from. It is not essential for the story, and not in the Bible, so one would like to know where Milton got it from, and what the source was likely to mean to him. Mr Grant McColley (*Paradise Lost, an Account of its Growth and Major Origins*, 1940), who shows that many of Milton's details are in "the hexameral tradition", reports it in the twelfth-century *De Victoria Verbi Dei* by Tuitensis, who it seems made Satan add the democratic argument that no one knows his own creation; also in Avitus, a bishop of Vienne who wrote hexameters on the First Things about A.D. 500. The poem of Avitus, which is in the *Patrilogia*, was published at Paris in 1508, 1545 and 1560, so it would be fairly available and well known, as well as interestingly old. Mr McColley feels that to follow the literary tradition was simply proper, but Milton was not so very conservative; he is more likely to have regarded this tradition as a kind of historical evidence, which needed to be traced to its sources. I expect he thought he knew where Avitus had got the idea that Satan denied his creation.

Professor Denis Saurat, as has been well said, roused us from our dogmatic slumbers about the sources of Milton (*Milton, Man and Thinker*, 1925; with additions and subtractions, 1944); his main position is that the Jewish mystical tradition of the *Zohar* was then broadening the mind of all Europe, therefore presumably also Milton's. This has not much to say about Satan; except that he will be saved at last like everyone else, a view which Milton ignores. But it claims to report the views of mystical rabbis of the second century A.D., a main period for the

Gnostics, who held rather similar views. They did have things to say about Satan, and to suppose Milton aware of the connection is only to make a further deduction from the evidence of M. Saurat.

Thus he remarks (p. 220 of 1944 ed.):

> *Areopagitica* (1644) contains a precious indication: "Who finds not that Irenaeus, Epiphanius, Jerome and others discover more heresies than they well confute, and that oft for heresy which is the truer opinion?" Irenaeus and Epiphanius having written mostly against the Gnostics, Milton thus seems not disinclined to approve the latter.

However, this is no great help for M. Saurat's argument that the God of Milton is extremely metaphysical, and thereby wholly justified:

> Milton had more sympathy for heretics than for Fathers of the Church, but it is difficult to see what he could derive from the Gnostics. Some of them, exaggerating the old notion that found some good in the Fall, came to worship the Serpent, the cause of the Fall, as the great benefactor. It was probably as a polemical device, and to confute these Ophites, that Epiphanius declared that the Serpent who had tempted Eve was no other than Satan. It is only then, about 380 A.D., that the tradition of the Fathers at last caught up with Jewish myth. The Jews had reached that conclusion during the first century. (p. 223.)

He adds that Chapter V of the nineteenth *Clementine Homily* says that the Devil had no beginning.

With one part of his mind, I would fully agree, Milton held views about God which make most of the scenes in his Heaven quite impossible; but he did not consider it meaningless or misleading to envisage the traditional story very fully. What is peculiar about this picture of God, as adapted to our feeble imaginations by a poem, is that it is so very like the God of the Gnostics—or like one of their ideas of God, as they did not impose uniformity by persecution. The *Encyclopaedia of Religion and Ethics*, under 'Gnosticism', calls it a slander by the Fathers to say they believed the Devil had created the world; instead, 'God was limited to the task of blind creation':

> As the agent of Creation, Gnosticism assumes a Demiourgos, who is usually represented as the son of Sophia. He is himself ignorant of the Pleroma above him, and governs the world created by him in the belief that he is the supreme God; but unconsciously he transmits the elements of light which have come to him through his mother. The Demiourgos is conceived not as an evil power, but rather as a cosmical force which acts unwittingly. But, since he represents a mechanical will, controlling the spiritual life of which he has been the unconscious vehicle, he becomes the tyrant from whose thraldom the soul claims deliverance.

Some Gnostics therefore thought it a duty to defy the ordinances of the law, and thereby throw off allegiance to the inferior God; Milton would probably regard this as merely a confusion about the New Dispensation of Christ. The whole position is very like Thomas Hardy, let alone Blake and Shelley; but then, these authors very likely derived it from the Gnostics too, even if remotely. It is clear anyhow that the Gnostics would have been a comfort to Satan upon Niphates' top. I happened to come across *The Western Response to Zoroaster* (J. Duchesne-

Guillemin, 1958), a very scholarly and rather sceptical survey, contemptuous of the *Encyclopaedia*, which should prevent my attempt at a report from being out of date. There was an element of truth, after all, in saying they believed that Satan created the world, because 'The Gnostics and some Hermetists . . . explain creation itself as the result of a fall' (p. 84), just as it is in Milton (VII. 150). Plotinus, though otherwise startlingly unworldly, called this idea coarse and blasphemous; as a result of his influence, Plato was not considered a Dualist after the third century, but in the second century he was. At this period Gnosticism 'radiated back' into Iran, says the author, letting himself assume for once that the whole line of thought had come from Persia:

> According to at least two texts, when the beings are given their material form this creation is motivated, with Ormuzd, by the need to counter Ahriman's attack. The first initiative to material creation, therefore, comes from the evil spirit. (p. 101)

This makes the tradition very early, so that it is likely to have cropped up in Milton's reading of the Fathers and their background; I do not mean that he had read these especially remote Persian texts, but that his historical judgement was right if he decided that the tradition was early, and therefore suitable for his epic. He took a learned interest in such heresies, and would not at all plume himself on being original for inventing one. When he made Satan deny that God created Satan, and when he implied that mankind were created as part of the divine reaction to Satan, he almost certainly considered these opinions not new but old.

However, the two cases are very different; always ready to defend himself, he could have boasted that he had taken a belief of the devils from the Gnostics, but could not have given the same source for a pronouncement of God. Maybe he had simply forgotten where it came from; in any case, it did not carry for him the implications which had rightly shocked Plotinus. Both can be fitted into a long-familiar pigeon-hole as 'Manichaean'; thus the translator of the *De Doctrina* remarks, in a footnote to Milton's proof that God created the angels: 'The opinion that the angels were not created, but self-existent, according to the Manichaean system, is with great propriety attributed to Satan in Paradise Lost.' I felt rather snubbed, after adventuring among such peaks of learning, to find that the point was obvious to a theologian in 1825, but perhaps it helps to show that the illiberal attitude to Satan is a recent one.

My object in giving this rather sketchy bit of background is to recall that Milton, being so learned a man, would not seriously despise Satan for disbelieving his creation; nor should we read that into the poem, because Satan is not meant to become contemptible until his character collapses after he has doubted his own thesis upon Niphates' top. Professor C. S. Lewis, on the other hand, jeers at him heartily for it, saying that he is beginning to incur the Doom of Nonsense, so he thinks he just growed, like Topsy. Lewis, I should make clear, considers that Milton subordinated the absurdity of Satan to his misery, so that as a whole Milton gives a tragic not a comic treatment of 'the satanic predicament'; but Lewis's account of Satan's moral absurdity is very impressive, and clearly true up to a point. Milton thought it proper to be sardonic about the enemy of mankind; but he was scrupulously careful to give him strong arguments for his fall. Here, I think, Lewis shows contempt for the beliefs of most of his audience (with something of the noble pride of Satan, perhaps); he treats creation by a personal God as the only theory of origin which is not mere jabberwocky, whereas the audience presumably accept the Darwinian account of the emergence of mankind. I too find that more numinous, more imaginatively stirring, than to say 'God just made us; and the earth stands on an elephant, and the elephant stands on a tortoise'; especially as, in the past, the argument has tended to continue 'if you ask me what the tortoise stands on I'll burn you alive'. Milton shows himself attracted by the idea that Nature somehow works of its own accord, which indeed followed from his basic theory of matter; and he would know that it is distinctly unusual in the history of human opinion to hold that the present ruler of the universe is also its creator. He did not automatically despise the thoughts of pagan philosophers; they could win Heaven by faith in God alone. As for myself, when I was a little boy I was very afraid I might not have the courage which I knew life to demand of me; my life has turned out pretty easy so far, but, if some bully said he would burn me alive unless I pretended to believe he had created me, I hope I would have enough honour to tell him that the evidence did not seem to me decisive. I dare not despise Satan for making this answer.

But the moral argument must not get detached from the literary-critical one, or I may appear to say that the poem is bad because Milton agrees with my opponents. Recent critics, especially in America where they are more energetic about theory than in England, tell us that we must accept the intellectual postulates inherent in the aesthetic form of a literary work, so that it is often merely bad taste to find in a poem more than its surface meaning. Hence, by a curious twist, they often feel that to do so must be an attack upon the poem. Somebody objected to some earlier remarks of mine about *Paradise Lost* that I was blaming a giraffe for not being a rabbit. That is, the *Ecstasie* of Donne is like a rabbit, the kind of poem whose form admits of our examining what it means, but when I picked on details of the epic which interested me, as evidence of the breadth of Milton's mind, this critic thought I was complaining at some lack of petty correctness, whereas the reader of an epic ought to admire the broad strokes of the brush. The theory would be hard to explain to Milton. I have tried to follow his whole account of the tragedy of Satan, and it seems to me a very large-minded one. I think that a critic who cannot follow it, because he thinks Milton wants us to pick small holes in Satan all the time, has been prevented either by a false theory or by some distressing want in his own nature from realizing the size of the giraffe.

Chapter 3

HEAVEN

DR JOHNSON, in his *Life of Milton*, refused to discuss the character of God in *Paradise Lost*, remarking that the topic was not proper for a slight occasion. Probably many present-day readers are in sympathy with this attitude, and as much on literary as on religious grounds. They feel: 'Milton here was trying to express the ineffable, so we cannot be very cross or surprised at having him fail; and there is not likely to be much profit in worrying over the causes of his failure, as we cannot tell what would have succeeded. It would be more sensible to make the best of the good parts, as one commonly has to do in English Literature.' I think his treatment of God so strange that it rewards inquiry. But, in any case, tactful reticence is no longer enough here, and firm treatment can at least I think counter one reaction which has become widespread. It is that of settled disgust, perhaps never more firmly expressed than by Professor Yvor Winters in the *Hudson Review* for Autumn 1956:

> It requires more than a willing suspension of disbelief to read Milton; it requires a willing suspension of intelligence. A good many years ago I found Milton's procedure more nearly defensible than I find it now; I find that I grow extremely tired of the meaningless inflation, the tedious falsification of the materials by way of excessive emotion. . . . [Comparison to the gods in Homer] . . . Milton, however, is concerned with a deity and with additional supernatural agents who are conceived in extremely

> intellectual terms; our conceptions of them are the result of more than 2000 years of the most profound and complex intellectual activity in the history of the human race. Milton's form is such that he must first reduce these beings to something much nearer the form of the Homeric gods than their proper form, and then must treat his ridiculously degraded beings in heroic language.

One can quite see that, read in this way, the poem is very bad. But reading it so is merely one of the harmful effects of modern literary theory; Milton would not be 'aesthetic' about God like that. We can be sure of it, because he is willing to lecture very drily in the poem when he needs to make the theoretical position clear, for example about the digestive system of an angel (v. 410). Also, he did not share the respect of Yvor Winters for the intellectual labours of the Schoolmen, or of Aristotle either, and was fond of saying that our only sound evidence about God is the text of Holy Writ. He was thus likely to feel that he was sweeping away nonsense, insisting upon reality, when he presented God in this simplified way; it would give him a certain fighting exhilaration, so far from what Yvor Winters denounced that the critic probably felt about his own bit of writing a pale echo of what the poet had felt about his epic. Milton would also consider that even this way of writing about God, though the best, was very limited because God is ineffable; in the *De Doctrina*, he is inclined to think that no man or angel could see God, and that God could only act through the agency of the Son. The feeling of this comes out, though perhaps not the literal meaning, when Raphael says:

> *Commission from above*
> *I have receiv'd, to answer thy desire*

Of knowledge within bounds; beyond abstain
To ask, nor let thine own inventions hope
Things not reveal'd which th'invisible King
Only Omniscient hath suppress in Night,
To none communicable in Earth or Heaven. (VII. 120)

Yet he was determined to present the whole of the relevant text of Genesis, however literally false in his own opinion; as by making God walk in the Garden, or punish the race of serpents. The surface effect is much what Yvor Winters described, but Milton had a very different purpose; the requirement made him give a grim picture of God, as he came to realize increasingly, one would think, while the work of detailed imagination went forward. Such, he considered, is the only kind of thing our minds can know about God; and the result is to give an exposure from the inside of what goes on in the minds of Christians. I think this at least saves the poem from the pompous fatuity which Yvor Winters would otherwise be very right to disapprove.

It seems to me that Milton leaves out only one major theological doctrine, and that he was right to, although the results are rather startling. The western half of the Eurasian land mass, unlike the eastern, has long regarded its supreme God or ultimate reality as a person; but has also long realized that this is a tricky belief which requires a subtle qualification. His Godhead must be mysteriously one with Goodness itself, so that he neither imposes the moral law by ukase as a tyrant nor is himself bound by it as external to him. As regards his Godhead, he is the impersonal Absolute of Hinduism; he is built into the moral structure of the universe so as to be quite unlike other persons, and his other unique powers (omnipotence, omniscience and absolute foreknowledge) are merely a result. If you deny that God is a person, as many people do, you will not agree with Yvor Winters that the western intellectual activity has been profounder than the eastern; but you have to agree that the western theologians were trying to handle a real difficulty. Milton in his poem, apart from a few bare assertions perhaps, does not handle it at all. This was partly because he thought that the profound intellectual activity had often cheated; but, in any case, if God is to be shown acting in a story, we have something better to do than take his status for granted. The fundamental purpose of putting elaborate detail into a story is to enable us to use our judgement about the characters; often both their situation and their moral convictions, or their scales of value, are very unlike our own, but we use the detail to imagine how they feel when they act as they do, so that we 'know what to make of them'. Understanding that other people are different is one of the bases of civilization, and this use for a story is as much a culture-conquest as the idea of God. Milton therefore could not have made God automatically good in the epic; God is on trial, as the Christian Mr Diekhoff well remarked; and the reason is that all the characters are on trial in any civilized narrative.

You may still say, even after accepting this argument, that Milton does not make God come out of the trial as well as he should; and the poet could answer that it was not his immediate business to invent a new theology. That a third of the angels reject the claims of God was inherent in the story; Abdiel tells them that God should be obeyed because he is good, and they deny that he is good; so it would be no use for Abdiel to tell them about the refinements of Aquinas. We are bound to be impressed by the weight of their testimony. Thus Sir Herbert Grierson soberly remarked (*Milton and Words-*

worth, 1937; p. 116) "if the third part of a school or college or nation broke into rebellion we should be driven, or strongly disposed, to suspect some mismanagement by the supreme powers"; he does not discuss how Milton could have avoided this effect, but I think one must agree that Milton's treatment draws attention to it, and that it is what is fundamentally wrong about the behaviour of his God. The initial error of Satan is that he doubts the credentials of God, and I, like Grierson, naturally think of a Professor doubting the credentials of his Vice-Chancellor; such a man would not be pursued with infinite malignity into eternal torture, but given evidence which put the credentials beyond doubt. To be sure, there could be no such placid solution when Milton doubted the credentials of Charles I, but the poem assumes that the cases were quite different, because God actually had got credentials. We know that he could have convinced Satan, because he actually does it when he reduces Satan to despair on Niphates' top. God need not have shown his credentials in the manner calculated to produce the greatest suffering and moral corruption for both the malcontent angels and ourselves; it is in this sense, to recall an objection of C. S. Lewis, that Shelley could reasonably call Satan's wrongs 'beyond measure'. Regarding *Paradise Lost* as written to justify God for creating a world so full of sin and misery, it surely deserves the astonishment with which so many critics have regarded it; and critics who argue otherwise, whether out of piety or not, seem to me to preach an immoral moral.

Part of the explanation has to be that Milton wanted us to imagine the temptation which made Satan fall, to realize how Satan might reasonably come to believe that God is a usurper, or at least what the belief would feel like. Surely this must have been his purpose in writing the very queer words of the Father to the Son at the beginning of the revolt:

Nearly it now concerns us to be sure
Of our Omnipotence, and with what Arms
We mean to hold what anciently we claim
Of Deity or Empire . . .
Let us advise, and to this hazard draw
With speed what force is left, and all employ
In our defence, lest unawares we lose
This our high place, our Sanctuary, our Hill. (v. 720)

Here we are actually shown God 'doubting his empire', which is what Satan began the poem by telling us God had done. Many a Christian reader must have been sufficiently unnerved here to wonder whether Milton's theology was going very wrong, till a few lines later the reply of the Son reassured him that this is merely one of God's jokes. The Son regards the strategy as a plan to restore his own badly shaken prestige:

Mighty Father, thou thy foes
Justly hast in derision, and secure
Laughst at their vain designs and tumults vain,
Matter to mee of Glory, whom their hate
Illustrates, when they see all Regal Power
Giv'n me to quell their pride, and in th'event
Know whether I be dextrous to subdue
Thy Rebels, or be found the worst in Heav'n.

It is an interesting point about our feelings, I think, that we feel no objection to this answer. One might point out that the Son can only be pretending to face a test, because the magic he is being given is all-powerful; so that really his jeering is as coarse as his Father's. The same kind of hole has been picked in the courage of the divinely equipped heroes of Homer, and feels off the point there too; perhaps because we need not expect the Bronze Age chieftains to believe quite completely in the magic of their weapons. Even if we call the Son simple-minded here, we don't feel that is to his discredit; the youth is eager to win his spurs. At this minor point, we can be content to read the poem like Yvor Winters as an imitation of Homer. But we cannot feel the same about the joke of the Father, and as Yvor Winters said the reason is a metaphysical one; though far short of the full horror of the story. The joke becomes appallingly malignant if you realize that God has a second purpose in remaining passive; to give the rebels false evidence that he is a usurper, and thus drive them into real evil. Milton himself necessarily understood that this was part of the meaning, but he did not care to thrust it upon all readers; he wanted, without yielding on his own convictions, to make the tremendous piece of engineering as broad in its appeal as he could, acceptable to all Protestant sects. Most readers, of course, have found no such horrible implication in God's joke; they have found it pretty flat, but thereby all the more jovial in an Old Testament manner. Even so, they have felt that such a joke, while natural enough from simple omnipotence, does not suggest a transcendent God whose Godhead is mysteriously identical with Goodness. Without quite noticing it, they are already regarding Milton's God rather as Satan does.

The force with which Satan's rhetoric hits the reader derives partly from the fact that the story makes him seem evidently right. Going through the first two books for the first time, a Christian is likely to feel that the Devil is merely trying to seduce his judgement in a striking manner; but as he goes on with the poem and encounters God he is almost bound, if at all instructed in his theology, to feel a secret resistance—'This can't be God.' Satan was intended to strike terror into the reader, not to be a figure of farce, and such a reaction would add to the terror, or indeed be the real basis for it—'Satan is so subtle that he is actually liable to seduce you while you read about him.' Milton would presumably become aware of this dramatic effect, but it would not be his reason for telling the story as he did. Even if he remained unaware I am not proposing a new way to read the poem, because I claim to point out what often went on in the minds of pious readers who were deeply impressed by it.

It is hard to make this claim about any view of the words by which God is made to start the whole action of the poem. All angels must henceforth obey the Christ, he says, on pain of eternal expulsion, because

> *This day have I begot whom I declare*
> *My only Son* (V. 600)

One would expect the readers to be shocked for several reasons. Mr Grant McColley is rather too smooth at this stage of his proof that the material of the poem was standard tradition:

> During Milton's era, the belief that the Exaltation (and Incarnation) occasioned Satan's rebellion enjoyed appreciable literary prestige. (p. 33)

On page 257 he admits that making the Exaltation the only cause is "unique among works closely related to *Paradise Lost*". Still, the Latin *Battle of the Angels* by Valamarana (1623) had made Satan revolt because God prophesied the Incarnation before he created man. The poet was using a reputable theory; Calvin, of all people, rejected it because the Incarnation could not be necessary till the Fall had occurred, so he maintained that Christ had always been King of the Angels (A. H. Gilbert, *The Composition of Paradise Lost*, 1947). Thus the theory would be well known among fit readers, and it would take them over the first jolt of accepting Milton's story. Both Mr McColley and Mr Gilbert explain the shocking part, so far as they recognize it, as due to the gradual growth of the epic from a drama; thus Mr McColley feels he is winning his case when he emphasizes

> the impropriety of describing God as twice exalting the Son, and commanding the angels to bow before him. Such a Divine Decree as the Exaltation was as irrevocable as it was eternal. (p. 316)

Books III and V, on this view, must report the same scene in Heaven, and different aspects of it were merely separated for the literary requirements of epic construction. This view lets you off attending to the story, and anything which does that ends by making you feel the poetry is bad. The poem exalts the Son a third time when he ends the war, and Milton might well think that the purposes of the Father though eternal were realized gradually in time. I am grateful to Mr McColley for showing that Milton did not decide on the order of the poem till he had composed a good deal of it; for example, I have long wondered why Beelzebub is not named as Satan's 'next subordinate' at v. 670, but now agree that Milton when he composed the lines thought he was giving the character a lead-in at the beginning of the story. But I do not believe that this idea of gradual development is enough to explain any important crux in the final version. Delighted by achieving the perfect order, Milton would have the whole text as far as it had got read over to him to make sure that the details clicked into place; the detail about Beelzebub would not need correcting, and of course to correct it might involve changing a lot of lines for their musical value. Raphael may just as well never mention Beelzebub. But we are not to think that Milton was careless about revision, like a collaborator in an Elizabethan play; he would only behave like that if he came to think that an accident due to his method of composition had been inspired. When he separates these councils in Heaven, he takes for granted that God foreknew the effects of the first exaltation of the Son, and indeed exalted the Son because he foreknew that the Son would choose the Incarnation. Hence the order of events in Milton could be seen as reconciling the opposed theories; it makes God look artful, but maybe only because Milton was trying to act as chairman. We should agree, I think, that the poem was written piecemeal and fitted together gradually, but not that this makes it 'merely episodic'; it records a prolonged effort to justify God.

Masson found that the Rev. T. Tomkins, then aged twenty-eight, was the official who licensed the poem for publication, and supposed with Victorian gaiety that he could not stand more than the first Book. But this was a time when the Anglicans really did persecute, and the poem must have been scrutinized. It is an effort to realize that Milton was fairly safe about this beginning to his story, because it used a familiar text which had always needed explaining away. "This day I have begot" comes in Psalms ii. 7, apparently as part of a prophecy that the Kings of the Jews will rule the uttermost parts of the earth, and St Paul reasonably supposes (Hebrews i. 5-8) that the passage had best be regarded as foretelling the Christ. At least, he recalls it to the Hebrews among other Old Testament quotations, but he may have believed that this one had been applied to Jesus directly. A Pelican Book *Beyond the Gospels* by Roderic Dunkerley (1957) gives the rather complicated textual background, much of which was available to Milton. When Jesus is baptized, explains Mr Dunkerley, the voice from Heaven is naturally enough made to complete the quotation: "Thou art my (beloved) Son; this day I have begotten thee" in a variety of the surviving records—

> in 'Bezae' and also in some early Church writers, including . . . the Ebionite Gospel. . . . Canon Streeter, a great authority on the Gospels, believed that this was the correct reading in Luke, because the tendency was for the scribes to bring the Gospels into harmony with each other.

Thus there is evidence of disagreement or embarrassment about the use of the phrase at the Baptism, which Milton would find interesting. Mr Robert Graves (*The Nazarene Gospel Restored*, 1953) gives authority for regarding the use in Psalm ii as a coronation formula (viii. a), but as one based on an older ceremony of adoption (vii. d). To regard it as an adoption formula seems enough; the literal absurdity of "This day I have begotten this man" drove home a specific meaning—'from now on, he is to count as my son in every way'. This fits the use in the Psalm, and the Synoptists would wish to fulfil the Scriptures; but, on second thoughts, you couldn't say it to a person who was already your son, so for God to say it to Jesus might be misunderstood. Milton in the *De Doctrina* (Chapter V) gives a rather lengthy analysis of the extended sense of *beget*, including the idea of giving a special honour, as in the final glorification of the Son. He accepts the Son as begotten before all worlds and as the Father's instrument for creating the angels, though not as equal or identical to him, and of course does not think that the Father begot the Son in a human manner. His Arianism must have been knocking about in his mind when he boldly transferred the phrase to the occasion of the fall of Satan, but the text was already so abstruse that the orthodox could hardly complain. I imagine that this gave him a certain sense of glee; but, in any case, it is hard to see what other device would have given him the necessary start at a point of time for his epic narrative. The technical difficulty had been in his mind, because he expressed it through the voice of Adam:

> *what cause*
> *Mov'd the creator in his holy Rest*
> *Through all Eternity so late to build* . . . (VII. 90)

But, however necessary the device may have been, it makes the case for Satan's revolt look much stronger. If the Son had inherently held this position from before the creation of all angels, why has it been officially withheld from him till this day, and still more, why have the angels not previously been told that he was the agent of their creation? Unless he had always deserved the position, as Milton at least believed when writing the relevant passages of the *De Doctrina*, the case as put by C. S. Lewis, for example, falls to the ground. Thirdly, to give no reason at all for the Exaltation makes it appear a challenge, intended to outrage a growing intellectual dissatisfaction among the angels with the claims of God. Whether or not a reader feels dissatisfied by this slight jolt in the narrative, Satan and his troops object to it so much that they find it sufficient ground for revolt. Even granting that Milton wanted to give Satan a real temptation, he was not wholly concentrated at the time on trying to justify God. But there is no need to regard this as a mistake; he would probably answer that he was telling us a deep truth about the nature of God, whose apparently arbitrary harshness is intended to test us with baffling moral problems. To give us this warning is clearly more important than simply to whitewash God; indeed that would be a very irresponsible thing to do. Such is the real defence; and one may also suspect that, in a more casual but more impulsive part of his mind, he was angry with the people of England for rejecting the Rule of the Saints, and would not have minded punishing them a bit himself; so far as that went, he could feel himself on the same side as his punishing God.

His God has in any case an authoritarian character, just what one would expect from a usurping angel, which can be felt all the time in Heaven, even in the relations of the angels with one another. Probably most readers recognize the trouble about him only in this diffused way, and the effect is that they merely blame the literary treatment. But why do the angels have to be organized into an elaborate hierarchy at all? Are they organized to do something, or is it merely what is called a 'pecking order' among hens? C. S. Lewis quotes some fine passages from Milton in both prose and verse to show that he had long loved the idea of a social order which can act perfectly because certain of loyal co-operation; he connects this with Milton's love of formal dignity in both life and art; indeed the idea that discipline secures freedom, he says, is 'perhaps the central paradox of his vision'. I cannot remember which critic extracted a mystical vision, surprisingly but I think justly, from the harsh words with which God begins all the trouble by promoting his Son:

> *Under his great Vice-regent Reign abide*
> *United as one individual Soul*
> *For ever happy; him who disobeys*
> *Mee disobeys, breaks union, and that day*

Cast out from God and blessed vision, falls
Into utter darkness, deep ingulft, his place
Ordain'd without redemption, without end. (v. 160)

The second line feels oddly like Wordsworth, and Milton did I believe envisage here something like the biological co-operation of innumerable cells to make a man. The eternal curses which follow make the idea very remote; indeed, for most of the time Milton rather labours, with firm good sense one would think, to make the angels very like men and evidently not parts of a universal soul. I agree that he loved the order and unity of Heaven, though the poetry about it never strikes me as haunting, but he also clearly found the idea hard to combine with the traditional story he was to tell. After all, the only leader in the poem who expresses affection for his subordinates is Satan, when he weeps before his troops to win their "firm accord, more than can be in Heaven".

It is convenient to bring in here, at the cost of a slight digression, another aspect of the lives of the angels, again best approached through the penetrating treatment of C. S. Lewis. Discussing why Eve should blush at the approach of love in the state of innocence (VIII. 510), he says splendidly that even an angel may feel a noble sense of doubt whether he is perfect enough for the scrutiny of the beloved. Her modesty can thus be welcomed, but Milton has got something else a bit wrong:

> His Eve exhibits modesty too exclusively in sexual contexts, and his Adam does not exhibit it at all. There is even a strong and (in the circumstances) a most offensive suggestion of female bodily shame as an incentive to male desire. (p. 120)

Still, if it is an essential duty for a man to keep control

over his woman, he must also hide from her any doubts he may feel that he is superior; indeed, he can hardly be permitted to love her unless she is showing consciousness of her inferiority. What Lewis rightly finds coarse here in practice seems to be merely the doctrine of Degree which he has been recommending in theory. Poor Adam does feel such modesty, though he manfully hides it from Eve; he confesses it to Raphael, who scolds him for feeling it at all, so it is hard to have Lewis scolding him for not exhibiting it. To be sure, Adam does not feel shame about sex, which the text of Genesis would be enough to forbid; but he feels the nobler shame described by Lewis, because he tells the angel that she can make him feel in the wrong when he disagrees with her. On being upbraided for this breach of hierarchy, and told that "Love hath his seat in Reason, and is judicious," he says in effect 'Come now, what do you know about this? Have you got any sex?' and Milton to his eternal credit makes the angel blush. Raphael explains that the angelic act of love is by total interpenetration (VIII. 620), a thing which human authors have regretted that they cannot achieve. Lewis decides that the idea is 'certainly not filthy' (p. 109), but does not explain why the angel blushes at a mere reference to the topic; it cannot be for the noble reason he has given.

A scholarly article in the *Journal of the History of Ideas* ("Milton's Angelological Heresies", Robert West, 1953) decides that Milton had no real theological authority for the belief, but might have been misunderstanding one of the Cambridge Platonists. Probably Milton would have answered that he had plenty of authority, except that his authorities had been too timid to understand their own meaning; to describe the bliss of Heaven in terms of human love is very ancient. But I agree that some recent bit of writing had probably impressed him before he took the bit between his teeth and re-interpreted the tradition about the loves of Heaven in a startling manner. So well-read a poet had certainly read the English poets who were prominent when he was young; I think his real 'authority' had been the love-poetry of Donne, published after Donne's death when Milton was aged twenty-four but famous and accessible beforehand, which frequently claims that the ideal human lovers make one soul by interpenetrating completely. As to the idea that Milton betrays homosexuality by letting angels love each other, which Robert Graves used as an accusation, and C. S. Lewis felt to need earnest rebuttal, I think that a sensitive man who took Milton's attitude to women, especially a classical scholar, would be bound to toy in fancy at least with the happiness of having an understanding partner who need not be continually snubbed. There is not much evidence that Milton felt so, but if he did it is to his credit. We know from the Divorce Pamphlets that he considered an understanding partner as the basic requirement for the ennobling of a physical act of love. Donne of course was not made homosexual by this high conception of love, because he believed he knew at least one woman who was adequate for the purpose; to present the belief as firmly as he did in *The Extasie* was inherently a blow at the doctrine of the inferiority of women. Milton would perhaps consider such love forbidden to our fallen condition, as to the devils, but he would find nothing in it to make an angel blush. The messenger may well feel that he has been caught out talking nonsense about love and the hierarchy of Degree, in obedience to his instructions; this is why the incident is found welcome nowadays, but Milton would need another explanation. He may simply have had unexpected feelings about blushes.

While at school I was made to read *Ecce Homo* by Sir John Seeley (1866), a life of Jesus which explains that, when he was confronted with the woman taken in adultery and wrote with his finger in the sand, he was merely doodling to hide his blushes; then the book makes some arch comments on his sexual innocence, as if by Barrie about Peter Pan. I thought this in such bad taste as to be positively blasphemous, which rather surprised me as I did not believe in the religion. Milton says in the poem that the rosy red of the angel is love's proper hue, so perhaps he did, in a Victorian manner, regard other people's blushes as a source of keen though blameless sexual pleasure. I am not sure whether this is the same as what Lewis calls offensive; Lewis may have confused it with the masculine sense of power through mastering an unwilling partner, though Milton roundly insists that Eve was willing (VIII. 485).

The question is thus rather muddling, and one would expect Milton to have a firm justification ready. I am now to offer a sublime one, which fits in with other important doctrines of the poem. The angels feel that their act of love, being a unification of only two divine natures, is a step away from making 'one individual soul' with God. God might be expected to be 'jealous', as he is ambiguously called in the Bible, but the poem makes him noticeably jovial about the matter. Thus, after prophesying a 'Union without end' which must include even the blessed among mankind, he dismisses the angelic regiment for a bit of comfort:

> *Meanwhile inhabit lax, ye powers of Heav'n.* (VII. 160)

They need not watch him creating the world, which they are expected to resent, but can go off and have some cosy interpenetration. Some of them take an interest in the return of the unsuccessful guard after the Fall (x. 25), but they are again at leisure when God summons them to hear his next proposal:

> *Th' Angelic blast*
> *Filld all the Regions: from their blissful Bowers*
> *Of Aramantine shade, Fountain or Spring,*
> *By the waters of life, where-ere they sat*
> *In fellowships of joy; the Sons of Light*
> *Hasted . . .* (XI. 80)

Milton gives the same haunting moan here as in his descriptions of the nuptial bower of Adam and Eve, though not nearly so well; then the first line of God's announcement of their Fall is:

> *O Sons, like one of us Man is become . . .*

M. Saurat considered this one of God's eerie jokes, and it certainly has a mysterious tone of connivance; though it was a safe enough thing for Milton to use, being simply quoted from Genesis iii 22.

Apart from this private act of love, which Raphael blushes even to mention, the good angels never have any fulfilment at all; that is, never feel they have carried through something they had undertaken. The sympathetic intelligence of C. S. Lewis was quite right to dive to the basis of any social structure, but there is nothing here for him to find. In human experience, we feel this pride in an organization when there is some purpose to be served, which all the subordinates want to help forward; as in a hospital, or an army at war, or even a farm getting in the harvest, where it commonly does not need a very elaborate hierarchy. If the angels have nothing to do, their aristocrats are not even ex-aristocrats, as in Proust. The crowds who go to the seaside on a public holiday would be annoyed if someone tried to organize them, because they want to sit around and let the kids make sand-castles; but in a Butlin camp or a ski-ing hotel people will put up with a surprising amount of being organized, because they see some point in it, such as learning a new trick. Heaven, surely, is not usually visualized as like a Butlin camp, let alone a hospital; a variety of mystical writers have said, always with beauty I think, that it is like being at the seaside. It is that immortal sea where the children sport upon the shore. Thus to describe the God of Milton as 'legalistic' is too charitable; what we are offered is a parody of legalistic behaviour, a thing in itself often necessary and reassuring, but also often suspected of being employed to gratify the privileged few; and it is evidently used in Heaven for that purpose alone. Such a Heaven was a forcing-house to develop the pride of Satan, which is described as his fundamental sin. C. S. Lewis jeers at him, in the course of the sustained proof that he is ridiculous, because though fighting for liberty against hierarchy he hedges by saying:

> *Orders and Degrees*
> *Jar not with liberty, but well consist.* (V. 790)

I have tried to show that this would not seem very shocking anyhow, but also Satan has a war on his hands, a situation in which everyone agrees that subordination is necessary. The only person who has imposed it where it is not necessary is God. As so often in C. S. Lewis's treatment, the accusation aimed at Satan comes smack in the face of God.

A member of the Welfare State need not feel puzzled by the mind of Milton here, let alone contemptuous of it; to love the idea of an ordered society, and then feel repelled on being confronted with the details of working it out, is an experience familiar to our age. Milton sometimes realized that he was describing the situation of the good angels as a miserable one, but he felt this through an immediate social judgement of what he had imagined, not as part of the structure of his argument. Thus Raphael remarks sociably to Adam that he would like to hear about Adam's first experiences, because he wasn't there "that day" (we need not deduce, like some critics, that he wasn't present at the Creation during the previous week). God had sent him with a troop to guard the gates of Hell:

Squar'd in full Legion (such command we had)
To see that none thence issu'd forth a spy,
Or enemy, while God was at his work,
Lest he incensed at such irruption bold
Destruction with Creation might have mixt.
Not that they durst without his leave attempt,
But us he sends upon his high behests
For state, as Sovran King, and to enure
Our prompt obedience. (VIII. 230)

They knew, and they knew that God knew that they knew, that this tiresome chore was completely useless. Apparently most of them did not want to see Adam emerge into consciousness, but Raphael says that he did, and also that he assumes God gave him a job at the time merely to disappoint him. I grant that Milton is on strong ground so far as the situation is a military one, because an army does get disciplined like this; but then, consider the morale of this army. They know that they failed to defeat the rebels, and that God need never have ordered them to try, indeed must have intended to humiliate them, because as soon as he chose he removed the rebels with contemptuous omnipotence. Similarly, when he chooses to let Satan out of Hell, he simply orders his troops out of the way. Raphael knows that Satan could not get out unless God let him out, but he cannot imagine the courage of Satan, so he presumes that Satan would not dare to come without knowledge that God had let him. Incidentally, Raphael also takes for granted that God hasn't enough control of his temper to carry through a plan if anybody happens to irritate him while he is working on it; a theologian might suspect that God only pretends to lose his temper on such occasions (God endorses this view at x. 625). It is a timid slavish mind that we get shown to us here, such as the conditions of service must be expected to breed. Milton imagines the type very clearly, however much against his overall intention, in a quaint bit of spite expressed by the less amiable Gabriel after Satan has been captured in Paradise:

> *thou sly hypocrite, who now would'st seem*
> *Patron of liberty, who more than thou*
> *Once fawn'd, and cring'd, and servilely ador'd*
> *Heavn's awful Monarch? Wherefore but in hope*
> *To dispossess him, and thyself to reign?* (IV. 960)

When I was a little boy, about eight I think, I read a story in my sister's *Girls' Own Paper* about a catty girl who accused another girl of tightlacing, whereas the truth was, the story explained, that all these girls, including the catty one, were ill and in pain because they had to tightlace. I crept away sweating with horror, but feeling I had learned an important truth about the way people behave. This quotation seems to me quite enough to prove that God had already produced a very unattractive Heaven before Satan fell.

But there is something much stranger than this about the activity of God in the poem. The most striking case was first pointed out I think by M. Paul Phelps Morand

(*De Comus A Satan*, 1939); it comes just afterwards, at the same scene of capture:

> *Fly thither whence thou fledst: if from this hour*
> *Within these hallowed limits thou appear,*
> *Back to the infernal pit I drag thee chain'd,*
> *And seal thee so, as henceforth not to scorn*
> *The facile gates of hell too slightly barrd.* (IV. 965)

Some critic has accused Gabriel of weakness here, taking him to mean "Don't you dare come again," but he might mean to grant Satan one hour for decision whether to go of his own accord or be dragged in chains; it is a statesmanlike proposal, though no use because Satan decides to fight at once. We know that the loyalist angels could not defeat Satan's army, though twice their number; but surely the entire angelic guard would have a fair chance to capture Satan alone. God however prevents them from trying, by hanging forth in Heaven the constellation of his golden scales:

> *Wherein all things created first he weigh'd,*
> *The pendulous round Earth with ballanc't Air*
> *In counterpoise, now ponders all events,*
> *Battles and Realms: in these he put two weights,*
> *The sequel each of parting and of fight;*
> *The latter quick flew up, and kickt the beam.* (IV. 1000)

Gabriel interprets this to mean that God forbids him to try, pointing out that he and Satan can only do what Heaven permits; so Satan escapes, 'murmuring', but free to continue with the Temptation. I do not see what the incident can mean except that God was determined to make man fall, and had supplied a guard only for show; as soon as the guards look like succeeding he prevents them. No doubt the Latin pun on *ponder* helps to emphasize that the whole incident is meant to be allegorical, but no translation of it into more spiritual terms can alter the basic fact about it. (This reflection is not from Bertrand Russell but from Milton himself in *De Doctrina* Chapter II.) Satan still has to be clever; he remains in darkness by flying round the world every day for a week, and so on; but God has saved his liberty at the crucial point. Milton does not pick up Satan's story again till four books later, and then remarks that he had 'fled before the threats' of Gabriel (IX. 55), a very official account of what had happened. However, at the time Milton gave a reason for God's action: that he stopped the fight because it might have spoiled his new-made universe (IV. 990). In the age of the Cobalt Bomb, one is inclined to find this rational and sympathetic of God; but still, if he is going to send nearly all of us to Hell as a result of Adam's Fall, we cannot be expected to agree with him that it was less important than the scenery. Yvor Winters' view that the poem is just an imitation of Homer is especially plausible here, but as a rule Milton can make his learned imitations fit his purpose, and we may be sure he would have claimed that this one did too. I think we are struck by the incident, when it is pointed out, merely because we refuse to notice that similar things are going on all the time; we can swallow the general layout of 'Fate' by which God arranges what he has preordained, but it feels different when he nips in and prevents his own troops from doing what he had ordered them to do. Afterwards he forgives them for their failure, remarking with his usual grinding contempt for them that they couldn't have been the smallest use anyhow (X. 35). Milton himself has just rubbed the point home here, using the insinuating hiss which he gives his Satan when particularly serpent-like; God of course knew at once about the Fall, he remarks,

for what can scape the Eye
Of God All-seeing, or deceive his Heart
Omniscient, who in all things wise and just
Hinder'd not Satan . . . (x. 5)

M. Morand well points out that God was quite right to forgive the angelic guard; if they were punished, there would be a danger of their considering who was the real culprit.

Satan in *Paradise Regained* makes the same point, though this may be irrelevant—perhaps Milton did not try to make Satan's development consistent in both poems:

Tis true, I am that Spirit unfortunate,
Who leagu'd with millions more in rash revolt
Kept not my happy Station, but was driv'n
With them from bliss to the bottomless deep,
Yet to that hideous place not so confin'd
By rigour unconniving, but that oft
Leaving my dolorous Prison I enjoy
Large liberty to round this Globe of Earth,
Or range in th' air, nor from the Heav'n of Heav'ns
Hath he excluded my resort sometimes.
I came among the Sons of God, when he
Gave up into my hands Uzzean Job
To prove him, and illustrate his high worth;
And when to all his Angels he propos'd
To draw the proud King Ahab into fraud . . . (I. 360)

and so forth; that God 'connives' with Satan is a rather striking accusation against him, and cannot be denied on the textual evidence which Satan quotes. We are often told nowadays that Milton's attitude to Satan must have been perfectly simple, but it is clear that when writing *Paradise Lost* he had plenty more evidence for God's connivance with Satan which he chose not to use. The reason why this game can be played, of course, is that the Old Testament is a rag-bag of material from very different stages of development; one would think Milton after his thorough study must have understood that, but his main allies were committed to relying on the text, to oppose the traditions of Rome. The furthest he went in writing was to conjecture that God allowed the text of his Word to become corrupt so as to force upon our attention the prior importance of our own consciences (*De Doctrina*, Chapter XXX).

No scholastic philosopher, said Sir Walter Raleigh, "could have walked into a metaphysical bramble-bush with the blind recklessness that Milton displays"; he seems to have been the first to make this very central point. But I do not think anyone who has read the *De Doctrina* will regard Milton's treatment as due to ignorance or stupidity. The effect is that of a powerful mind thrashing about in exasperation. Perhaps I should have recognized earlier a scholastic position which he would consider elementary; we are not to think that God forces the will of individuals merely because he foreknows what they will do. God's foreknowledge was universally admitted, even by believers in free will, such as Milton had become when he wrote the epic. The idea in itself is not remote from common experience; many a mother has felt with horror that she can 'see' her son is going to take to bad courses. We find a greater difficulty in the case of a Creator, as was said in lapidary form by Aquinas:

> Knowledge, as knowledge, does not imply, indeed, causality; but, in so far as it is a knowledge belonging

> to the artist who forms, it stands in the relation of causality to that which is produced by his art.

This too is not beyond our experience, especially if we firmly regard the Creator as a Father; who will often fear, without even blaming Mother, a recurrence of his own bad tendencies or perhaps those of the wicked uncles. Besides, an ancient tradition allows us to say that an author may be too inspired quite to foresee what he is producing by his art. But a parent who 'foresaw' that the children would fall and then insisted upon exposing them to the temptation in view would be considered neurotic, if nothing worse; and this is what we must ascribe to Milton's God.

Waldock, I think, first remarked that he seems anxious to prove he does not cause the Fall; "indeed, never to the end of the poem does he succeed in living down this particular worry". I had perhaps better document this argument. God says in his first speech:

> *So without least impulse or shadow of Fate,*
> *Or aught by me immutably foreseen,*
> *They trespass, Authors to themselves in all*
> *Both what they judge and what they choose; for so*
> *I formed them free, and free they must remain,*
> *Till they enthrall themselves.* (III. 120)

All this upbraiding of them is done before they have fallen, and God again protests his innocence as soon as they have done it:

> *no Decree of mine*
> *Concurring to necessitate his Fall,*
> *Or touch with lightest moment of impulse*
> *His free will, to her own inclining left*
> *In even scale.* (X. 45)

Can it be the uneasy conscience of God or of Milton which produces this unfortunate metaphor of the scales, actually reminding us of the incident when he forced his troops to expose mankind to the tempter? Before the Creation, he gives what is perhaps a slightly different account of his power:

> *Boundless the Deep, because I am who fill*
> *Infinitude, nor vacuous the space.*
> *Though I uncircumscribed myself retire,*
> *And put not forth my goodness, which is free*
> *To act or not, Necessity and Chance*
> *Approach not mee, and what I will is Fate.* (VII. 170)

This is one of the main bits used by M. Saurat to show the profundity, or the impersonality and pantheism, of Milton's God; and God's claims do feel better if we identify him with Fate and the Absolute and the primeval matter of Chaos. But surely the story we are reading inspires a simpler reflection. Chaos is also a person, and though he acts out of resentment, so that God would not need to tip him off about the situation, he does exactly what God wants of him; he lets Satan pass for the corruption of mankind. As for making Sin and Death the guardians of Hell Gate, Sir Walter Raleigh remarked with casual elegance:

> No one has plausibly explained how they came by their office. It was intended to be a perfect sinecure; there was no one to be let in and no one to be let out. The single occasion that presented itself for a neglect of their duty was by them eagerly seized. (p. 108)

—though later he approves of the absurdity, because "they are the only creations of English poetry which approach the Latin in grandeur" (p. 238). Surely the explanation is very simple; God always intended them to let Satan out. Critics somehow cannot bring themselves to recognize that Milton does this steadily and consistently, after announcing that he will at the start. As a believer in the providence of God, Milton could not possibly have believed in the huge success-story of Satan fighting his way to Paradise. The chains of Hell, Sin, Death, Chaos and an army of good angels hold Satan back, but all this stage machinery is arranged by God to collapse as soon as he advances upon it, just as the fire cannot harm Siegfried when he has courage enough to walk through it to Brunhild. Chaos indeed jeers at the heroic piece of space-travel when he directs Satan to the newly created world:

If that be your walk, you have not far. (II. 1010)

(By the way, Yvor Winters could not have called this line 'meaningless inflation'.) We have thus no reason to doubt that Milton also intended the final paradox of the series, after Satan has reached Eden, when God cheats his own troops to make certain that the Fall occurs. As to what God means by saying that none of his busy activity affects their free will, I suppose he means that he does not actually hypnotize them, as Svengali did Trilby; though he lets Satan do to Eve as much as a hypnotist really can do.

A particularly impressive example of this poetic technique is given by a detail about the chains, which I think must have made Mr T. S. Eliot decide that the treatment of the chains is not sufficiently imagist. The first words of God in the poem insist that he cannot control Satan, and mention these chains as among the things that Satan has escaped from. We might indeed suppose that Milton has 'made a slip', forgotten his story and his theology, whether from lack of imaging or not. The reason why this will not do, I think, is that he is writing so frightfully well; his feelings are so deeply involved that the sound effects become wonderful. *Wide interrupt can hold* is like the cry of sea-mews upon rocks; it has what I think is meant by the term 'plangency'. We have to suppose it meant something important to him.

> *Only begotten Son, seest thou what rage*
> *Transports our adversary, whom no bounds*
> *Prescrib'd, no bars of Hell, nor all the chains*
> *Heapt on him there, nor yet the main Abyss*
> *Wide interrupt can hold; so bent he seems*
> *On desperate revenge, that shall redound*
> *Upon his own rebellious head. And now*
> *Through all restraint broke loose he wings his way*
> *Nor far off Heav'n, in the Precincts of Light,*
> *Directly towards the new created World,*
> *And man there plac'd . . .* (III. 80)

The only consistent view, after the firm statement at I. 210 for example, is that this is the first of God's grisly jokes. The passage, I think, is the strongest bit of evidence for the view of C. S. Lewis, that Milton intended Satan to be ridiculous; but even so it does not feel very like a joke. Milton might have some wish to confuse his simpler readers, and God to confuse the loyalist angels, who have been summoned to hear him; one might think God could not want to look weak, but he may be wanting to justify his revenge. Nobody says that it is a joke, as the Son does after God expresses fear of losing his throne; but there is no opportunity, because what God goes on to say is so lengthy and appalling. His settled plan for punishment comes steadily out, and the verse rhythm becomes totally unlike the thrilling energy of this first sentence. In his first reply to the Son, we find him talking in rocking-horse couplets, using the off-rhymes which were re-invented by Wilfred Owen to describe the First World War, with the same purpose of setting a reader's teeth on edge:

> *This my long sufferance and my day of grace*
> *They who neglect and scorn, shall never taste;*
> *But hard be hardened, blind be blinded more,*
> *That they may stumble on, and deeper fall.* (III. 200)

This is also where we get the stage-villain's hiss of "Die he or Justice must". God is much at his worst here, in his first appearance; but he needs to be, to make the offer of the Son produce a dramatic change. I do not know what to make of his expressing the Calvinist doctrine that the elect are chosen by his will alone, which Milton had appeared to reject (185); it has a peculiar impact here, when God has not yet even secured the Fall of Adam and Eve. One might argue that he was in no mood to make jokes; and besides, the effect here is not a sardonic mockery of Satan, which can be felt in the military joke readily enough, but a mysterious and deeply rooted sense of glory. A simple explanation may be put forward; Milton felt that this was such a tricky bit to put over his audience, because the inherent contradictions were coming so very near the surface, that he needed with a secret delight to call on the whole of his power. This is almost what Shelley took to be his frame of mind; and it is hard to accept, with the *De Doctrina* before us, without talking about Milton's Unconsciousness. But we may be sure that there is a mediating factor; if he had been challenged about the passage, he would have said that he was following the Old Testament scrupulously, and allowing God to mock his foes.

This has often been said about the jokes of Milton's

God, or at least about the one which can't be ignored because it is explained as a joke (V. 720); and one can make a rough check from the Concordance at the end of a Bible. The only important case is from Psalm ii; here again we meet the ancient document in which the King of Zion is adopted as the son of God:

> Why do the heathen rage . . . ? The kings of the earth set themselves, and the rulers take counsel together, against the Lord, and against his anointed. . . . He that sitteth in the heavens shall laugh; the Lord shall have them in derision.

This is echoed in Psalms xxxvii. 13 and lix. 8, and perhaps in Proverbs i. 26, where Wisdom and not God mocks the worldly rather than a powerful aggressor; but after trying to look under all the relevant words I do not find that the Concordance ever ascribes the sentiment to the Prophets. It was thus an ancient tradition but one treated with reserve, as Milton would understand. Naturally his intention in putting so much weight on it has been found especially hard to grasp.

The views of M. Morand about the divine characters have been neglected and seem to me illuminating. In the same year as *De Comus A Satan* he published a pamphlet in English, *The Effects of his Political Life on John Milton*, concerned to show that a certain worldly-mindedness entered Milton's later poetry as a result of his rather sordid experience of government, politics, and propaganda. What chiefly stands out in this lively work, I think, is an accusation that Milton himself had smuggled into a later edition of *Eikon Basilike* the prayer, derived from Sidney's *Arcadia*, for which he then so resoundingly denounced King Charles in *Eikonoclastes*; we are given a shocking picture of an English expert getting the evidence of a

Dutch researcher ignored by gentlemanly bluff. Mr Robert Graves used the main story in *Wife to Mr Milton*, but I had not realized that the evidence for it was so strong; indeed, Mr Graves often seems too disgusted by Milton to be convincing—disagreeable in many ways he may have been, but surely not a physical coward. I don't feel that the action is too bad for Milton; he would think the divine purpose behind the Civil War justified propaganda tricks, and need not have thought this a particularly bad one. The King was dead, and the purpose of the cheat was merely to prevent the people from thinking him a martyr. He hadn't written any of the book really, and Milton suspected that at the time, so it was only a matter of answering one cheat with another. Milton must in any case have been insincere in pretending to be shocked at the use of a prayer by Sidney, given in the story as that of a pagan, but so Christian in feeling as to be out of period (it assumes that God may be sending us evil as a test or tonic for our characters, which even if to be found in Aeschylus or Marcus Aurelius is not standard for Arcadia). Milton might comfort himself with the reflection that he wasn't even damaging the man's character in the eyes of fit judges, only making use of a popular superstition—as Shelley expected on another occasion. However, M. Morand finds that this kind of activity brought about a Fallen condition, as one might say, in the mind of the poet, and such is what *De Comus A Satan* examines throughout the later poetry.

There is an assumption here that to do Government propaganda can only have a bad effect upon a poet's mind, and I feel able to speak on the point as I was employed at such work myself in the Second World War, indeed once had the honour of being named in rebuttal by Fritzsche himself and called a curly-headed Jew. I wasn't in on any of the splendid tricks, such as Milton is accused of, but the cooked-up argufying I have experienced. To work at it forces you to imagine all the time what the enemy will reply; you are trying to get him into a corner. Such a training cannot narrow a man's understanding of other people's opinions, though it may well narrow his own opinions. I should say that Milton's experience of propaganda is what makes his later poetry so very dramatic; that is, though he is a furious partisan, he can always imagine with all its force exactly what the reply of the opponent would be. As to his integrity, he was such an inconvenient propagandist that the Government deserve credit for having the nerve to appoint and retain him. He had already published the Divorce Pamphlets before he got the job; well now, if you are setting out to be severe and revolutionary on the basis of literal acceptance of the Old Testament, the most embarrassing thing you can be confronted with is detailed evidence about the sexual habits of the patriarchs; it is the one point where the plain man feels he can laugh. Milton always remained liable to defend his side by an argument which would strike his employers as damaging; his style of attack is savagely whole-hearted, but his depth of historical knowledge and imaginative sympathy keep having unexpected effects. He was not at all likely to feel that he had forfeited his independence of mind by such work. M. Morand therefore strikes me as rather innocent in assuming that he was corrupted by it, but I warmly agree that it made his mind very political. Professor Wilson Knight has also remarked that Milton wrote a political allegory under the appearance of a religious poem, though he did not draw such drastic consequences from the epigram.

On the Morand view, God is simply a dynastic ruler

like those Milton had had to deal with; Cromwell had wanted his son to inherit, no less than Charles. M. Morand does not seem to realize it, but the effect is to make Milton's God much better. His intrigues and lies to bolster his power are now comparatively unselfish, being only meant to transfer it unimpaired to his Son, and above all he feels no malignity towards his victims. His method of impressing the loyalist angels will doom almost all mankind to misery, but he takes no pleasure in that; it simply does not bother him. The hypocrisy which the jovial old ruffian feels to be required of him in public has not poisoned his own mind, as we realize when he permits himself his leering jokes. This does, I should say, correspond to the impression usually made by the poem on a person not brought up as a Christian, such as my Chinese and Japanese students. The next step is to regard the debate in Heaven, where the Son, but no angel, offers to die for man, as a political trick rigged up to impress the surviving angels; the Son is free to remark (III. 245) that he knows the Father won't let him stay dead, so that the incantationary repetition of the word *death* comes to seem blatantly artificial. (We find in the *De Doctrina* Chapter XII that Milton includes "under the head of death, in Scripture, all evils whatsoever" . . .). Nobody is surprised at the absence of volunteers among the good angels, whereas Satan, during the parallel scene in Hell (II. 470), has to close the debate hurriedly for fear a less competent rebel put himself forward. Otherwise the two scenes are deliberately made alike, and the reason is simply that both are political:

> Ce qui frappe, c'est le parallelisme des moyens employées, conseils, discours. Même souci de garder pour soi tout gloire. (p. 145)

On reaching *Paradise Regained*, M. Morand is interested to learn how the Son grew up. In *Paradise Lost* he often seems half ashamed of the autocratic behaviour of his Father, because his role is to induce the subject angels to endure it; but when he is alone on the earth-visit which has been arranged for him we find he has merely the cold calculating pride which we would expect from his training. However, we already find this trait, decides M. Morand, at the early public moment when he offers his Sacrifice; he is unable to avoid presenting himself as solely interested in his own career (p. 169). As the Creation for which he was the instrument has already happened, he might at least speak as if he could tell a man apart from a cow, but he says that his Father's grace visits "all his creatures" (III. 230). Satan, on the parallel occasion, was at least genuinely concerned to get the job done, whoever did it; and M. Morand decides that the ringing repetition of ME in the speech of sacrifice of the Son is a little too grotesque, however perfectly in character. Milton

> n'eût pas pensé à ce que peut contenir de ridicule ce martellement du moi.
>
> De personnages extra-terrestres, le moins éloigné de la modestie est encore Satan. (p. 171)

This is at least a splendid reply to the argument that pride is the basic fault of all the characters who fall.

The Morand line of argument can be taken an extra step, to argue that the Son too is being cheated by the Father; and this excites a suspicion that there is something inadequate about it. He says nothing of the means of his death, and speaks as if he is going to remain on earth till the Last Day:

> *Behold mee then, mee for him, life for life*
> *I offer, on mee let thine anger fall;*

Account mee man; I for his sake will leave
Thy bosom, and this glory next to thee
Freely put off, and for him lastly die
Well pleas'd, on me let Death wreck all his rage;
Under his gloomy power I shall not long
Lie vanquisht; thou hast giv'n me to possess
Life in my self for ever, by thee I live,
Though now to Death I yield, and am his due
All of me that can die, yet that debt paid,
Thou wilt not leave me in the loathsome grave
His prey, nor suffer my unspotted Soul
For ever with corruption there to dwell;
But I shall rise Victorious, and subdue
My Vanquisher, spoild of his vaunted spoil;
Death his death's wound shall then receive, and stoop
Inglorious, of his mortal sting disarm'd.
I through the ample Air in Triumph high
Shall lead Hell Captive maugre Hell, and show
The Powers of darkness bound. Thou at the sight
Pleas'd, out of Heaven shalt look down and smile,
While by thee rais'd I ruin all my Foes,
Death last, and with his Carcass glut the Grave:
Then with the multitude of my redeemd
Shall enter Heaven long absent, and return,
Father, to see thy face, wherein no cloud
Of anger shall remain, but peace assur'd,
And reconcilement; wrath shall be no more
Thenceforth, but in thy presence Joy entire. (III. 240)

Our chief impression here, surely, is not that he is too little interested in mankind but that he does not know what is going to happen, except for a triumph at which he can rejoice. If the Jews had not chosen to kill him, he would presumably have remained on earth till the Last

Day, making history less bad than the poem describes it as being; and what they will choose can be foreknown by the Father only. The Son expects to find no frown upon the face of God on Judgement Day, the *Dies Irae* itself, so we can hardly doubt that he expects things to turn out better than they do. His prophecy appears to be a continuous narrative: "not long lie . . . rise victorious . . . then . . . then", as if he will lead the blessed to Heaven very soon after the Resurrection. Among human speakers 'lastly die' is a natural way to express pathos, though a tautology; but a meaning which would make it a correct description of the career of the Son is hard to invent. It may be possible to interpret the whole speech as a true forecast, and Milton may have planned to leave this alternative open; but it is a more natural reading to suppose the Son ignorant, and Milton denies him foreknowledge in *De Doctrina* Chap. V.

We must compare the speech to what Michael tells Adam at XII. 410, not long after hearing it. The angel has now been told of the Crucifixion, and explains that soon after it, while ascending to Heaven, Christ will surprise Satan in the air and drag him in chains, then resume his seat at God's right hand till the Second Coming. This clears up part of the Son's narrative; and if he is to remain on earth after the Second Coming for the Millennium, finally returning with his Saints, that explains 'long absent'. Milton seems rather doubtful about this doctrine, as Michael says that Christ will receive the faithful into bliss 'whether in Heaven or Earth'. *De Doctrina* Chapter XXXIII says that the glorious reign of Christ on earth will begin at the start of the Last Judgement and 'extend a little beyond its conclusion'; then the chapter goes on to name the thousand years, then it gives a still grander interpretation. Only the blessed will be revived for the Millennium (Revelation xx. 5), which might explain why the Son expects no frown when he leads them to Heaven after a thousand years. At any rate, if he expects to labour so long for mankind, we can hardly agree with M. Morand that he betrays lack of interest in them.

It often happens with a formative piece of criticism that one needs to consider why it seemed so true, after apparently refuting it. The mere repetition of *me* when offering oneself for sacrifice cannot be enough to prove self-centredness, even in the style of Milton, because Eve does it in a speech of splendid generosity. Surely the reason why Milton's treatment here seems cold, compared to a Good Friday service which is the natural comparison, is that no one throughout the long 'scene in Heaven' ever mentions that the Son is to die by torture. Even Michael does not describe the Cross to Adam as painful, only as 'shameful and accurst'. Death for a day and a half any of us might proffer, but we would find slow torture worth mentioning even given a doctor in attendance who guaranteed recovery after unconsciousness had finally supervened. I do not know whether there is a standard explanation for this lack in the poem, and do not remember to have seen it noticed. The reason for it, surely, is that Milton would not dirty his fingers with the bodily horror so prominent in the religion. We need not be surprised, because all his heroes fiercely refuse to let the prospect of pain so much as enter their minds while deciding what they ought to do; his devils are so superior to pain that we actually cannot remember they are all the time in bodily agony. This steady blaze of moral splendour must I am afraid be called unreal but at least makes the religion feel a good deal cleaner. The son regularly talks like a young medieval aristocrat eager to win his spurs, and like him is not expected to mention pain. No doubt the singing angels (III. 375) would mention the Crucifixion if they had been told of it, but it could mean little to them as they have never experienced pain; God has only just invented it, and only applied it to rebels. Clearly God has given at least Michael further information before he speaks to Adam. But there is no dignified enough procedure by which God could tell the angels that he has made a huge increase in his demand upon the Son after accepting the Son's offer. To cheat his own Son into death by torture would be too bad even for the God of M. Morand; it would be bad propaganda. Thus I think we should apply here too the principle of Mr Rajan, that the correct interpretation is always the sublimest one; Milton considered death by torture such a trivial sacrifice that he thought the Son must have offered a longer mission than the Father decided to require of him. Even if the Son does not know about the Crucifixion, he knows a good deal about the consequences of his offer; if we suppose the Father to have told him this beforehand we must still picture them, as M. Morand does, hammering out in private the scene of propaganda dialogue which they will present to the assembled angels. But their background is impossible for us to envisage, and the Father may simply put into the mind of the Son as much foreknowledge as he chooses on the instant, so that the Son acts, as we would call it, spontaneously. The process might let the Son presume the happier alternative for mankind, out of a bold confidence in his power to convert them; but, even so, he must be above feeling wronged when he finds that the Crucifixion has been incurred. We need not after that join M. Morand in blaming him for hoping to deserve praise. Milton if he intended this high detail would have to regard it as visible only to very fit readers, such as could cross-question his text like M.

Morand; the broad literary effect is rather one of tactfulness in keeping the Crucifixion out of sight. The motive of the Father in crucifying the Son is of course left in even deeper obscurity.

Milton did however I think mean to adumbrate a kind of motive by his picture of the Last Things. Professor C. S. Lewis once kindly came to a lecture I was giving on the half-finished material of this book; and at question time, after a sentence of charitable compunction, recognizing that the speaker wasn't responsible for this bit, he said "Does Phelps Morand think God is going to abdicate, then?" I tried to explain that M. Morand regarded this as the way Milton's dramatic imagination worked, after it had been corrupted by his patriotic labours, not as part of his theological system. The answer felt weak, and soon afterwards another difficulty drove me back to the book of M. Saurat, which I had probably not read since I was an undergraduate; I thus suddenly realized, what M. Saurat was not intending to prove, that Milton did expect God to abdicate. At least, that is the most direct way to express the idea; you may also say that he is an emergent or evolutionary deity, as has been believed at times by many other thinkers, for example Aeschylus and H. G. Wells.

There has been such a campaign to prove that only the coarsely worldly Victorians would even want the world to get better that I had better digress about that, or I may be thought to be jeering at Milton. We are often told that *In Memoriam* is bad because Tennyson tries to palm off progress in this world as a substitute for Heaven. But he says in the poem that he would stop being good, or would kill himself, if he stopped believing he would go to Heaven; it is wilful to argue that he treats the progress of the human race as an adequate alternative. Indeed, he seems rather too petulant about his demand for Heaven, considering that *Tithonus*, written about the same time (according to Stopford Brooke) though kept from publication till later, appreciates so nobly the hunger of mankind for the peace of oblivion. But the underlying logic of *In Memoriam* is firm. The signs that God is working out a vast plan of evolution are treated as evidence that he is good, and therefore that he will provide Heaven for Tennyson. To believe that God's Providence can be seen at work in the world, and that this is evidence for his existence and goodness, is what is called Natural Theology; it is very traditional, and the inability of neo-Christians to understand it casts an odd light on their pretensions. Tennyson has also been accused of insincerity about progress because in another poem he expressed alarm at the prospect of war in the air; but he realized the time-scale very clearly; while maintaining that the process of the suns will eventually reach a good end, it is only sensible to warn mankind that we are likely to go through some very bad periods beforehand. Now, when mankind seems almost certain to destroy itself quite soon, we cannot help wincing at a belief that progress is inevitable; but this qualification seems all that is needed. I think that reverence *ought* to be aroused by the thought that so long and large a process has recently produced ourselves who can describe it, and other-worldly persons who boast of not feeling that seem to me merely to have cauterized themselves against genuine religious feeling. The seventeenth century too would have thought that so much contempt for Providence verged upon the Manichean. Milton claimed to get his conception of progress from the Bible; but he would have found corroboration, one would think, in the *Prometheus*, which was well known. There is only one reference to the myth in the epic, and it is twisted into a complaint against women (IV. 720); but Mr R. J. Z. Werblowsky, in his broad and philosophical *Lucifer and Prometheus* (1952), may well be right to think that Milton tried to avoid direct comparison between Prometheus and his Satan.

At the point which seemed to me illuminating, M. Saurat was calling Milton 'the old incorrigible dreamer' (p. 165, 1944 edition), apparently just for believing in the Millennium on earth, though that only requires literal acceptance of Revelation xx; but he was quoting part of Milton's commentary in Chapter XXXIII of the *De Doctrina*, "Of Perfect Glorification", and no doubt recognized that Milton was somehow going rather further. Milton says:

> It may be asked, if Christ is to deliver up the kingdom to God and the Father, what becomes of the declarations [quotations from Heb. i. 8, Dan. vii. 14, and Luke i. 33] "of his kingdom there shall be no end". I reply, there shall be no end of his kingdom . . . till time itself shall be no longer, Rev. x. 6, until everything which his kingdom was intended to effect shall be accomplished . . . it will not be destroyed, nor will its period be a period of dissolution, but rather of perfection and consummation, like the end of the law, Matt. v. 18.

The last clause seems to recall the precedent of an earlier evolutionary step, whereby the New Dispensation of Jesus made the Mosaic Law unnecessary; it is clear that the final one, which makes even the Millennium unnecessary, must be of an extremely radical character. The Father, I submit, has to turn into the God of the Cambridge Platonists and suchlike mystical characters; at present he is still the very disagreeable God of the Old

Testament, but eventually he will dissolve into the landscape and become immanent only. The difficulty of fitting in this extremely grand climax was perhaps what made Milton uncertain about the controverted time-scheme of the Millennium. The doctrine of the end of time, if one takes it seriously, is already enough to make anything but Total Union (or else Total Separateness from God) hard to conceive.

The question which Milton answers here is at least one which he makes extremely prominent in the speech of rejoicing by the Father after the speech of sacrifice by the Son (III. 320). The Father first says he *will* give the Son all power, then in the present tense "I give thee"; yet he had given it already, or at least enough to cause Satan and his followers to revolt. Without so much as a full stop, the Father next says that the time when he will give it is the Day of Judgement, and the climax of the whole speech is to say that immediately after that "God shall be All in All". The eternal gift of the Father is thus to be received only on the Last Day, and handed back the day after. This has not been found disturbing, because the paradox is so clear that we assume it to be deliberate; nor are interpretations of it hard to come by. But Milton would see it in the light of the passage in the *De Doctrina*; there "God shall be All in All" ends the Biblical quotation which comes just before Milton's mystical "reply":

> Then cometh the end . . . but when he saith, all things are put under him, it is manifest that he is excepted which did put all things under him; and when all things are subdued unto him, then shall the Son himself also be subject unto him that put all things under him, that God may be all in all. (I Corinthians xv. 24-28)

St Paul is grappling with earlier texts here in much the same scholarly way that Milton did, which would give Milton a certain confidence about re-interpreting his results even though they were inspired because Biblical. After hearing so much from M. Morand about the political corruption of Milton's mind, one is pleased to find it less corrupt than St Paul's; Milton decided that God was telling the truth, and that he would keep his promise literally. At the end of the speech of the Father, Milton turns into poetry the decision he had reached in prose:

The World shall burn, and from her ashes spring
New Heav'n and Earth, wherein the just shall dwell . . .
Then thou thy regal Sceptre shalt lay by,
For regal Sceptre then no more shall need,
God shall be All in All. But all ye Gods
Adore him, who to compass all this dies,
Adore the Son, and honour him as me. (III. 340)

I grant that the language is obscure, as is fitting because it is oracular; and, besides, Milton wanted the poem to be universal, so did not want to thrust a special doctrine upon the reader. But the doctrine is implied decisively if the language is examined with care. St Paul presumably had in mind a literal autocracy, but Milton contrives to make the text imply pantheism. The O.E.D. records that the intransitive use of the verb *need* had become slightly archaic except for a few set phrases; the general intransitive use needed here belongs to the previous century—e.g. "stopping of heads with lead shall not need now" 1545. But a reader who noticed the change of grammar from *shalt* to *shall* could only impute the old construction: "Authority will then no longer be needed"—not, therefore, from the Father, any more than from the Son. There is much more point in the last two lines quoted if the

Father has just proposed, though in an even more remote sense than the Son, that he too shall die. *All* is rather a pet word in Milton's poetry but I think he never gives it a capital letter anywhere else, and one would expect that by writing "All in All" he meant to imply a special doctrine, as we do by writing "the Absolute". Then again, this is the only time God calls the angels Gods, with or without a capital letter. He does it here meaning that they will in effect become so after he has abdicated. The reference has justly been used as a partial defence of Satan for calling his rebels Gods, but we are meant to understand that his claim for them is a subtle misuse of the deeper truth adumbrated here. Taking all the details together, I think it is clear that Milton wanted to suggest a high mystery at this culminating point.

There was a more urgent and practical angle to the question; it was not only one of the status of the Son, but of mankind. You cannot think it merely whimsical of M. Morand to call God dynastic if you look up the words *heir* and *inherit* in the concordance usually given at the end of a Bible. Milton was of course merely quoting the text when he made the Father call the Son his heir (as in VI. 705); but the blessed among mankind are also regularly called 'heirs of God's kingdom' and suchlike. The word *heir* specifically means one who will inherit; it would be comical to talk as if M. Morand was the first to wonder what the Bible might mean by it. The blessed among mankind are heirs of God through their union with Christ; Milton's Chapter XXIV is 'Of Union and Fellowship with Christ and the Saints, wherein is considered the Mystical or Invisible Church', and he says it is 'not confined to place or time, inasmuch as it is composed of individuals of widely separated countries, and of all ages from the foundation of the world'. He would regard this as a blow at all priesthoods, but also regard the invisible union as a prefiguring of the far distant real one. We can now see that it is already offered in the otherwise harsh words by which the Father appointed the Son:

> *Under his great Vice-regent reign abide*
> *United as one individual Soul*
> *For ever happy* (v. 610)

As a means of achieving such unity the speech is a remarkable failure; but God already knew that men would be needed as well as angels before the alchemy could be done. When the unity is complete, neither the loyal angels nor the blessed among mankind will require even the vice-regency of the Son, still less the rule of the Father; and only so can they become 'heirs and inheritors of God's Kingdom'.

The texts prove, I submit, that Milton envisaged the idea, as indeed so informed a man could hardly help doing; but the poetry must decide whether it meant a great deal to him, and the bits so far quoted are not very good. Milton however also ascribes it to God in the one really splendid passage allotted to him. This is merely an earlier part of the same speech, but the sequence III. 80-345 is full of startling changes of tone. The end of the speech happens to let us see Milton's mind at work, because we can relate it to the *De Doctrina*, but the main feeling there is just immense pride; Milton could never let the Father appear soft, and his deepest yielding must be almost hidden by a blaze of glory. Just before advancing upon thirty lines of glory, he has rejoiced that his Son:

> *though thron'd in highest bliss,*
> *Equal to God, and equally enjoying*
> *God-like fruition, quitted all to save*

A world from utter loss, and hast been found
By Merit more than Birthright Son of God,
Found worthiest to be so by being Good,
Far more than Great or High; because in thee
Love hath abounded more than Glory abounds,
Therefore thy Humiliation shall exalt
With thee thy Manhood also to this Throne;
Here shalt thou sit incarnate, here shalt Reign
Both God and Man, Son both of God and Man,
Anointed universal King; all Power
I give thee, reign for ever, and assume
Thy Merits; under thee as Head Supreme
Thrones, Princedoms, Powers, Dominions I reduce : (III. 305)

It is a tremendous moral cleansing for Milton's God, after the greed for power which can be felt in him everywhere else, to say that he will give his throne to Incarnate Man, and the rhythm around the word *humiliation* is like taking off in an aeroplane. I had long felt that this is much the best moment of God in the poem, morally as well as poetically, without having any idea why it came there. It comes there because he is envisaging his abdication, and the democratic appeal of the prophecy of God is what makes the whole picture of him just tolerable.

I may be told that I am simply misreading; the Father is not giving Man his own throne, but the Son's, and Milton has made this clear just previously by recalling that the Son too is throned; indeed I think this is the only place in the poem where he is said to be 'throned' at the right hand of God. (When the Father tells the Son to rise and drive out the rebels, Milton mysteriously says that he addresses 'The Assessor of his Throne' VI. 680; but I can deduce nothing from that.) But the grandeur of the position of the Son needed emphasizing here in any case, and Milton is inclined to 'plant' a word in this way soon before it is used especially sublimely. The effect of repeating the word *throne* is not so obtrusive as to exclude the more tremendous meaning. Besides, the Father could not say that the Son will be exalted as a reward to the throne which the Son already occupies; and the sequence is "this throne . . . here . . . here . . . Head Supreme", very empty rhetoric if it does not refer to the supreme throne. I grant that the meaning is not obvious unless one realizes how much support it is given later in the speech.

Wondering where to stop my quotation, I was struck by how immediately the passage turns from generosity to pride of power. The distinction is perhaps an unreal one; all the lines are *about* pride. God is generous to give his throne, but Milton exults in the dignity given to Man. The last line of my quotation, except that it omits the Virtues for convenience, gives the same roll-call of the titles of the angels as Satan does in his rabble-rousing speech; no doubt this was the standard form in Heaven, but the effect is to make the reader compare the two offers. One must agree with M. Morand that it is all weirdly political; temporary acceptance of lower-class status is what the Son is being praised for, a severe thing in his mind, just as it is beneath Satan's class to become incarnate as a snake. As to torture, that might come your way in any class, and would only be a minor thing to boast about afterwards. But one dare not call this mode of thought contemptible, if it elevates, or makes proud enough to act well, all classes of the society in which it operates.

I can claim that this account gives the thought of the epic a much needed consistency. Thus it may be objected that Milton's own temperament, because of the pride so evident in his style, would be quite unattracted by an ideal of total union. But certainly; he presents it as very unattractive even to the good angels. Abdiel can only translate it into terms exasperating for Satan; and the blushing of Raphael now acquires considerable point, which after all one would expect so bizarre a detail to have. Though capable of re-uniting themselves with God the angels do not want to, especially because this capacity lets them enjoy occasional acts of love among themselves. It is fundamental to Milton's system that angels, like all the rest of the universe, are parts of God from which God willingly removed his will; these highest forms of life, he finds it natural to suppose, have an approximation to the divine power among themselves, so that they can love by total interpenetration. Presumably God can gobble them up as soon as look at them, which would make him an alarming employer, and perhaps they are relieved that he never expresses any affection for them—though even interpenetration with God would not actually mean death; the Son, like Satan, doubts whether any life can be totally destroyed, III. 165; so does Milton, *De Doctrina* Chapter VII. Thus they put up a timidly evasive but none the less stubborn resistance to dissolving themselves into God, like a peasantry under Communism trying to delay collectivization; and here too the state has the high claim that it has promised eventually to wither away. God must abdicate, in the sense of becoming totally immanent or invisible, before the plan of Total Union can seem tolerable to them; and it is bitter for them that this transcendence cannot be achieved without stirring into the brew the blessed among mankind. Exactly why the angels are so inadequate that God's programme is necessary remains obscure; Milton quotes in *De Doctrina* Chapter VII from Job iv. 18 "he put no trust in his servants, and his angels he charged with folly", which perhaps he felt to give authority to his picture. But it is intelligible that a stern period of training may be required before transcendence, and at any rate the story is a great boast for ourselves; we are not inclined to blame God for deciding that he needed us before he could abdicate conscientiously.

Thus, by combining the views of M. Saurat and M. Morand, the one attributing to Milton thoughts beyond the reaches of our souls and the other a harsh worldliness, we can I think partly solve the central problem about the poem, which is how Milton can have thought it to justify God. I think the 'internal' evidence of Milton's own writing enough to decide that he meant what I have tried to describe, because it makes our impression of the poem and indeed of the author much more satisfactory; but, even so, external evidence is needed to answer the objection that Milton could not have meant that, or could not have thought of it. I had best begin by saying what I learned from M. Saurat and where I thought his view inadequate. His main interest, as I understand, was to show that the European Renaissance could not have occurred without an underground influence from Jewish mystics beginning two or three centuries before Milton; the main reason for supposing that Milton had read the *Zohar*, even after textual evidence had been found, was that he was a man who habitually went to the sources of the ideas which he had already found floating about. The doctrine that matter was not created from nothing but was part of God M. Saurat considered fundamental to the Renaissance, because it allowed enough trust in the flesh, the sciences, the arts, the future before man in this world. Milton undoubtedly does express this doctrine, but it does not strike me as prominent in other poets of the time, except for the paradoxes of Donne's love-poetry.

However, I want to answer a rebuttal of the Saurat position which I happened to come across in an informative and strictly philological work by G. N. Conklin, *Biblical Criticism and Heresy in Milton*, 1949. He says that Milton could not have been influenced by the *Zohar*, or by the mystics around him in the Commonwealth such as Fludd either, because he was "a Puritan, a logician, and, whatever else, assuredly no theosophist", and furthermore that it is mere justice to admit that Milton extracted his beliefs from the ancient texts of Holy Writ by scientific philological techniques, as he steadily claimed to do. Thus his crucial decision that matter was not created from nothing turned simply on an analysis of the Biblical words for *create*, chiefly but not only in Hebrew. Admittedly, this is what Milton claims in Chapter VII of *De Doctrina*, but he was accustomed to defend a position rhetorically, to convince other people, after arriving at it himself by a more conscientious assessment of the evidence. The philological argument here is only, and could only be, that previous uses of the word had not meant this unique concept before the attempt at expressing it was allegedly made; thus the word in the Bible does not have to mean what theologians say, and is never redefined by the Bible in a phrase or sentence as meaning that. Milton goes on to give other reasons for his conclusion that 'create' in the Bible does not mean 'from nothing', and by doing so he has in effect enough sense to admit that his negative argument does not make a positive one. These problems about sources are often very subtle, because a powerful mind grabs at a hint of what it needs; admittedly, the *Zohar* was not the only possible source of these large mystical ideas; and one could explain the verbal correspondences found by M. Saurat by supposing that Milton got some other learned man to answer his questions about the *Zohar*, and read some crucial bits out to him, after he had become blind.

All the same, such ideas undoubtedly were floating about. The trouble with M. Saurat's position, I think, is that he welcomes the liquefaction of God the Father, making him wholly immanent in his creation, and argues that Milton intended that in his epic, without realizing that Milton and his learned contemporaries would think the liquefaction of all the rest of us a prior condition. The idea of the re-absorption of the soul into the Absolute does get hinted at a good deal in the literature, if only in the form of complete self-abandonment to God; whereas the idea that God himself is wholly immanent in his creation belonged mainly to the high specialized output of the Cambridge Platonists. Marlowe's Faustus, in his final speech, desires to return his soul like a rain-drop to the sea rather than remain eternally as an individual in Hell, and this is a crucial image for grasping the Far-Eastern position; the same idea is quite noisy in the supposedly orthodox peroration of *Urn-Burial*: "if any have been so happy as truly to understand Christian annihilation . . . liquefaction . . . ingression into the divine shadow". When Lovewit at the end of *The Alchemist* rebuffs a superstitious fool by saying "Away, you Harry Nicholas" (the founder of the mystical Family of Love which maintained that any man can become Christ), the now remote figure is presumed to be familiar to a popular audience. The ideas which Milton hinted at in the bits of his epic which I have picked out were therefore not nearly so learned and unusual as they seem now; indeed, he probably treated them with caution because they might suggest a more Levelling, more economic-revolutionary, political stand than he in fact took. But the Cambridge Platonists were not dangerous for property-owners in this way; they were a strand of recent advanced thought which deserved recognition in his epic; also they allowed of a welcome contrast to the picture of God which the Bible forced him to present, and gave a bit more body to the mysterious climax of the Fortunate Fall. The abdication of the Father was thus quite an important part of his delicately balanced structure, and not at all a secret heresy; and of course not 'unconscious' if it needed tact. At bottom, indeed, a quaintly political mind is what we find engaged on the enormous synthesis. Milton knows by experience that God is at present the grindingly harsh figure described in the Old Testament; after all, Milton had long been printing the conviction that his political side had been proved right because God had made it win, so its eventual defeat was a difficult thing to justify God for. But it was essential to retain the faith that God has a good eventual plan; well then, the Cambridge Platonists can be allowed to be right about God, but only as he will become in the remote future. It seems to me one of the likeable sides of Milton that he would regard this as a practical and statesmanlike proposal.

M. Saurat, on the other hand, wanted Milton to use the *Zohar* to drive the last remnants of Manichaeism out of Christianity, and therefore argued that God in the epic is already an ineffable Absolute or World-Soul dissolved into the formative matter of the universe. After a timid peep into one volume of a translation of the *Zohar*, I am sure that Milton would not find it as opposite from the Gnostics as black from white, which is what the eloquence and selection of M. Saurat lead us to suppose. Milton would regard it as further evidence that the Fathers had slandered the Gnostics, as he had been sure when he was young, just as Rome had behaved very wickedly to the Cathars; all these heretics probably had something to be said for them, though of course one must expect most of their stuff to be dead wood. And the Gnostics are reported as believing, no less than the Cabbalists of the *Zohar*, in an eventual reunion of the many with the One. The Saurat interpretation of the epic makes nonsense of most of its narrative, but that is better than giving it an evil sense; the point where one ought to revolt comes when the interpretation drives poor M. Saurat into uneasy brief expressions of bad feeling. He praises God's jokes (p. 192, 1944 edition) because the only relation of the Absolute to its creation which a poet can present is 'irony', and here the protean word has to mean mean-minded jeering. M. Saurat deserves to be released from this position; the idea of God as the Absolute is genuinely present in the poem, but only when God is adumbrating the Last Things.

The well-argued view of M. Morand, that the purblind Milton described God from his experience of Cromwell, also allows of an unexpectedly sublime conclusion. Milton's own political record, as I understand, cannot be found contemptible; he backed Cromwell and his Independents in the army against the Presbyterians in Parliament because he wanted religious freedom, but always remained capable of saying where he thought Cromwell had gone wrong; for example, in refusing to disestablish the Church. However, on one point Cromwell was impeccable, and appears to be unique among dictators; his admitted and genuine bother, for a number of years, was to find some way of establishing a Parliament under which he could feel himself justified in stopping being dictator. When Milton made God the Father plan for his eventual abdication, he ascribed to him in the high tradition of Plutarch the noblest sentiment that could be found in an absolute ruler; and could reflect with pride that he had himself seen it in operation, though with a tragic end. Milton's God is thus to be regarded as like King Lear and Prospero, turbulent and masterful characters who are struggling to become able to renounce their power and enter peace; the story makes him behave much worse than they do, but the author allows him the same purifying aspiration. Even the lie of God "Die he or Justice must", we may now charitably reflect, is partly covered when Milton says that Satan

with necessity
The Tyrant's plea, excused his devilish deeds. (IV. 395)

It must be added at once that we cannot find enough necessity; the poem, to be completely four-square, ought to explain why God had to procure all these falls for his eventual high purpose. Such is the basic question as it stood long before Milton handled it; but he puts the mystery in a place evidently beyond human knowledge, and he makes tolerably decent, though salty and rough, what is within our reach.

This I think answers the fundamental objection of Yvor Winters, with which it seemed right to begin the chapter; Milton's poetical formula for God is not simply to copy Zeus in Homer but, much more dramatically, to cut out everything between the two ends of the large body of Western thought about God, and stick to Moses except at the high points which anticipate Spinoza. The procedure is bound to make God interesting; take the case of his announcing to the loyal angels that he will create mankind to spite the devil. God must be supposed to intend his words to suggest to the angels what they do to us, but any angel instructed in theology must realize that God has intended throughout all eternity to spite Satan, so that when he presents this plan as new he is telling a lie, which he has also intended to tell throughout all eternity. No wonder it will be 'far happier days' after he has abdicated (XII. 465). Milton was well able to understand these contradictions, and naturally he would want to leave room for an eventual solution of them.

Perhaps I find him like Kafka merely because both seem to have had a kind of foreknowledge of the Totalitarian State, whether or not this was what C. S. Lewis praised as his beautiful sense of the idea of social order. The picture of God in the poem, including perhaps even the high moments when he speaks of the end, is astonishingly like Uncle Joe Stalin; the same patience under an appearance of roughness, the same flashes of joviality, the same thorough unscrupulousness, the same real bad temper. It seems little use to puzzle ourselves whether Milton realized he was producing this effect, because it would follow in any case from what he had set himself to do.

Chapter 4

EVE

A POST-GRADUATE student at Peking National University, when I went back there shortly after the war, was examining the Fall of Eve with growing indignation on her behalf, and seemed to me to have made an important discovery; I took his essay to the Summer School at Kenyon College, Ohio, in 1948, but failed to place it with a magazine, and he was unlikely to follow it up in later years. So when I at last got round to reading M. Morand I was relieved from an old sense of guilt; Mr Chang Chin-Yen would in any case not have had the priority. Rather little of this book is my own invention. These two critics are very unlike, except in their sense of justice and a certain independence of current critical fashion; and what occurred to both of them, not to me, was that Adam and Eve would not have fallen unless God had sent Raphael to talk to them, supposedly to strengthen their resistance to temptation. Merely cheating his own troops to get Satan into Paradise would not have been enough.

They are both hard to tempt; Eve at least wants to get to Heaven, and this is the point which is exploited, but Adam is so free from ambition as to be almost impenetrable. Even so, when Satan first tempts Eve, whispering ill dreams disguised as a toad, she wakes up determined to resist. I cannot sympathize with the view of Dr Tillyard, that her flushing and her anxiety show her already not quite innocent before her Fall; if it is lack of innocence to want to go to Heaven, and to find a need to distinguish between different methods of getting there, our fallen minds seem unable to distinguish innocence from imbecility. I expect Milton would have considered it a sin not to want to go to Heaven, and he makes her able to resist a temptation to use a wrong method till she had been subjected to the discourse of Raphael. She imagines herself in the dream as consenting, but Milton regards it as within the powers of Satan to give her such a dream. Hypnotists have long been saying, as I understand, that one cannot make people do by 'suggestion' anything they deeply resist, a random murder for example, but can put any ideas into their heads; thus agreeing with Milton on both points. In the dream Satan appeared to her as an angel, ate the apple, told her it was the food of angels and the way to get to Heaven, and suggested that she positively ought to acquire knowledge and become divine:

> *Taste this, and be henceforth among the gods*
> *Thyself a goddess; not to earth confin'd*
> *But sometimes in the air, as wee, sometimes*
> *Ascend to Heav'n, by merit thine, and see*
> *What life the Gods live there, and so live thou.* (v. 80)

The Bible says she was tempted by the savour (the smell, as she had not yet tasted it); Milton ascribes this mainly to the dream he has invented, which helps to make the real temptation less trivial. She is given a space-flight, and 'wonders' at it, but

> *O how glad I wak'd*
> *To find this but a dream!*

The comforting Adam remarks that the shock of an imaginary acceptance is more likely to strengthen her resistance than otherwise (120), and this view seems as plausible as Dr Tillyard's. We need not assume that the reason why she acts on the same arguments later is that they have been working underground upon her passions; Milton does not decide for us; they have also been rationally supported by the discourse of Raphael.

It occurs rather often to Raphael that he is not sure how much God will allow him to tell (v. 570, vii. 120, viii. 175); this is to be expected from the emissary of a tyrant, and we need not blame him if the effect is to tempt them to speculate about God's intentions. But he has no doubt that he can give them a more practical piece of information at the start, while moralizing over his need and capacity to eat the fruit and nuts which Eve has provided. By the way, I do not know that anyone has answered the comment of Bentley on the passage: "If the devils need feeding, our author has made poor provision for them in his Second Book, where they have nothing to eat but Hell Fire, and no danger of their dinner cooling." One can't deny that Milton is careless on the point, but a reader who is troubled by it may conclude that God sustains the rebels by miracle, and thus deludes them into believing they have gained magical power. Otherwise the details about food are consistent with the Great Chain of Being; indeed we learn around xi. 50, when God is remarking innocently that Nature herself now compels Adam and Eve to leave Paradise, that before the Fall they had a less crude metabolism, and were perhaps actually better fitted to eat with Raphael than with ourselves. In any case, Raphael says:

time may come when men
With angels may participate, and find
No inconvenient Diet, nor too light Fare:

And from these corporal nutriments perhaps
Your bodies may at last turn all to Spirit,
Improv'd by tract of time, and wingd ascend
Ethereal, as wee, or may at choice
Here or in Heav'nly Paradises dwell;
If ye be found obedient . . . (v. 495)

The subject has been exhaustively discussed, but I think I am the first to point out the startling repetition of 'as wee', again surrounded by commas and given Milton's double 'E' for emphasis, only four hundred lines later. Eve is meant to prick up her ears at this, and so are we (a flashback would be needed in the film version); the voice of the mysterious dream and the spokesman of God are not merely saying the same thing (that God expects them to manage to get to Heaven, and that what they eat has something to do with it) but even using the same tricks of speech. We may be sure that Raphael does not know what Satan has whispered, because he is not wicked enough to cheat Eve in such a way; but it is merely a matter of theology that Milton's God has arranged the correspondence—all such accidents lie within his Providence. He has thus made it baffling for her to gauge his intentions.

Dr Tillyard, who was the first I think to point out that Milton scrutinizes the approach to the Fall like a novelist, remarked very fairly that the reason why she says she wants to 'work' apart from her husband is that she feels the need to flap her wings a bit; after hearing Raphael on her future expected début, she may well want to obtain a tiny change in her experience, and indeed could hardly be admired if she had no impulse to react at all. This then is why Satan can catch her alone. The critics who blame Adam for letting her go, after giving her every warning, seem to me to preach an immoral moral; certainly, Milton thought that men ought to control women, but that would make him feel all the more outraged when Eve turns round and blames Adam for having let her go. Adam merely behaves well there, as Dr Tillyard I think proves without quite meaning to.

Before following the story further, I must consider a point about Milton's intentions. He remarks in the 'argument' to Book V (my italics):

> God *to render man inexcusable* sends Raphael to admonish him of his obedience, of his free estate, of his enemy near at hand; who he is, and why his enemy, and whatever else may avail Adam to know.

This sounds like an exasperated confession that he has failed to justify God, and that M. Morand is right; but one needs to look for some other explanation. Perhaps the sentence feels harsh merely because of its order; after the first phrase it offers a rather liberal programme, but the tone has already been set as by the foreknowledge of God. The programme indeed is not fully carried out; Raphael does once let drop, in his lengthy discourses, that Satan "now is plotting how he may seduce" Adam (VI. 900), but he never once says the practical thing which would be really likely to prevent the Fall, that Satan is known to have reached the Garden and spoken to Eve in her sleep, and will probably soon address them again in disguise. God tells Raphael that Satan has already "disturb'd / This night the human pair", but does not tell him to tell them so (V. 230). We are told that God felt pity for them before giving this instruction to Raphael, and he reaffirms their free will in it; at the end of the speech he treats the visit as merely a legal precaution, but this order of presentation does not strike one as presuming throughout that they will fall:

this let him know,
Lest wilfully transgressing he pretend
Surprisal, unadmonisht, unforewarnd. (245)

Thus the 'argument' only gives a wrong summary in the words *near at hand*, which is not why it feels shocking. These prefaces were added a year after first publication, which meant some years after composing the poem (I see no reason to believe the theory that they were directives for the author composed beforehand); Milton might by then be regarding our parents more severely, with some forgetfulness of his poetic balance of judgement, or simply wanting to put more emphasis on the severity of God. Also he might want to insist that in giving a long reported narrative he had not merely imitated the epic formula but made it serve an important function. Even so, the brutal phrase is liable to excite the doubts of the justice of God with which he had so long wrestled, and might fairly be called a Freudian slip of the tongue.

However, as so often with Milton, fuller information brings in a mediating factor rather hard to allow for; the phrase has been explained as a reference to Romans i. 19-21. One might answer that the text is misapplied. St Paul is telling the Romans, adroitly enough, that Gentiles can be saved but also damned; God will punish them for unnatural behaviour (sodomy comes in further down) because they already know right from wrong by the natural law, even if without the help of the Gospel or the Mosaic Law. Such at least has long been the interpretation of his impressive but cloudy language. Calvin argued from this text that we derive no benefit from the manifestation of God in his works, but only further condemnation, because we are unable to discern from Nature what we ought to be able to; whereas a simpler view would be that the passage rather clears up the apparent injustice of God towards the Red Indians.

> Because that which may be known of God is manifest in them (marg. 'to them'); for God hath shewed it unto them. For the invisible things of him from the creation of the world are clearly seen, being understood by the things that are made, even his eternal power and godhead; so that they are without excuse.

On the face of it, St Paul is being liberal or at least philosophic, so that Milton cheats by applying the text to such a different case; but he may have found an interesting likeness. He consistently treats angels as very like men; now Adam and Eve, though created with the vast foreknowledge implied by their language, lack that 'experience of the world' which rather mysteriously teaches to a good character Natural Law; instead, then, they ought to have the experience of hearing about the affairs of Heaven, which are quite sufficiently rough. Raphael is not bearing an official message, because he doubts what he is allowed to tell; he acts like a gossip or a historian. His account of what happened to Satan, one may agree, ought to have taught Eve that God cannot be trusted to interpret a person's motives generously. Exactly what Natural Law may be, and whether it would tell you not to eat the apple, also whether it is the same as God's Grace which is the same as Right Reason, would strike Milton as the chief point of theoretical interest all along. Such I think is what pokes up its head behind the cool harshness of this bit of prose summary; he always did see all round the issues that were being raised. The explanation in a sense clears the good feeling of Milton, though necessarily not of God.

Ever since the development of monotheism Eve has been blamed for wanting to become a God, and Milton accepts that accusation against her from the text of Genesis, but his language is not arranged to vilify her for it much. We are told that Raphael has 'divine effulgence' just before he encourages Eve to try to get to Heaven; and God himself has called the angels Gods, though perhaps only to encourage them to become so in a special sense. Eve was not taught like us about the classical gods at school, and Milton affects to believe they were devils in disguise; thus, one way and another, he feels free to use the noun and adjective with the looseness natural to a linguist and historian. What Eve means by becoming a God, on the other hand, is quite specific; she means becoming able to do space-travel, like the modest angels whom she habitually hears singing (IV. 680); thus she says she wondered in the dream at "my flight *and change* / To this high exaltation" (V. 90). Milton added topical interest to the space-travel inherent in the story by repeatedly suggesting that there may be life on other planets; for example III. 565, 670; V. 260; VII. 620; VIII. 145, 175 and 150, where he also envisages other solar systems with inhabited planets. Various critics, feeling they ought to blame Eve in any way they can, have scorned her as a social climber trying to wangle an invite to Heaven. In any case, a Christian has no business to be too refined to try to go to Heaven; but also the reader is encouraged to feel, and Eve is twice positively told, that for her it is a straightforward matter of space-travel technique, rather like improving the ships till they could discover America. On the other hand, Professor Lewis finds it particularly bad of her to bow to the Tree after eating the apple:

> She who thought it beneath her dignity to bow to Adam or to God, now worships a vegetable. She has at last become 'primitive' in the popular sense.

But she bows "as to the power / That dwelt therein" (IX. 835); and Milton himself has to argue that the tree was sacred, when he is struggling in Chapter XI of the *De Doctrina* to justify God for punishing the whole of her posterity (p. 198). We may be content, I think, to blame her for disobedience only.

Another echo of Satan by Raphael concerns the phrase 'thought himself impaired', which C. S. Lewis used as a kind of slogan to sum up the case against Satan. Raphael says it around V. 660, in his description of the angels' revolt, and does of course mean that Satan fell through pride and envy. But Satan had whispered to Eve in her dream, shortly before,

> *And why not Gods of Men, since good, the more*
> *Communicated, more abundant grows;*
> *The Author not impair'd, but honourd more?* (V. 70)

When the accredited Raphael tells Eve that Satan is despised in Heaven for this grudging impulse, she may naturally conclude that it cannot also actuate God; the argument of the mysterious voice is again confirmed. But God does think himself impaired when she eats the apple, unless indeed he only pretends to, for some political motive. Milton insists ruthlessly throughout the poem, whenever he pronounces about the motives of God, even when the incidental effects might be described as good, that God acted for his own glory. Indeed, he gives Satan a powerful joke about this in *Paradise Regained*, after the Saviour has rejected glory out of contempt for mankind,

Of whom to be dispraised were no small praise. (III. 55)

Therein least
Resembling thy great Father; he seeks glory (III. 110)

and so on through a very damaging speech. It is an intelligible view that God cannot work except for his own glory, because he includes all value in himself; but this makes it hard to feel that both Eve and Satan deserved all their punishments because they too wanted glory. They had been taught in a hard school.

Among the possible influences on her mind we should also consider the refusal of Raphael to explain astronomy, early in Book VIII. It is true that she has left the table at the end of his narrative, before the males begin general discussion, but we are told she will hear about it from Adam (50) and she admits later to overhearing some of it (IX. 275). Dr Tillyard pointed out that the effect on the reader is splendidly architectural; he has been flying to Heaven and Hell, but now he finds himself confined to earth and the domestic drama of one couple. This is very fine, but Adam and Eve would feel it differently. At lunch the angel practically offered them their wings, and towards evening he sharply refuses to answer a question relevant to way-finding, which is asked by Adam as soon as the narrative is concluded. Adam accepts the snub with adroit good humour, but they are bound to feel it as another bit of calculated bafflement. Raphael then suggests that God made astronomy difficult so as to be able to jeer at astronomers. He describes the Copernican controversy, refusing to tell the answer, for another hundred lines.

Mr Grant McColley, in his survey of the sources, gives quotations to show that the speech echoes a book by Wilkins, expressing belief in life on other planets, and also a pious rebuttal by an Alexander Ross (*The New Planet No Planet*, 1646). Thus the material was more than twenty years old when Milton published. Mr McColley remarks that Wilkins, and other scientists such as Oldenburg, had been on good terms with Cromwell but readily made their peace with Charles at the Restoration; he deduces that Milton had wanted to attack the new astronomy earlier, on religious grounds, but had been afraid of irritating his master. Thus Milton felt liberated by the Restoration on this issue:

> he was a human being who now was untrammelled by considerations which not unfrequently have softened the utterances of mankind. (p. 322)

Milton appears very mean-minded in this account, but we should not deduce that Mr McColley is too. He may be a freethinker who expects Puritans to be narrow, or a neo-Christian who thinks it a religious duty to prove that seventeenth-century poets hated and despised science, imputing bad motives for a high spiritual purpose. I have to admit that Milton ascribes almost all our technical skills to the devils—Mr Werblowsky (op. cit.) is very good on the psychological background of this tradition; but Milton may have found it useful for his poem without being obsessed by its psychology. The idea that he disapproved of believing in life on other planets, I think, is refuted by his repeated gratuitous suggestion of it—"but who dwelt happy there / He stayd not to inquire" (III. 570)—every time he takes an interest in one of the space-trips required by his story. His theological position removed some of the reasons for disapproving of it, and we have no evidence that he did; we only know that he toys with it readily. What does seem peculiar about the discourse of Raphael is that he does not mention the halfway theory of Tycho Brahe, which still held the field, on the existing evidence, at the date of publication. But it was wrong, and Milton would deserve praise if he felt that no halfway theory could satisfy the mind, or at any rate his own very all-or-none mind. The subject was still in a muddle, and we need not blame Milton for sticking to the old sharp alternatives; we do not know that he had any narrow motive for it. All he required for his poem was a snub for presumption, and while supplying that he positively insinuated that there is more in the universe than we know.

It seems only fair to distinguish between Milton and his God; I readily agree that his God does appear mean-minded. Alexander Ross did not say that God would laugh, only that anybody would laugh, if he read the rival astronomers. The heroic labours of seventeenth-century astronomers were considered often to blind them, chiefly because Galileo went blind when very old; and Milton considered that he too had been driven blind by devoted work in another field. A certain puckish humour is being aimed at all through Book VIII, but Milton must have been aware that even this echo of a joke by God carries the same Quilp-like malignity as his actual jokes in the poem. Also, the long description of the alternative theories is likely to drive the curiosity of our parents in the direction which Raphael forbids. Here again, a detached observer may blame Eve for not deducing that God must be very ungenerous, but Milton could hardly blame her for continuing to trust him. Her own generous mind would lead her to think that, though perhaps rather nasty, he cannot be quite so nasty as she is being persistently told; well then, he must be trailing his coat, and wanting her to display her courage. A bullfighter of course does praise a bull if it is brave, but he means to kill it anyhow.

I do not have to deny that she is confronted at the crisis with a variety of arguments, some of them less worthy than others. She is typically a woman in that her decision is intuitive; at least, Milton would hardly have said so, because it was angels who were intuitive, meaning that their minds worked too fast to need the discursive reason (not always, v. 490); but Eve is intuitive in the modern sense that she lumps the arguments together and cannot afterwards pick out the one that decided her. Nowadays a critic is expected to pick it out, thus defining his position; but probably Milton would have said that she did not know, any more than all we critics do. I think it was the following argument of the serpent:

will God incense his ire
For such a petty trespass, and not praise
Rather your dauntless virtue, whom the pain
Of Death denounc't, whatever thing Death be,
Deterred not from achieving what might lead
To happier life, knowledge of Good and Evil? (IX. 695)

That is, she feels the answer to this elaborate puzzle must be that God wants her to eat the apple, since what he is really testing is not her obedience but her courage, also whether her desire to get to Heaven is real enough to call all her courage out. I think this the most likely motive because it is the most sublime, thus again following the principle of Mr Rajan that the characteristic virtue of the poem is sublimity.

The thought, indeed, is not prominent in her soliloquy just before she eats; if it had been, Milton would have had to call her justified. Instead, she has moved on to feel a certain impatience with the God who has set her such a difficult puzzle about his intentions; but this is very understandable, once you admit that she recognizes them as a puzzle.

In plain then, what forbids he but to know,
Forbids us good, forbids us to be wise?
Such prohibitions bind not. (760)

This means that you ought not to obey a God if your conscience tells you that his orders are wrong; and that, if your God then sends you to Hell for disobeying him, you were still right to have obeyed your conscience. Any Christian missionary might find himself saying this when wrestling for the soul of a pagan, and a critic who jeers at it seems to me simply immoral. Nor does Eve take the further step of deciding that her God must be bad; if she did that, she might fairly be blamed for impatience and perhaps for disloyalty, in jumping ahead of the evidence before her. As so often in human affairs, her problem is one of Inverse Probability. Thus a candidate in an Intelligence Test often has to think 'Which answer is the tester likely to have thought the intelligent one?', and this tends to make him irritated with the whole test. In this case, if God is good, that is, if he is the kind of teacher who wants to produce an independent-minded student, then he will love her for eating the apple; her solution of the problem will be correct because she has understood his intention. But if he didn't mean that, then he has behaved rather queerly, and it doesn't appear that he deserves to be obeyed; for one thing, he hasn't even behaved as generously as the Serpent, who might have been tempted to use his new powers to contrive equality with mankind (770). If one considers intermediate hypotheses about the character of God, the penalties he has threatened are at least extremely vague, or even unknown.

Hence, on any hypothesis, considering that God himself admits that eating the apple would provide something they need (755), to eat it is probably the best thing to do.

C. S. Lewis said truly enough that the poem's moral of obedience has the 'desolating clarity' of what we were taught in the nursery, adding that he cannot understand why modern scholars have missed it; but he also insisted very finely that we are not to regard Adam and Eve as ignorant savages—nor, therefore, as children. I too think that children should be taught to obey, and consider that the fashion has swung rather too far against smacking them; but Milton knew very well that if he had punished his own children for a trivial act of disobedience as God proposes to do here he would be lucky if he were taken to jail, because that would protect him from the just anger of his neighbours. We keep being told nowadays about the deep belief of the seventeenth century in the natural hierarchy; but Milton had not got the legal power to kill his children held by an Ancient Roman, and even those famous aristocrats regarded torture as only applicable to slaves, so that they too would not be allowed by their fellows to torture their children indefinitely. One expects the morality of a God to be archaic, but this God seems to be wickeder than any recorded society. The myth might indeed be justified as a warning that Nature is unjust, for example when innocent actions give us shocking diseases; but Milton insists that there was no magic about the apple, and that it was chosen by God as a random test of obedience. A father may reasonably impose a random prohibition to test the character of his children, but anyone would agree that he should then judge an act of disobedience in the light of its intention. Still more is this true of adult and responsible characters, because they ought to be expected, indeed have to be expected, to interpret an order rationally. It is an intelligible view about kids, though a very wild one, that if they have been told to stay in bed they ought to do it even though the house is burning down; because somebody is always responsible for looking after them, and they are less bother in a crisis if they don't rush about. A similar view is often taken of soldiers, and the boy who stood on the burning deck satisfied both criteria. But this is evidently an unsuitable way to treat Adam and Eve, as they point out themselves; indeed Milton would feel he was restoring dignity to mankind, as he went on imagining their speeches, by showing how very marginal the original ground of our fall had been. I admit that Eve herself claims to be something like a child at the moment before she falls, that is, she claims a justification from her admitted ignorance of good and evil; but that powerful stroke from the mind of Milton is in a way a very adult thing for her to do. I cannot think it morally wise for pious critics to try to turn this against her:

> *What fear I then? Rather, what know to fear*
> *Under this ignorance of good and evil,*
> *Of God or Death, of law or penalty?*
> *Here grows the cure of all, this fruit divine . . .* (775)

That is, she does not know the moral sanction behind this law, or even the meaning of the repeated obscure threats of a penalty. You might think that nothing needed 'curing' in Paradise, but she has already protested that it is too miserable to live in such terror of the unknown that they dare not spend half an hour apart. 'Divine' need only mean 'teaching divinity'. It seems to me odd of Dr Tillyard, whom I greatly revere for his work on Milton, to have described this turn of thought as 'triviality of mind'.

The effect of the speech is simply that she decides she *ought* to eat the apple, think God what he may.

One of the most difficult parts of the assignment Milton had set himself was to make it credible that she would eat the apple at all, after he had turned the figures of the briefly recorded myth into high-minded intelligent characters. Nothing happens in Eve's life except pleasure and being warned not to eat the apple, so how can she do it without appearing fatuous? The point was cleared accidentally by C. S. Lewis, while rebuking us for our modern notions; we ought not to think of her as 'primitive', he said, but as a great lady, the ambassadress of mankind. Yes indeed, but more; as a medieval great lady, for example Eleanor of Aquitaine who was Queen both of England and of a French Court of Love. A puritan disapproved of these powerful females, including the Queen of Heaven; but they were still felt to be staggeringly grand, and Milton was set to turn all human culture into an expression of the grandeur of the Fall. A modern reader tends to have the same mixed feelings as the author; we can understand well enough that he was not merely vilifying Eve when he depicted her so. She thinks: 'The reason why all the males keep on saying I mustn't eat the apple, in this nerve-wracking way, is obviously that they are longing for me to do it; this is the kind of thing they need a queen to have the nerve to do'; so she does it. It is a splendid bit of invention by Milton; true to life, and the only way to make sense of her story; and he makes her later behaviour support it. In effect, she presumes that God will love her for eating the apple, at any rate later on, when he has realized that that was what he had wanted her to do at bottom. So he would have done if he had been better, but the story is that he gives nearly all her descendants eternal torture for it.

M. Morand, who first drew attention to the curious effect of the visit of Raphael, deserves all the more credit because he finds difficulty in imagining the lady his argument requires; indeed, he seems to have been written off by the English and Americans as a cynical Frenchman. He revolts at the phrase 'virgin majesty' for this honeymoon figure, and finds that '*le lecteur peut rester perplexe*' about the sexual pleasures of Paradise; these are '*fautes de gout*', indeed '*nous sommes gènés par le côté didactique et toute une lourdeur bourgeoise dont le jeune poète etait bien loin*'. The young poet, he means, had been both celibate and untainted by Government propaganda. Cardinal Newman had felt the same, and perhaps Mr T. S. Eliot was echoing Newman on the point in his essay of 1936; so we need not think that M. Morand was being peculiarly French about the matter in 1939; it was just part of the anti-romantic movement. The praise of licit sex in the poem feels to me a splendid bit of nerve, so that I am only amused by critics who boast of being embarrassed there and call love bourgeois. Having been irritated in this way, M. Morand jeers at her savagely when she pleads to work alone: '*C'est là une bien petite creature qui juge ainsi, une très petite femme banale, sans jugement*' (p. 187). But his sense of justice is all the more outraged at the intellectual difficulty of the problem with which God confronts this fool, so that his build-up of hissing contempt greatly adds to the drama when she wins him over. At the moment of the Fall he becomes convinced, having considered the alternatives before her, that she decides nobly like Prometheus for the ultimate benefit of mankind: '*il n'y a donc pas sottise ou vanité de sa part à accepter ce but*'. We should salute M. Morand, and respect his earlier hesitation, when he steps out and restores the natural dignity of the Mother of Mankind.

This praise is also deserved by Dr Tillyard. The most important gain for my own understanding of the poem from his work on it, and probably for many people though we should be ashamed at having needed to be told, is to recognize the central splendour of the speech of pleading by Eve (X. 920) which wins back Adam and secures the reproduction of mankind. Critics used to be fond of saying that Milton was gloating in the passage over how he had humiliated his first wife, when she begged to return to him, after it had become plain that her royalist family was on the losing side in the Civil War. The idea is probably not false, but then the drama of that scene might well grow afterwards in his mind; to think he was merely satisfying an old grudge ceases to be entertaining when you realize what the speech achieves in the story. It is true that Adam has just been expressing the most extravagant hatred of women in all Milton's work. He says 'It spoils everything to have women about, and why should God saddle *us* with them? Angels don't get distracted by females.' Milton had experienced such feelings, but he is dramatic when he puts the wildest tantrum just before the overwhelming answer. Compared to this victory through the generosity of a woman, all the nagging against women in Milton, though much the best reason why so many people dislike him, reduces to a family grumble.

To talk about Eve's dignity will not appease those who dislike Milton for unvarying pomposity, so I had better recall the purpose of writing an epic. The Greeks liked to say that they had learned all their virtues from Homer, and the Renaissance deduced that each modern nation needed an epic of its own to live nobly. Milton thought that the English no longer deserved a patriotic epic, but badly needed making nobler somehow. It was thus of the first importance not to let us think meanly of our first parents, or even of the hand by which they fell; they could be made to argue absurdly, but must always keep a certain rock-bottom splendour. This indeed was a practical reason why the epic had to treat the justice of God as hard to defend. On the other hand, the stock accusation of pomposity of style, too Latinized to be able to give body-feeling or a natural movement of thought, cannot be made at all against this appeal by Eve.

Forsake me not thus, Adam, witness Heav'n
What love sincere, and reverence in my heart
I bear thee, and unweeting have offended,
Unhappily deceiv'd; thy suppliant
I beg, and clasp thy knees; bereave me not,
Whereon I live, thy gentle looks, thy aid,
Thy counsel in this uttermost distress,
My only strength and stay: forlorn of thee,
Whither shall I betake me, where subsist?
While yet we live, scarce one short hour perhaps,
Between us two let there be peace, both joining,
As join'd in injuries, one enmity
Against a Foe by doom express assign'd us,
That cruel Serpent: On me exercise not
Thy hatred for this misery befall'n,
On me already lost, mee than thyself
More miserable; both have sin'd, but thou
Against God only, I against God and thee,
And to the place of judgement will return,
There with my cries importune Heaven, that all
The sentence from thy head remov'd may light
On me, sole cause to thee of all this woe,
Mee mee only just object of his ire.

One might think it a tiny point in favour of Milton's God that he lets this count as repentance, though it contains nothing to gratify his vanity; but Adam, though his heart is melted, begins his answer by treating the speech as further ground for rebuke, and only gradually argues his way to the correct solution, which is prostration before God; so Milton intends it to be clear that God would not regard her as repentant until Adam had re-directed her impulses. He begins:

> *Unwary, and too desirous, as before*
> *So now of what thou knowst not, who desir'st*
> *The punishment all on thyself; alas,*
> *Bear thine own first, ill able to sustain*
> *His full wrath whose thou feelst as yet least part,*
> *And my displeasure bearst so ill. If Prayers*
> *Could alter high decrees, I to that place*
> *Would speed before thee, and be louder heard,*
> *That on my head all might be visited,*
> *Thy frailty and infirmer Sex forgiv'n,*
> *To me committed and by me expos'd.*

It was all right, as literary criticism goes, for C. S. Lewis to discover that Eve envisages murdering Adam as soon as she has eaten the apple, but the same searchlight ought also to be turned upon her husband. His immediate determination to beat her at the new game of generosity, despising her for not enduring his displeasure, even accusing her of greediness for trying to get ahead of him, and assuring her he can shout her down, is likeable of Adam but just as fit to be called satire by Milton as anything said by Eve. M. Saurat remarked, with so much depth that he too almost deserves the title of restoring the dignity of the Mother of Mankind:

> Here Milton happily forgets his theories of the predominance of reason, and the influence of 'female charm' on Adam is this time his salvation.

Very true, except that we have no reason to think Milton had forgotten. It is the high point of his structure that Adam and Eve recover sufficiently to decide to produce the race of man in spite of their Fall. Yet her first repentance is towards Adam only, and she regards God as someone she might badger till he let Adam off; it is all God's fault really because he assigned them the serpent by 'doom express', she remarks with much truth. Hence it is important to realize, as various critics have remarked, that there is a total absence of heavenly aid at this crucial point. Milton had come to insist, as against the Calvinists, that our nature was not totally corrupted by the Fall, but I do not think this entailed believing that we can ever do good except by Divine Grace. He makes the Son remark, while rejoicing over the repentance of Adam and Eve, that God's 'implanted Grace' in man is already producing fruit (XI. 25). It is thus presented as like a seed, presumed to grow by itself after being planted; both God's grace and his curse act in a kind of biological way. Indeed this may explain why the Son made the tactless remark that God sends his Grace to 'all his creatures', not only to mankind (III. 230). The belief has a decisively good effect on the literary technique. If the melting of Eve begins the solution of the whole drama, ordinary Christian sentiment would expect at least a Guardian Angel at work; and, from the point of view of imitating Homer, it is positively breach of epic formula to have no divine intervention. Eve is never more absolutely alone, and it seems clear that any other treatment would have been painfully unconvincing. Sir Walter Raleigh said that Milton could not have brought a child into *Paradise Lost*, because one sensible remark would have destroyed the whole crazy piece of engineering; and it is true that the thought of a mind like Milton's having anything to do with a child is rather painful. But he was enabled to get something near the effect by his conception of Woman.

This, I think, is also the way to understand his treatment of the innocence of both Eve and Adam. C. S. Lewis, in the course of maintaining that the poem is not heretical, gave a useful summary of the position of St Augustine about sex before the Fall. The saint decided that the erection of the male organ was then under direct control of the will, and therefore could have been performed sinlessly, although for other reasons it was not. Milton was thus not essentially wrong, though no doubt tactless and so forth, when he presented our parents as actually making love without sin. I think that, as God tells them to multiply before the Fall in Genesis i. 28, the Saint's insistence upon their chastity was a slanderous accusation of disobedience. But Augustine is in another much deeper heresy about the conditions of life, because the spontaneity of a sexual emotion is like that of any other, love towards God for example. The sexual condition he considers holy is that of an acrobatic prostitute; naturally enough, because he believes his own salvation to depend on being able to turn on his love for God 'with a tap' (as the limerick says), however appalled he may become at the behaviour of this God. But to achieve that degree of saintliness would only make his love not worth having. The independence of our feelings from our will, which he regards as the essence of being fallen, is our basic protection against the lethal convictions which so often capture our brains. If Milton had presented Adam and Eve as 'self-controlled' to this extent they would have seemed like insects and been unable to fall. In any case, he could not have presented them so, because he accepted enlightened views of the relations of soul and body. The idea that he fakes the Fall a bit, by making our parents rather fallen from the start, may make readers think but underrates the depth of his treatment; or perhaps one need not call 'deep' what an Elizabethan playwright and a modern novelist take for granted, but Milton had theoretical support for it.

Adam and Eve had to be spontaneous even before their Fall, because a chain of partly rational 'spirits' with a partly independent life are always at work in mankind relating soul to body; and this was not an upsetting discovery, because matter was part of God from which God had willingly removed his will. The doctrine was part of the confused challenge of Paracelsus, which had made a great flutter, so that Milton had no need to search the *Zohar* for it. He treats this view of matter as basic to his whole position, and probably came to do so when he broke with Calvinism by denying that Total Depravity is entailed upon us by Original Sin. Mr Walter Pagel's treatise (*Paracelsus*, 1958) struck me as full of echoes of the problems raised by Milton:

> Until the nineteenth century, Paracelsus was charged with 'Arian and Gnostic heresy'. Pantheistic speculation is indeed evident in his idea that the 'virtues' and 'arcana' in Nature are direct emanations from divinity and 'uncreated' (p. 42). There is a distinct materialistic ring about Paracelsus' concept of higher and lower soul—which are in need of food: 'For leaven and ferment are Christ, and verbum domini is the word of the father that has become matter and is the material food of the soul' (p. 118). It was a gnostic thought that the soul of the world flows constantly into us with our food, for it is the same soul that dwells in plants, animals, and men. The idea that man 'is what he eats' is Paracelsan (p. 208).

So far from wondering where Paracelsus could get such ideas, Mr Pagel finds them rather hard to distinguish from the 'popular pantheism' of the Middle Ages. This, he thinks, came from the monistic theory of Stoicism and was transmitted by Salomo ibn Gebirol, whose work was recognized by Europeans early in the thirteenth century (p. 230). I feel more at home when learning that Bruno in a philosophical dialogue of 1584 quoted Gebirol

> first together with Democritus and the Epicureans as the authority for the assertion that matter is the only substance of things and at the same time the divine essence . . . the fountain of all being and becoming which sends forth the forms from its bosom—an eternal principle, a divine virtue (p. 232).

Bruno was setting out to praise the views of Paracelsus, whom he called 'medicorum princeps'; and Milton could hardly ignore Bruno, because he had been martyred by Rome.

A literary reader such as myself finds the love-poetry of Donne unique for its paradoxes about the relations of soul and body, and is rather unwilling to regard them as commonplaces of his time. Surely they were at least 'advanced', if not 'left-wing'. The young Donne is uneasy about his mystical doctrine, sure that it is an important truth somehow but also that it is hard to fit into respectable theology, and therefore needs witty paradoxes. But it was only the sexual implications of the doctrine which the love-poets felt might become embarrassing; Spenser has the same earnestness, together with the same uneasiness, about his 'sensuous idealism'. The mere belief that soul and body are related by a subtle hierarchy of 'spirits', so that their relations are complex, was one that Donne felt free to expound in sermons; as Grierson pointed out in his great edition (1912; Vol. II, p. 45). The N.E.D. gives the first use of 'materialism' as Restoration, no doubt in opposition to Hobbes; the position of Milton had perhaps come to seem bolder than when he was young by the time he published *Paradise Lost*, but it was not complained of till long afterwards.

Nowadays pious authors take for granted that materialism is the bad thing, whereas everything spiritual is good; thus any religion, Thuggee for example, would be better than none. But Marlowe in *Faustus* treats the word 'spirit' as meaning a devil; for example the tempter tells Faustus, "Thou art a spirit; God cannot pity thee." In the same way, a modern reader tends to feel that the confusion of matter and spirit in *Paradise Lost* is part of the general bogusness of Milton's style; but after you have defined spirit as a subtle form of matter, as at any rate Lucretius had done, it is not contradictory to continue to use the word with that meaning. The modern pious use of 'materialism' and 'spirituality', which involves such a gross distortion of human experience, would have been considered mere ignorance in the seventeenth century. I grant that if you translate this use of *materialist* as 'selfish' the sentence usually makes sense, but then, it often tells a lie.

Dr Tillyard said in his *Milton* (1930) that, if Milton had been in the Garden, he would have eaten the apple at once and written a pamphlet to prove that it was his duty. This has always seemed to me very profound; but Dr Tillyard repented of it, and the chapter 'Adam and Eve in Paradise' of his *Studies in Milton* (1952) gives the rather beautiful spectacle of a man trying to expunge his joke without making the tactical error of repeating it. His very thorough reading in Milton publications was perhaps what made him tired of such remarks; indeed,

Studies in Milton gives the only reference I have found to the work of M. Morand, though with no reference to its thesis (I found the work itself because M. Morand presented it to Sheffield University, having taught there earlier). They were going to have children anyway, Dr Tillyard sensibly pointed out, and the spectacle of their honeymoon is no reason for supposing that if they hadn't fallen they would have become bored. Thus Raphael's first words to Eve are "Hail, Mother of Mankind", and he tells her that her sons will fill the world (v. 385). Michael, while nagging Adam about the results of the Fall, says that he might have had all future generations coming to pay him their respects at his capital seat in Paradise (XI. 345). The generous imagination of C. S. Lewis was stirred by this picture of Adam as the reality of which our Kings and Popes are a pale shadow, reminded perhaps of the Chief Selenite in *The First Men in the Moon*; it is clear from the word *generations* that the rest of us would still be dying, out of courtesy to our children, as we do now, whereas Adam could last on without public inconvenience. But surely, all we learn from these remarks is what use the two angels make of their briefing by God when they speak to mankind. Michael is a pig about it, whereas the affable Raphael is embarrassed; but both of them have heard God say beforehand (III. 95) that the Fall is certain, therefore no great weight need be attached to their estimates of the alternative. The third quotation given by Dr Tillyard is the operative one, from the speech by God to the loyal angels after the rebels have been evicted, in which he announces that he will at once create the world (VII. 150). This announcement (though reported to us later in the poem) was made about ten days earlier than the speech of God in Book III, when he sees Satan approaching the newly created world and prophesies the Fall. Raphael, when he is sent to exhort Adam and Eve to stand firm, has just recently heard the speech of Book III, which made clear that his work can have no use except 'to render Man inexcusable'; no wonder he seems rather oddly anxious not to let drop anything he mustn't tell them, because is it an essential part of his assignment not to tell them that they are certain to fall. God has set him an extremely unpleasant bit of work here, which more than anything recalls the earlier loyal activities, presented in a flash-back from before his imprisonment, of the hero of *Darkness at Noon.*

I grant that the speech of God in Book VII, as Raphael reports it, appears not to expect the Fall. It is fair to reflect that, if God had then said he foresaw it, Raphael could not have reported his speech to Adam and Eve in full. However, the reader is no doubt expected to believe the report, and it is dramatically convincing. God makes the speech 'beholding the multitude' who have just returned from pursuing the rebels into the deep, and the good angels sing in praise of it, so though addressed to the Son it must be intended for them to overhear. To be sure, he remarks, many angels have joined Satan in trying to dethrone me, but 'at least' he has failed; "far the greater part have kept, I see, / Their stations", says God, looking coolly round as if he hadn't bothered to inquire before (the two-thirds rule of course makes the statement correct); anyhow, enough of them are left to do the only essential thing, that is, perform incessant ceremonial songs and dances to praise himself. Satan indeed has carried off quite a lot of them,

But lest his heart exalt him in the harm
Already done, to have dispeopl'd Heav'n,
My damage fondly deem'd, I can repair

That detriment, if such it be to lose
Self-lost, and in a moment will create
Another world, out of one man a Race
Of men innumerable, there to dwell,
Not here, till by degrees of merit rais'd
They open to themselves at length the way
Up hither, under long obedience tried,
And Earth be chang'd to Heav'n, and Heav'n to Earth,
One Kingdom, Joy and Union without end. (VII. 150)

As usual, God is struggling to make the necessary excuses without admitting that there is anything to excuse; we would find the absurdity more obvious if we were not so accustomed to hear it from our own political leaders. The theory that he doesn't yet know mankind are going to fall is an attractive way to read the passage; one must add that he does know it immediately after he has created them (III. 95). The change could only come because he knows he has created them badly, and this would explain his explosive resentment against Adam ('Ingrate!') before Adam has fallen. The irritation of an artist against a bad piece of his own workmanship is a sympathetic thing, and would be one of the few decent feelings ever allowed to God by Milton, even though farcically unjust. I think he might have put it in 'unconsciously', in the sense that to imagine the detailed behaviour throughout a dramatic narrative of a person with absolute foreknowledge is inherently impossible; but there is no need to accuse Milton of any slip here. If God had admitted to the angels that all but a tiny remnant of his creation would be captured by Satan, it would not have sounded such a clever way to get the better of Satan, but rather a way of reinforcing him. It may be thought that God has no duty to do propaganda, but in his last scene he says himself that he has. Summon all angels, he says, to hear what I will do to fallen man:

from them I will not hide
My judgements, how with Mankind I proceed,
As how with peccant angels late they saw;
And in their state, though firm, stood more confirm'd. (XI. 70)

He will not admit that they were not firm, but says it was right to make them firmer. In the speech before creation he seems to run into a more urgent problem; 'not here' is thrown in with hurried decisiveness because he can see that the angels are becoming restive again about the hierarchical issue which has already cost him a third of them. To have a lot of earthly men put over their heads would be too much even for the loyalists; indeed one might think, were God capable of a shadow of turning, that this was the moment when he decided that mankind must fall. Such is the only intelligible effect of *not here*; however he reconciled it with his theology, Milton imagines God to make up his speech as he goes along by estimating the reaction of his audience, as Satan does, and as Mr Eliot thought Satan could not do. When God goes on to claim that he hasn't lost anything really because it is only 'self-lost', that is, lost by his own unreasonableness and bad temper, he fits exactly the Lewis description of Satan, which Satan does not till late in the poem. However, what God goes on to say about the future of mankind cannot be called either false or ignorant; like most official language it is evasive, but the reassurance it gives on the urgent hierarchical issue is not misleading; nor is the speech even timid, as the unpopular programme of eventual 'union' is still put forward at the end. To realize that it secretly envisages the Fall, we may interpret the grammar as 'they will not come here *unless* they have passed long tests' or as 'only *some* of them will pass their tests'; I think both feel natural and combine to give enough suggestion of the truth. Only a tiny proportion of mankind will get to Heaven, so the angels need not be upset; but God does not care to say so outright because he also needs to boast against Satan. This at any rate makes the speech hold water, whereas Dr Tillyard's view has to deny the foreknowledge of God. What would have happened if Adam and Eve had irritated God by refusing to do what he foreknew is too horrible to imagine.

We cannot help feeling a baffled desire to know what Milton thought about it all himself, though the main answer has to be that he had trained his mind to see all round the question. One important answer has been given by the splendid detective work of Sewell on the manuscript of the *De Doctrina*; at the time when Milton was writing the poem, his beliefs were coming so near to the position taken by Eve that it is actually hard to say where he thought he differed from her. When Dr Tillyard made his joke, he did not realize that it was literally true; I expect indeed that having read Sewell (1939) helped eventually, by a noble paradox, to make him decide to renounce it. Milton had come to believe that even a Jew living before Christ did not literally have to obey the Mosaic Law, though God had pronounced it specially for the Jews; clearly then, Adam and Eve did not literally have to obey the apple prohibition made specially for them, either. This makes even greater nonsense of the assertion by God 'Die he or justice must'.

As one would expect, the idea feels less startling when expressed in its own technical terms. Milton had long believed that the modern Elect do not literally have to obey the Word of God, including the Ten Commandments, though they must attach great importance to it as their defence against human traditions, such as those of Rome. Even Rome agreed that the new dispensation of Christ had fulfilled the Law by the Gospel. But the texts in which Jesus speaks in favour of the Law were found hard to get round, and the Old Testament was the sanction, especially among Puritans, for such duties as Sabbath-keeping and maltreatment of witches; thus the firmness with which the earlier Milton argued our freedom from it might already seem bold. On the Sewell interpretation of the manuscript, the blind man never made a final revision all through, because the labour would only have been worth while for publication, which remained impossible; thus we get his earlier view in Chapter IV, where he says that salvation was offered "under the condition of obedience in the Old Testament, and of faith in the New". About the time of the Fall of the Commonwealth, he was saying in Chapter XV that

> Jews and others who lived before Christ, and many also who have lived since his time, but to whom he has not been revealed, should be saved by faith in God alone.

It had long been thought, as seems natural, that Milton allowed considerable latitude to the individual conscience in his early Divorce Pamphlets but became 'legalistic' during and after the Fall of the Commonwealth, in the grim mood when he turned to his epic. We now find that his mind did not react so obviously, and that he turned to his highest fling of theoretical generosity at the time of despair when there was nothing left to describe but the Fall of Man. Thus in the *Treatise of Civil Power* (1659) he is saying

> if we be not free we are not sons, but still servants adopted; and if we turn again to those weak and

> beggarly rudiments [such as 'Thou shalt not kill'] we are not free; yea though willingly and with an unrequired conscience we desire to be in bondage to them.

A reader of Sewell is tempted to take a less high-minded view, and say that Milton became tolerant just then, not because his mind was so wonderfully unexpected, but because he was afraid of being persecuted himself; and he must have reflected that he might save his life by taking ship to America, as some of the regicides actually did, so that the fling of theory in favour of the Red Indians becomes intelligible. The answer is that he was bringing out pamphlets so fast that he was almost like a modern 'columnist'; and to go on printing such things meant practically asking for death when Charles II was restored. The increasing fierceness of the writing makes clear enough that he expected the Restoration.

Sewell writes very well, so far as I can judge, about the generosity and moral depth of this phase of Milton's work, in which he conceives of the State of Grace as one which makes man entirely free, as a son not a servant of God, because it is "a reconciliation between man and God whereby man's understanding should be illuminated and his will enfranchised by a knowledge of the nature of God, or of spiritual things" (p. 213). Yes indeed, but this position, which Sewell has eloquently illustrated (from p. 192) with quotations from the Cambridge Platonists (whom Milton would not only know about but probably have to hear preaching to Parliament as part of his official duty), shows all the time by the choice of subtle grammar for its expression that it is an attempt to dissolve God into Goodness itself, instead of letting him be an archaic personal tyrant who issues laws. Sewell is echoing the style of the Cambridge Platonists when he writes "knowledge of the nature of God, or of spiritual things"; what they really meant by God is almost precisely what Fielding meant by the good impulses of Tom Jones. Milton is following this, instead of forgetting his principles as M. Saurat thought, when he makes Eve give her decisive speech of repentance without any epic machinery.

He thus believed when he wrote the poem that Eve would have been justified if she had eaten the apple with sufficient faith that God wanted her to do it, in spite of God's repeated instructions to the contrary. This would make Milton less likely to describe her as falling through triviality; and his account can only blame her, I think, for trusting Goodness rather than God, one side of the divine nature rather than the other. She does indeed take a rather petulant tone towards God, but only (so to speak) if he is not good. There is a lack of tact in the presence of the All-Knowing, but Milton could not seriously regard this as enough reason for the appalling consequences to all mankind.

It has been remarked that Milton went almost straight on from finishing *Paradise Lost* to starting *Paradise Regained* or *Samson Agonistes* (which were published together), so that there is little reason to expect a change of mind in between. But Sewell seems plainly right in saying that Milton abandoned his struggle towards a humanistic attitude in that brief interval. Milton no longer feels in *Samson*, as he nearly does in describing Eve, that your own conscience must come first; he now feels that you must do whatever God inspires you to think his will, however bad the rest of your conscience tells you this action to be. Considering how many crimes have been committed by fanaticism, the distinction is a practical one. Sewell never seems to realize how striking his conclusions are, but I think the epic feels much better if you accept them. They amount to saying that Milton drove himself into a corner when he settled down to imagine the Fall of Eve, and found the result profoundly disturbing.

We should now be able to reconsider the echoes of the advice of Satan in the advice of Raphael. Milton would design the parallel as part of the structure of the epic, and would expect it to produce dramatic ironies; their first business is to affect the readers, and he might well not consider how they would affect the evidence confronting Eve. Still, it is not clear how they should affect the readers, either. We ought to be imagining the dramatic story; and the echoes are pointless unless one sees them as evidence—that is why most readers ignore them. However, as has been well known since the ancient Greeks, to leave dramatic ironies lying about is a powerful means of giving an Atmosphere of 'sinister fatality' or what not; it derives from actual belief in Fate but is not thought of so definitely. Milton might therefore use it without feeling much responsibility for it; but, as soon as these echoes are allowed to mean anything, they are a striking addition to the grim and oppressive picture of the plans of his God. Though capable of humbug in a good cause, Milton was impatient of humbug; he is not likely to have hidden from himself what the echoes implied.

Chapter 5

ADAM

I AM next to consider the Fall of Adam, which has long been considered very defensible; here most readers would agree, probably, that Milton intended to heighten the moral paradox or present the Fall as partly noble. There is not much to discuss about the incident itself, so that what Adam thinks about its effects on his children, and what Milton thinks, are the main topics for the chapter.

The poetry ascribed to Adam on first learning that Eve has fallen is a private reflection and not spoken to her, perhaps because he will not boast to her of his high-mindedness, perhaps to keep better control over her by not confessing his enslavement. Its beauty at least proves that Milton could understand both sides of the case:

some cursed fraud
Of Enemy hath beguil'd thee, yet unknown,
And mee with thee hath ruind, for with thee
Certain my resolution is to die;
How can I live without thee, how forgo
Thy sweet Converse and Love so dearly join'd,
To live again in these wild Woods forlorn?
Should God create another Eve, and I
Another Rib afford, yet loss of thee
Would never from my heart; no, no, I feel
The Link of Nature draw me: Flesh of Flesh,
Bone of my Bone thou art, and from thy State
Mine never shall be parted, bliss or woe. (IX. 905)

Such is the state of mind which Milton is soon to explain as:

> *he scrupl'd not to eat,*
> *Against his better knowledge, not deceiv'd,*
> *But fondly overcome with Female charm.* (IX. 1000)

Waldock found this assertion by Milton merely a lie; Milton's imagination had revolted against his own doctrine when he composed the first passage, and later he coldly put his face straight with a false accusation. But *female charm* need not mean that Eve leered at Adam and waggled her hips. What Adam has recently confessed to the angel (VIII. 550) is almost the same: 'The trouble is, when she wants me to do something, I tend to think that it's actually the right thing to do.' Such is more or less what now happens; all that Milton insists upon by his comment is that Adam, even at the moment of this whole-hearted decision, was aware of the objections to it. Only in this rather remote sense does Milton consider Adam to be overcome by female charm, but he finds it sufficient. The difficulty only arises if we do not realize that Milton, here as in all the other cases, pitches a temptation staggeringly high.

C. S. Lewis, considering the case, or defending the Christian position, said:

> If conjugal love were the highest value in Adam's world, then of course his decision would have been the correct one. But if there are things that have an even higher claim on a man, if the universe is imagined to be such that, when the pinch comes, a man ought to reject wife and mother and his own life also, then the case is altered, and then Adam can do no good to Eve (as, in fact, he does no good) by becoming her accomplice.

Like most people, I would readily agree that such a pinch often has come; the question is whether it comes for Adam here. His relations with God are rather hard for us to envisage; Milton had to follow the Bible in describing God as speaking to Adam, but it appears from the *De Doctrina* that he considered this only a figure of speech—at most the Son could have been speaking to him; but the Bible, he decides, sometimes uses the term merely for a visiting angel. Even so, Adam must believe that he has met God, as he is told he has, and will thus make a more direct estimate than we can of God's intentions in an unreasonable command. The eighth Book, with great poignancy just before the Fall, shows us both Raphael and God in a uniquely matey relation to Adam; he recounts in it his talk with God immediately after his creation, and ends it by making Raphael blush. We are made to feel that he regards God not as an absolute lawgiver but as a human father; as when God answers the petition of Adam by saying, in effect: 'What d'you want a woman for, hey? *I* don't want a woman.' Adam says he then 'used freedom' in defending his petition; the words as he reports them seem very tactful, but at any rate God said he was pleased (VIII. 440). He is bound to think of God as a jovial though pompous old buffer here; the incident is pointless unless translated like that, though the language retains its grandeur. When we consider the whole story, this joke by God is as sinister as all his others, because by supplying the temptress he is machining the Fall; but Adam does not know this, and is shown in a mood of trustful gaiety. He may well feel that he has handled even the angel's warning against uxoriousness with considerable success.

When Eve has returned to him after her fall, and he has made his choice in silence, he speaks to her 'as one . . .

submitting to what seemd remèdiless', says she has been bold and provoked great peril, but perhaps will not die; there is 'inducement strong / To us' (after fifteen lines) to eat the apple, and perhaps God will not destroy 'us' for it (after twenty lines). He ends with a firm statement, and she in her reply is well aware that he has passed a glorious trial of love, but by this delicate use of the plural he has done his utmost to take for granted that they face the danger together. He at once looks round for hope; they are subject to a boss with an incalculable temper, but his own interests may keep him from exploding here. To kill them would be

Not well conceiv'd of God, who though his Power
Creation could repeat, yet would be loath
Us to abolish, lest the Adversary
Triumph and say: Fickle their state whom God
Most favours, who can please him long? Me first
He ruin'd, now Mankind; whom will he next?
Matter of scorn, not to be giv'n the Foe.

This strikes the reader as so probable, especially after God's remark that he will create mankind to keep Satan from exulting (VII. 150), that Adam cannot appear as betraying 'the highest value in his world'. There is no question of harming God by eating the apple, only a question of how best to handle his vanity and bad temper. Neither in Adam's secret despair nor in his practical and generous counsel do we find any 'pinch' of the kind C. S. Lewis meant, any recognition that obedience to God is a higher 'value'. You might say that Adam betrays this awareness at his trial before God (X. 140), when he tries to put the blame on Eve; but his fine words only say that he is afraid he may get all the punishment. The incident is in Genesis, so we need not think Milton would have chosen to make his Adam act so meanly; indeed he contrives to twist it into a defence for both of them. Adam says that he ought not to expose his wife to blame (though this is before her love has won him back) but that God knows the truth here anyway. God should therefore realize that:

> *This Woman whom thou mad'st to be my help,*
> *And gav'st me as thy perfect gift, so good,*
> *So fit, so acceptable, so Divine,*
> *That from her hand I could suspect no ill,*
> *And what she did, whatever in itself,*
> *Her doing seem'd to justify the deed;*
> *She gave me of the Tree, and I did eat.*

He is lying so far as he implies that she persuaded him at the time (and the lie, as Waldock remarked, seems to become Heaven's official version of the story), but his broader complaint is what he had made in a milder way to the angel before the fall; and to stretch the truth like this might be an advantage for both, now that their punishment is being calculated, by letting him blame God for making human nature what it is. Undeniably this is fallen behaviour from Adam, but Milton struggled to give it a good interpretation. God then blames him for letting her 'rule' him; this was wrong because she was created his inferior; and then God makes her his inferior, presumably from the first time (195). There is a possible way round this farcical injustice: that the words 'made of thee' (150) give the reason why he ought not to have obeyed her, whereas the later curse upon her is that she must henceforth obey him. But what the angel had said when consulted on the problem was that the more Adam has 'skill to manage his self-esteem' the more Eve will 'acknowledge him her Head' (VIII. 570); and on this count he has not been blameworthy. In any case, God does not consider the real question, which is whether Adam was wrong to disobey him so as to share her punishment.

Modern critics often talk as if Shelley invented all this fuss about women, because he was so sentimental and romantic; before Shelley, the men all simply harnessed their wives to the plough. It is sometimes answered that Milton makes Adam Cavalier rather than Roundhead, or medieval rather than puritan, and I said much the same myself about Eve; but we need not strain ourselves to allow Milton this tiny bit of breadth. He had only to copy out the Bible, which makes Adam say 'Therefore shall a man leave his father and his mother, and shall cleave unto his wife, and they shall be one flesh' (Genesis ii. 24). The chapter-headings of the Authorized Version list this as 'Marriage Instituted', but the discussion by St Paul which quotes it is only optional in the Anglican Marriage Service. Adam said it before the Fall, at her creation (as in Milton, VIII. 495), and had had no experience of human parents, so that St Paul and others have evidently rather doubted how much weight to put on his opinion. Still, if it is a rule, and if God is his father, he must be admitted to keep the rule. In presenting both sides of the question, Milton would feel that he was only giving the full drama of the sacred text, and could not be blamed if God appeared unsympathetic.

After eating the apple Adam becomes jolly, and Sir Walter Raleigh (I think) called him the father of all bright epigrammatic wasters for saying:

> *if such pleasure be*
> *In things to us forbidden, it might be wisht*
> *For this one Tree had been forbidden ten.* (IX. 1025)

Still, after deciding to eat for high motives, there would be no merit in pulling a long face about it; what he has set out to do is to comfort his wife by his solidarity with her. Also the fruit has made them both 'as with new Wine intoxicated', and this brings on sexual desire, which is explained to be now of a low kind. Milton thus follows St Augustine in believing that the Fall produced a bad kind of sex, though he insists that it is not the only kind. Evidently there is some broad human truth here, but it is hard to say what; I fancy we have a large number of different grounds for arriving at the strong plain emotive reactions, for and against, to which so many words bear witness. Here as in Spenser and in D. H. Lawrence I feel uncertain even about what the difference was, let alone why it made one action good and the other bad. However, after Milton has said they were drunk (whether or not with the remote support of a rabbinical tradition), he has safeguarded himself against being thought to insult love in some technical way, and readers can invent adequate distinctions for themselves. There is also an interesting question about the mode of action of the fruit. Milton sometimes denies that it had any magical powers, regarding it as chosen at random for a test of obedience; but it has its 'power', and indeed an intoxicant would be a sensible plant for God to choose. This does not solve the puzzle about the plants in the last utterance of God, explaining why he will remove our parents from Paradise:

Lest therefore his now bolder hand
Reach also of the Tree of Life, and eat,
And live for ever, dream at least to live
For ever, to remove him I decree . . . (XI. 95)

It seems particularly absurd for God to take care not to let the angels know whether even this tree really worked, and eating it was never forbidden to Adam and Eve; but Milton of course is merely concerned to include Genesis iii. 22. without either imposing his own conclusion or ratting on it. Even so, the verse in the Bible looks very much as if both trees did have some kind of magical power; one realizes here that the text was pretty difficult to handle. To make them drunk after eating the apple was a piece of chairmanship, and ought to have been satisfactory to all parties.

C. S. Lewis also remarked that Adam has no reason to suppose he will help Eve by copying her sin, and that as the story goes he doesn't; if he had beaten her in private and stood up for her at the trial, also blaming himself perhaps for letting her out of his sight, she might for all we know have got off. But Adam never says that he expects his action to help her; he merely will not take the risk of having to live without her. The poem somehow does not encourage us to think of an alternative plan; Milton would perhaps have said that Adam's failure to think of one proves his lack of trust in God, but his God is as usual peculiarly unfitted to inspire trust. I doubt whether the practical thoughts of C. S. Lewis are much help here; it seems inevitable for Adam to do the most sublime thing available, so that there is a Greek fatality about the tragedy. We cannot help regarding this as next door to saying that the Fall was Fortunate, as Milton seems to have felt in more ways than he expressed; and in any case it makes Adam harder to blame.

The doctrine of the Fortunate Fall has been so splendidly taped down by Professor Lovejoy from its invention by St Augustine that his brief essay leaves one feeling an affection for the topic, and no doubt Milton with his immense information would feel in a similar way that the ancient paradox required to be used. But it meant a great deal more to him than that; his adventurous intelligence expected it to give a real justification of God, and at any rate it made the story he had to tell hang together; it set him free to insist, with harsh and startling logic, that God was working for the Fall all along. The glumness of the last two Books may be partly a result of finding this solution, when fully imagined, to be no great comfort; but he had evidently planned to make it clinch his case for God with a triumphant end to the poem; it is approached and handled so continuously that one can hardly say whether it occupies the last three hundred or four hundred lines. We must consider the situation, so far as our powers allow. The generosity of Eve has restored the courage of Adam; he is sufficiently recovered to invent the use of fire in a scientific harangue (x. 1070), and is almost prepared to leave Eden. But first he must be depressed again; the dreadful sight of the animals of Paradise starting to eat each other, a very imaginative stroke (xi. 190), is the first sign of the harm he has done to all the world, and now Michael must show him a vision of future history to make him realize the harm he has done to all his descendants. The history of mankind, though varied and sometimes thought cheerful by Adam (590), is explained by the angel to be monotonously horrible, and all the result of eating the apple. For the second edition Milton divided the last book into two, perhaps to make it less heavy, but added very little except three lines about madness; he had forgotten that Adam ought to have his nose rubbed in having caused all that horrible madness too (xi. 485). On the other hand, Michael considers that all diseases are a punishment for over-eating, and it seems only Eve started that (xi. 515). History has been adequately covered when we reach the birth of Christ; it is enough to remark, without mention of the Reformation, that afterwards the world will go on sinning against the light:

> *To good malignant, to bad men benign,*
> *Under her own weight groaning, till the day*
> *Appear of respiration to the just*
> *And vengeance to the wicked . . .* (XII. 540)

Perhaps the narrative stops not from lack of interest but merely because the birth of Christ causes a natural interruption. Poor Adam starts crying and says he's sure it's going to be all right after all (375); Michael snubs him and proceeds to a more exact statement of the doctrine of Atonement, undoubtedly to the glory of the Son, but as regards Man ending with a suggestion that even the elect will perhaps never be allowed into Heaven (465). Adam is positively broken by so much graciousness:

> *O goodness infinite, goodness immense!*
> *That all this good of evil shall produce,*
> *And evil turn to good; more wonderful*
> *Than that which by creation first brought forth*
> *Light out of darkness! Full of doubt I stand,*
> *Whether I should repent me now of sin* (470)

—or rather rejoice at having sinned. But come now, we need not pretend we have never heard of real justice; surely it is obvious that Adam had better put his affairs in the hands of a steady family lawyer. He is in no condition to stand up to all this police bullying. What he is really saying, apart from the emotional condition he has been reduced to, is 'Oh, so you did want us to eat the apple, after all? Well, I'm pleased to hear that, because Eve rather thought you did, at the time.' It would mean that there is no reason for all the evils Adam has just been shown on earth, let alone the pains of Hell. The doctrine of the Fortunate Fall, it seems clear, removes from God the last rag of excuse for his plot to corrupt the whole race of mankind. I can well understand that the paradox fascinated good men for generation after generation, because they were desperate to escape from the suspicion that they were committed, under threat of torture here and hereafter, to worshipping a devil; indeed to doubt that God wishes one to be saved was an unforgiveable sin, as Faustus remarks in the source-book though Marlowe left it out. In the chapter on Heaven I tried to show Milton struggling to find good enough motives for God, and maybe in the wide mind of Milton there also lurked a more raffish feeling, often expressed rather desperately by Dylan Thomas, that it is actually better to live in a fallen world. But none of this can seriously justify the Christian God, and I am not sure what the modern apologists mean by a 'paradox' when they suggest that their God is all the better for including such contradictions.

The most interesting part of the moral development of Adam and Eve, as Dr Tillyard well pointed out, comes after their Fall when they have begun to worry about the position of their descendants. Modern critics are fond of saying that Adam is brought to admit the justice of the curse laid by God upon all his children, though of course in ordinary moral terms God behaves disgracefully; and I am keen to point out that the conscience of Milton was not quite as corrupt as a neo-Christian's. To start with, we do not know how Adam has come to learn that all his posterity are now cursed, as he laments throughout x. 720-840; nor yet why Eve is at once certain of it on the hint of one line from Adam (965). This is not Milton's fault, as the text of Genesis, which he is following carefully, says nothing about it either. We should perhaps expect that the Son told them about it after the trial while he was dressing their shame in animal skins (x. 215); Milton seems interested but reserved here. Not caring to have the Son encourage their bodily shame, he explains that in the fallen world they will need something warmer than figleaves; but he doubts whether the Son would kill an animal for its skin, because the animals themselves had not yet been started killing each other by God. The Son also, with his Robe of righteousness, covered their inward nakedness from his Father's sight (220); this is hard to envisage, but might involve telling them how to pray. The passage does not suggest that he maintained a terrifying silence. The next 500 lines concern supernatural characters, and then we meet Adam in despair. In a set debate after emerging from hatred, Adam and Eve agree to trust God so far as to allow themselves to have children. Hope for revenge upon Satan, as that might be the meaning of the obscure prophecy, is the first reason Adam gives for having children; also it is probably their safest plan, as the prophecy at least implies that God has ordained it (1030). Michael has not yet shown Adam in a vision the full misery which their descendants have incurred. Their new assumption that the curse is upon our whole stock perhaps feels more natural in the poem because we have just been shown the devils being turned into snakes, but we are not told how to interpret the corresponding activity of God among mankind. The point where God should have warned Adam of the threat to his descendants is reported in the jovial Book VIII, and the sequence of God's remarks is positively misleading:

The day thou eat'st thereof, my sole command
Transgrest, inevitably thou shalt die;
From that day mortal, and this happy State

Shalt lose, expelled from hence into a World
Of woe and sorrow. Sternly he pronounc'd
The rigid interdiction, which resounds
Yet dreadful in mine ear, though in my choice
Not to incur; but soon his clear aspect
Returnd and gracious purpose thus renewd.
Not only these fair bounds, but all the Earth
To thee and to thy Race I give; as Lords
Possess it, and all things that therein live . . . (VIII. 330)

Next Adam names all the creatures, as they pass him 'two and two'; next he asks for a woman so that he also may 'beget like of his like' (425). Here, even more than in the first two chapters of Genesis, the positive gift to his children seems to exclude any threat against them; in Milton's account, Adam himself asks for children as a direct result of being told of the good prospects before them. A keenly suspicious lawyer might ask after these words of God whether all Adam's children would be cursed as well as himself, but it cannot be called fair warning. Milton discussed the Fall in Chapter XI of the *De Doctrina*, and early in it gives a standard rhetorical list proving that to eat the fruit included in itself all sins, among them 'an insensibility to the welfare of their offspring'; but later in the gradually accumulated chapter, in a brief but complex argument which I take to be against the Calvinist doctrine of Total Depravity, he remarks that Original Sin can hardly be attributed to our first parents:

> At any rate, it was a consequence of sin, rather than sin itself; or if it were a sin, it was a sin of ignorance; for they expected nothing less than they should lose any good by eating the fruit, or suffer harm in any way whatever.

When he wrote this, he surely meant also that they did not know they were harming their descendants; a man who did not count that as 'losing any good' could hardly be the author of Book X.

There is indeed one warning on this point in the poem; to Adam only, by Raphael just as he is leaving:

> *take heed lest Passion sway*
> *Thy Judgement to do aught, which else free Will*
> *Would not admit; thine and of all thy Sons*
> *The weal or woe in thee is plac't; beware.* (VIII. 635)

Milton was highly conscious of the question, and no doubt used his invention of an angelic visit to say this because he found it so notably lacking in the sacred text. Perhaps he felt afterwards that he should not put any weight on his own addition; also it comes just after Adam has made the angel blush, so that Adam might think of the threat as merely an attempt to recover dignity; and what a vast amount of woe the sons will inherit is not suggested by dragging a reference to them into an obscure and packed piece of grammar during the hurried farewell. Whatever the cause, Milton does not present the warning as effective; it does not occur to either Adam or Eve while they are deciding to eat, and we must suppose from their immense self-reproaches afterwards that they would not have eaten if it had done. Adam clearly feels that to stand by his wife is a danger to himself only; that is why he feels that his honour demands taking the risk. Such indeed is the reason why the 'pinch' of C. S. Lewis has not come, and Milton would have falsified the sacred text if he had made it come.

Adam in the speech described as his recantation asks for all the punishment on himself, reminds God that he did not ask to be created, demands why he may not be annihilated instead of causing misery in his turn, and says 'Inexplicable / Thy justice seems' (x. 755). He next admits that he failed to reject the conditions of life when first proposed (apparently in the speech of God which he reported earlier), also that he would want his own sons to obey him, and to that extent would behave like God the Father—but does not discuss what penalties he would himself choose to inflict. After an apparent digression, pointing out the unnaturalness and injustice of eternal torment for himself, he returns to drive home how much more unnatural and unjust it is for his descendants.

Ah, why should all mankind
For one man's fault thus guiltless be condemn'd,
If guiltless? But from mee what can proceed,
But all corrupt, both Mind and Will deprav'd,
Not to do only, but to will the same
With me? how can they then acquitted stand
In sight of God? Him after all Disputes
Forc't I absolve; all my evasions vain
And reasonings, though through Mazes, lead me still
But to my own conviction: first and last
On mee, mee only, as the source and spring
Of all corruption, all the blame lights due;
So might the wrath. (x. 825)

Surely it is an interesting point that God, so far from having 'disputed' with this man about the question at all, has not even pronounced any penalty against his children, either in the poem or in the sacred text it is assumed to copy. A doctor could only suppose that Adam is in a hangover condition of neurotic guilt. Milton's readers were to suppose that Adam had somehow arrived at the truth; but even so the kind of 'force' that God can use here is plainly not moral or logical. It is some kind of corruption of the whole stock, such as we may expect in future wars, and ought not to be confused with rational argument. The word *conviction* when Milton wrote had the head meaning 'being found guilty by a law-court', and did not as now mean 'inner certainty'. Thus the main effect of this use of the word by Adam would be that further arguing against God is only liable to bring a heavier penalty, as seems very probable. However, an intermediate sense 'making a person feel guilty' was coming up when Milton wrote, and he used it earlier in the same book. The Son is remarking that Satan need not be present at the trial (held by the Son, as Milton believed, though following the Bible in calling him God):

> *the third best absent is condemn'd,*
> *Convict by flight, and Rebel to all law,*
> *Conviction to the Serpent none belongs.* (x. 80)

The divine justice is particularly shocking here, because the serpent *is* present at the trial and *does* get punished, without deserving it at all; thus making the remark nonsense twice over. Milton is hampered because the first books of Genesis do not mention Satan, and presume that the actual serpent was guilty; thus it was particularly hard for him to make any moral sense of this bit of the text, and his only way out was some kind of joke. What was to him the more recent or slang meaning of 'conviction' gets imposed because the sentence requires a meaning for the word different from *convict*: 'it is useless to try to make Satan conscious of guilt by haranguing him as a judge, though legally he has confessed guilt by flight'. The bad pun is a way of making the treatment of the snake appear vaguely symbolical, a retort to Satan in his own sordid terms. After this use of the word *conviction*, I do not think the use of the word later in the same Book by the 'forc'd' Adam need mean he thought that God had produced moral reasons for his decision to corrupt the entire stock of mankind.

Much interest therefore attaches to Milton's attempt at justifying God on this point in Chapter XI of the *De Doctrina*, where it is at least clear that he felt the difficulty:

> If all did not sin in Adam, why has the condition of all become worse since his fall? Some of the modern commentators reply, that the deterioration was not moral, but physical. To which I answer, that it was as unjust to deprive the innocent of their physical, as of their moral, perfection; especially as the former has so much influence on the latter, that is, on the practical conduct of mankind.
>
> It is, however, a principle uniformly acted upon in the divine proceedings, and recognized by all nations and under all religions from the earliest period, that the penalty incurred by the violation of things sacred (and such was the tree of knowledge of good and evil) attaches not only to the criminal himself, but to the whole of his posterity, who thus become accursed and obnoxious to punishment.

Milton easily proves this with a long series of references to the Old Testament, also Thucydides and Virgil, and then recalls modern custom in cases of high treason; besides, 'we all know what are the recognized rights of war' against innocent persons such as women and children (he means nothing is too bad for them). 'God declares this to be the method of his justice.' It is hard to believe that Milton could avoid wincing when he included high treason, under which his own children might have suffered. In recent times we have heard much jeering at the idea of progress, but it is clearly a moral help in dealing with ancient sacred texts, which are always liable to give divine authority to some barbarous habit which was merely normal when they were written. Even so, we need not think the prophets so very barbarous; Ezekiel was civilized enough to denounce, in the name of the Lord, the custom of punishing the sons for the sins of the fathers (Chapter xviii), and Milton would have done better to list the passage among the relevant texts. I suppose he thought it would only be confusing, or raise false hopes, as there was such decisive authority against it. He knows very well that he would be wicked if he did this himself (at least, on God's scale; one can imagine him finding arguments for killing Charles II if Cromwell had caught him); but he is arguing steadily from the Word of God, and its texts force him to admit that this is what God calls justice—so then he argues for it bravely. He would feel in such cases that he was sweeping away soft-minded nonsense, and he always enjoyed the energy of his logic; thus he lays down generally in Chapter II that subtle theologians have no business to refine away the picture of God given in the Bible:

> In a word, God either is, or is not, such as he represents himself to be. If he be really such, why should we think otherwise of him? If he be not such, on what authority do we say what God has not said?

It was of course a standard Reformation position to claim the original text of the Bible as the true guide to correct the accumulated errors of Rome; and no wonder a man like Milton would come to feel slightly appalled during prolonged study of the Bronze Age literature to which he had nailed his conscience. We should recognize, what the *De Doctrina* makes very clear I think, that he was himself a man of civilized conscience, and that the reason why he was labouring so hard was to make his God appear a bit less morally disgusting. The fallen state of man seems to him (unlike our modern neo-Christians) essentially a problem about the justice of God. Thus he goes on:

> The difficulty is solved with respect to infants, by the consideration that all souls belong to God; that these, though guiltless of actual sin, were the offspring of sinful parents, and that God foresaw that, if suffered to live, they would grow up similar to their parents. With respect to the others, it is obviated by the consideration, that no one perishes, unless he himself sin.

The textual proof which follows must I think be a piece of double-talk, by his own argument as just quoted from Chapter II; if we are really only punished for our own sins, why should Milton struggle to defend the letter of so scandalous a doctrine? But he regarded his explanation here as a settled one, since he uses it in the poem:

> *suffering death,*
> *The penalty to thy transgression due,*
> *And due to theirs which out of thine will grow,*
> *So only can high Justice rest appaid.* (XII. 400)

I take it that a similar explanation comes in handy to justify God for corrupting the whole race of serpents:

> *To Judgement he proceeded on th'accus'd*
> *Serpent though brute, unable to transfer*
> *The Guilt on him who made him instrument*
> *Of mischief, and polluted from the end*
> *Of his Creation; justly then accursed*
> *As vitiated in Nature; more to know*
> *Concerned not Man . . .* (X. 165)

If it does not concern Man to know that Satan is their tempter it is hard to understand why Milton wrote his epic, let alone why Raphael explained the matter at such length to Adam and Eve; besides, Adam is given the credit of guessing the answer at X. 1030.

It is also puzzling that God was unable to transfer the guilt to the person guilty. The reason why all serpents eat dust and go upon their bellies is that they were 'vitiated in nature' when the original serpent was possessed by Satan for a brief performance; or rather when God cursed them for it, since we must not suppose that he only pretended to utter an efficient curse, whereas the natural cause was already in operation. We may notice that the actual curse on the serpent does not mention its descendants, any more than the curses upon Adam and Eve do.

It seems hardly fair to blame Milton for having to struggle in the coils of this serpent, out of determination to stick to his text. But the parallel does I think help to make clear the importance to his mind of the Mortalist Heresy, mainly expounded in Chapter XIII. Sewell seems evidently right (p. 182 ff.) in thinking that Milton adopted this theory, which had already been knocking about among the bold thinkers of the Commonwealth, because it improved God's moral position. The doctrine says that the soul dies with the body, and that both will simply be reconstituted by God on the Last Day (usually of course for eternal torture); also that 'the human soul is not created daily by the immediate act of God, but propagated from father to son in a natural order' (vii). One might think this already inherent in a sentence of Aquinas, that 'the risen creature must be an animal, if it is to be a man'; but Milton would also feel that it suited the organic unity of soul and body, interconnected by a hierarchy of 'spirits'. Recent science thus made the doctrine easier to argue for; but its chief merit for Milton was to make God less tirelessly spiteful. If in each fertile human act of sex God chooses to create a distinct personality, usually certain of damnation, and always corrupt, just to punish Adam, God seems too 'laboriously vile', to recall the Chinese name for Lord Napier; besides, as Milton points out, God would often be working on a Sunday (Chapter VII). If we can regard the whole human stock as tainted by the Fall, body and soul together in some biological way, the process seems more natural; it might even allow a resolution of the paradox that though inheriting the guilt of Adam we are only punished for our own sins. It strikes me as rather a marginal point, but Milton needed anything to make God better there.

The same problem, of course, arose over predestination, but that he came to give up, on the specific ground that it made God so wicked as to cause scandal (end of Chapter XII):

> There can be no doubt that for the purpose of vindicating the justice of God, especially in his calling of mankind, it is much better to allow to man . . . some portion of free will in respect of good works, or at least of good endeavours. . . . If he [God] inclines the will of man to good or evil according to his own pleasure, and then rewards the good, and punishes the wicked, the course of equity seems to be disturbed; and it is entirely on this supposition that the outcry against divine justice is founded. It would appear, therefore, that God's general judgement of the universe, to which such frequent allusion is made, should be understood as relating to natural

> and civil concerns, to things indifferent and fortuitous, in a word, to anything rather than to matters of morality and religion.

This seems an attractively light-hearted attempt to keep God under decent control, but perhaps the coolness of the tone was meant to help in hushing the 'outcry'. One has often to consider why Milton sounds comically tart about God, and sometimes it would be enough to say that he merely enjoys arguing:

> But, it is objected, God has no regard to the less depraved among the wicked in his choice, but often selects the worse rather than the better (Deut. ix. 5; Luke x. 13). I answer, that it cannot be determined from those passages what God regards in those whom he chooses; for, in the first place, I have not argued that he has regarded righteousness in the least degree.

However, this explanation cannot be felt as enough when he is gravely summarizing a fundamental position; for example, in Chapter II, after maintaining that there must be a supreme power, and that it cannot be Nature or Fate.

> In short, many visible proofs, the verification of numberless predictions, a multitude of wonderful works have compelled all nations to believe, either that God, or that some evil power whose name was unknown, presided over the affairs of the world.

Even Voltaire could hardly have written that icy sentence. The argument from prediction, one should remember, continued to be used as the unbeatable one for a plain man all through the eighteenth century; I understand that it has been so thoroughly confuted that no seminary still teaches it. I must carry the quotation straight on, because otherwise it would give a false impression:

> Now that evil should prevail over good, and be the true supreme power, is as unmeet as it is incredible. Hence it follows, as a necessary consequence, that God exists.
>
> Again, the existence of God is further proved by that feeling, whether we term it conscience or right reason, which even in the worst of characters is not altogether extinguished. If there were no God, there would be no distinction between right and wrong.

Such no doubt was the rock-bottom reason why Milton, like many other good men, continued to struggle to defend a God whose actions were revolting to his own conscience or right reason.

I hope these extracts will be enough to make clear that Milton genuinely considered God in need of defence, and indeed that, when Milton said at the beginning of his epic he intended to justify God, he was so far from expecting a reader to think the phrase poetical rhetoric that he was not even stepping out of the usual procedure of his prose. A curious trick has been played on modern readers here; they are told: 'Why, but of course you must read the poem taking for granted that Milton's God is good; not to do that would be absurdly unhistorical. Why, the first business of a literary critic is to sink his mind wholly into the mental world of the author, and in a case like this you must accept what they all thought way back in early times.' I think this literary doctrine is all nonsense anyhow; a critic ought to use his own moral judgement, for what it is worth, as well as try to understand the author's, and that is the only way he can arrive at a 'total reaction'. But in a case like this the argument is also grossly unhistorical. No doubt Milton would only have snorted if a Victorian had come up and praised him for making Satan good, but anyone who told him he had made God wicked would find his mind surprisingly at home; there would be some severe cross-questioning (is this a Jesuit or merely an Arminian?), but if that passed off all right he would ask the visitor to sit down and discuss the point at length. Nor was it only the later Milton, after the disillusion of the Fall of the Commonwealth, who felt God to need defence; he can be shown feeling it both before and after a major change in this theology. In *The Doctrine and Discipline of Divorce* (1643), writing as a believer in predestination, he remarks of Jesuits and Arminians that, if they could only understand the argument he has just propounded, 'they might, methinks, be persuaded to absolve both God and us' (*us* meaning the Calvinists). Near the end of Chapter III of the *De Doctrina* we find he has abandoned predestination, and his reason for it is still that he is anxious to absolve God:

> free causes are not impeded by any law of necessity arising from the decrees or prescience of God. There are some who, in their zeal to oppose this doctrine, do not hesitate even to assert that God himself is the cause and origin of evil. Such men, if they are not to be looked upon as misguided rather than mischievous, should be ranked among the most abandoned of all blasphemers. An attempt to refute them would be nothing more than an argument to prove that God was not the evil spirit.

This exasperation against his opponents, this extreme readiness to see that they are making God into the Devil, while the point of distinction he wants to insist upon is really so very slight, makes evident that Milton himself was sensitive and anxious about the danger of finding that he too was worshipping the Devil. When Milton gets round to his own pronouncement on this point, in Chapter VIII, after listing the crucial texts, he is hardly able to do more than issue a rule of decorum:

> But though in these, as well as in many other passages of the Old and New Testaments, God distinctly declares that it is himself who impels the sinner to sin, who binds his understanding, and leads him into error; yet, on account of the infinite holiness of the Deity, it is not allowable to consider him as in the smallest instance the author of sin.

What first struck me, when I began to nose about in the English translation of the *De Doctrina*, rather belatedly, was that its tone is very unlike what the learned critics who summarize it had led me to expect. But maybe, I thought, having no judgement of Latin style, this is only a result of translation; the work was done by Sumner, later an Anglican bishop, who must have been working fairly rapidly; it was printed (and reviewed by Macaulay) in 1825, two years after the Latin text had been discovered. One can imagine a translator making it sound like Gibbon, partly because that was an easy formula but also through feeling a certain impatience with this heretic. But the following passage, from Chapter VII, 'Of the Creation', another discussion of the effects of the Fall, seemed to me enough to refute the suspicion; it rises above the variations of tone available to a translator:

> But, it is contended, God does not create souls impure, but only impaired in their nature, and destitute

> of original righteousness; I answer that to create pure souls, destitute of original righteousness,—to send them into contaminated and corrupt bodies,—to deliver them up in their innocence and helplessness to the prison house of the body, as to an enemy, with understanding blinded and with will enslaved,—in other words, wholly deprived of sufficient strength for resisting the vicious propensities of the body—to create souls thus circumstanced, would argue as much injustice, as to have created them impure would have argued impurity; it would have argued as much injustice, as to have created the first man Adam himself impaired in his nature, and destitute of original righteousness.

Surely, in the face of this burning sense of the injustice of God, which Milton only just manages to drag into line, it was rather absurd of C. S. Lewis to say that nobody had ever doubted Milton's account of the Fall until the Romantics made rebellion fashionable. A sympathetic reader of Milton's prose is accustomed to feel that he writes like a lawyer or a politician, concerned to convince his reader by any argument which would serve, though really more humane or enlightened arguments are what have made Milton himself choose the side he is arguing on. But in discussing the justice of God Milton admits that the conscience of every decent man is against what he has to maintain; there is an 'outcry' against it; but what he has found in the Bible is the horrible truth about the justice of God, and men had much better learn to face it.

I shall end these quotations from the *De Doctrina* with an example which seems to me coldly hair-raising, though Sewell does not appear to find it so, and perhaps Milton did not either. In Chapter XVI, 'Of the Ministry of Redemption', the section *By Payment of the Required Price* consisted of a list of texts and then one sentence claiming that they refute any Socinian view, that is, any theory that Christ died not to pay for us but merely to set us an example to follow. The idea of payment is indeed deeply embedded in the system, as we too are paying all the time for Adam; what Satan reaches as rock-bottom, after abandoning his suspicion that God is a usurper, is that he could not in any case submit to a God who is a usurer. Some while after writing this section, Milton must have told his secretary to read it out to him, and then he dictated one further Latin sentence:

> At the time I confess myself unable to perceive how those who consider the Son of the same essence with the Father can explain either his incarnation or his satisfaction.

Maybe the shock comes partly from putting the sentence into English; the English word *satisfaction* has its own suggestions beside the central achievement of the Christ, 'a full oblation, remission and satisfaction for the sins of the whole world'. But these seem to me to act as a just satire. What Milton is thinking has to be: 'God couldn't have been satisfied by torturing himself to death, not if I know God; you could never have bought him off with that money; he could only have been satisfied by torturing somebody else to death.' Until I tried to follow the mind of Milton, I did not realize why the doctrine of the Trinity had been considered so important. Surely, if you regard God the Father as Milton had come to do here, he cannot possibly be justified. Milton when he embarked upon his epic was exactly in the position of the Satan he presents, overwhelmingly stubborn and gallant but defending a cause inherently hopeless from the start.

It is a difficult matter to try to sum up. The quotations I think make clear that Milton only just managed, after spiritual wrestling and the introduction of a certain amount of heresy, to reconcile his conscience or keep his temper with his God. When he says that the Holy Spirit dictated the poem to him, we can readily believe that, as the problems at issue had been gone over so long and anxiously, it was by a fairly direct process that the blind man at once invented and learned by heart a whole paragraph, commonly at night, and then waited as he said to be 'milked' of it; what is surprising is that the parts of the narrative fit together as well as they do. Even so, it is clear that he could have recognized the more alarming aspects of the narrative, merely by switching his attention; and his character makes him unlikely not to have recognized them. I should think that, with his usual nerve, he just refused to be rattled. Perhaps the main point is that when composing he felt like a defending counsel; such a man is positively wanted to realize at what points his client's case is weak, and he does not feel personally disgraced if his client still loses after he has gone as far as he can. Adding a little human interest to the admittedly tricky client God, by emphasizing his care to recover the reputation of his son, and giving a glimpse of the deeper side of his nature which makes him prepare for his latter end, is about all that can be done to swing the jury when the facts of the case are so little in dispute. On the other hand, when he made the case as strong as he could for Satan, Eve and Adam, he somehow did not mind driving home the injustice of God, because God was not at the moment his client. This picture is very inadequate because the problems about God are never out of sight in the poem; but still, being such a good advocate was what made the poetry so dramatic and in a way so broad. He understood how all contemporary sects would react to the words and situations he arranged for God, or the contradictions with which he had himself wrestled; it seems fair to add, he knew what he could get away with in the poem, even when it was necessarily very dickey. Though apparently isolated, he thus became an echoing-chamber for the whole mind of his period. The fact that he went on to make out a strong case for Delilah, even though in a narrower and fiercer frame of mind, proves I think that the moral generosity of *Paradise Lost* is not due to accident, muddle-headedness or split personality.

Chapter 6

DELILAH

HENCE I am now to defend the fall of Delilah in *Samson Agonistes*, though she is not usually regarded as a moral problem. Most of this book has been taken from previous critics, though their deductions have sometimes been pushed further; but here I think I may claim to be original. Any number of people have defended the Devil, in their various ways, but I do not know that anyone has defended Delilah; and yet her case is even easier to defend than Adam's—it is a push-over. I was led to the attempt, not because I was hungry for greater absurdity, but from wanting to be consistent; and perhaps the result, though in a way it makes my whole argument more plausible, also makes it more trivial. We are not tempted to suppose that Milton's Unconsciousness was working in favour of Delilah; or rather, we would expect to have to dig some way down in his Unconsciousness before getting underneath his settled hatred for her. We must respect his firm sense of justice when he makes the case for her so strong. But this is not a thing he would need to struggle to do; he wanted to present the problem inherent in the story of Samson, which was traditionally recognized as a moral paradox, and thus to present the very strange picture of our relations with God which it conveys. Critics have become accustomed to say that the poem shows a deep trust in God; but they would be shocked if they read the story in their newspaper, and a modern jury would at once regard Delilah as a deeply wronged wife.

The case has also the advantage of dealing with mundane affairs, so that our judgement sees round it more confidently than the cases of Eve and Satan. I would look ridiculous here if I presented myself as an indignant member of the bourgeoisie; Nietzsche and Bernard Shaw, if they had chosen to implement their principles in this case, would have been strongly in favour of Samson. The whole point of his story is that the common judgements of the world are wrong. What is briefly told about him in the Bible makes clear that his name attracted demigod-rogue legends, a type to be found as I gather in most of the surviving literatures, and in Negro, Red Indian and South Sea Island oral tradition. Milton's concern with the nature of God required him to ignore this comic aspect of Samson, but treating him as a moral problem brings out what had always at bottom been the point of the joke. The problem for the medieval mind, it seems, had merely been whether he was right to commit suicide; this would not be a pressing difficulty either to our own heroic age or to that of the ancient Hebrews. A man who volunteered in modern war for a desperately dangerous but not certainly fatal action, much to the advantage of his own side if he died in achieving it, would not be accused of proposing suicide by the padre of his regiment. Some recent critic has argued that Milton defends Samson against the charge of suicide in lines 1580-90, but the Messenger hardly does more than report the facts. Milton seems to have felt, as most readers do now, that other moral problems are more prominent in the story; and he was in the mood to be rather rough about telling 'the world' that the ways of God are not as our ways. Screwing the moral case up tighter, as he always liked to do, he made just one important addition to the text of the Bible; he made Delilah Samson's wife.

The poem begins with Samson blaming himself intensely, and struggling not to blame his God, for his failure to carry out the political duty to which he had been dedicated:

> *Promise was that I*
> *Should Israel from Philistinian yoke deliver;*
> *Ask for this great Deliverer now, and find him*
> *Eyeless in Gaza . . .* (40)

and so on through the famous hammer blows, all applying to Milton himself. I take it Milton would also realize that his play in a sense completed the great series of Elizabethan Revenge Plays; they too had usually been considered to deal with a moral problem which was also a political one. Our own moral ideas are perhaps unreasonable here, but they were already traditional for Milton. In a declared war between nations, a man may be wanted to do a good deal of cheating and killing civilians, and will commonly do it without remorse; but in an internal political struggle, not even recognized as a civil war, the same behaviour will be thought plainly criminal. Milton goes out of his way to suggest that Samson acts for an underprivileged class or minority group rather than a separate nation, and makes plain that only Samson is still fighting. Some of this may be called dramatic convention; thus, it is usual in a play to make opposing nations talk the same language; but in Milton the well-to-do father of Samson is lobbying among the Philistine lords to have his son's imprisonment converted to a fine, and this makes the whole society feel more settled. Samson himself boasts that the Philistines became his enemies because he provoked them (640). In effect, he is what the 1890s called a Nihilist, so that few of the literary critics who praise him would be on his side if they met him nowadays.

Naturally, Samson himself talks of the Philistines as an enemy nation, for example when he says to Delilah:

> *Why then*
> *Didst thou at first receive me for thy husband?*
> *Then, as since then, thy country's foe profest:* (880)

but his words to her soon after, as he tries to argue the case, show at least that he finds it to need arguing carefully:

> *if aught against my life*
> *Thy country sought of thee, it sought unjustly,*
> *Against the law of nature, law of nations,*
> *No more thy country, but an impious crew*
> *Of men conspiring to uphold their state*
> *By worse than hostile deeds, violating the ends*
> *For which our country is a name so dear;*
> *Not therefore to be obeyed.*

In modern English 'their state' chiefly means their country, but in Milton's time it still chiefly meant their position of rule, over Hebrews and lower-class Philistines alike presumably; though Milton could have wanted to leave open for Samson the modern meaning. And when a reader meets the sequence *thy country*—'you have no longer a country'—*our country*, he can hardly presume that Samson means to exclude his legal wife from 'our'. He is so nationalist that he may, but if so there is no persuasiveness in this bit of his argument; it must be meant as an appeal to her knowledge of what they have both grown up among, the moral traditions of the land of Palestine. The language suggests that the Philistine lords have practically become a wicked political party or ruling class. She next tells him that she betrayed him out of religious conviction, and Milton could not but realize that the answer takes us into the familiar archaic world of the pot calling the kettle black:

SAM. *But zeal moved thee:*
To please thy gods thou didst it. Gods unable
To acquit themselves and prosecute their foes
But by ungodly deeds, the contradiction
Of their own deity, Gods cannot be. (895)

The scansion requires an ironical stress on *thee*, implying 'You claim to be dedicated, do you; but I really am'; and maybe this preserves the logic of justice between Delilah and Samson. But it cannot do the same between Jehovah and Dagon; Samson's own God admittedly needs to be helped by deeds which are at least unlawful and such as Dagon would call ungodly. (I have put a full stop instead of Milton's semi-colon before *Gods unable*, because the modern reader expects the stops to bring out the grammar.) It is in his next debate, with the enemy champion Harappa, not from Delilah naturally enough, that we hear the political case against Samson; and here the retort is made plainly:

HAR. *Fair honour that thou dost thy God, in trusting*
He will accept thee to defend his cause,
A Murderer, a Revolter, and a Robber.
SAM. *Tongue-doughty giant, how dost thou prove me these?*
HAR. *Is not thy nation subject to our Lords?*
Their magistrates confest it, when they took thee
As a League-breaker and delivered bound
Into our hands: for hadst thou not committed
Notorious murder . . . (1180)

I grant that, in this quarrel, Harappa calls the Philistines and Hebrews two nations, but that does not prove he would admit it in more diplomatic moments. The reader is evidently meant to imagine the position as like the results of the Norman Conquest; a gradual settlement is in progress, and we know that the rulers permit intermarriage. (It came to be thought that Samson broke a law of Jehovah there, but the Bible does not say so, and the Hebrew regulation may be a later one.) Samson answers with what we already know to be a lie:

SAM. *Among the daughters of the Philistines*
I chose a wife, which argued me no foe;
But your ill-meaning Politician Lords,
Under pretence of bridal friends and guests,
Appointed to await me thirty spies,
Who threatning cruel death constrain'd the bride
To wring from me and tell to them my secret,
That solv'd the riddle which I had propos'd.
When I perceived all set on enmity,
As on my enemies, where ever chanc'd
I used hostility . . .

The Bible does say (Judges xiv) that they threatened the bride they would 'burn thee and thy father's house with fire', but we gather that they were only trying to avoid paying on the bet, whereas Samson's motive in proposing the bet was to boast of a portent from his God. They were nasty guests even for their own people, but only Samson had come as already a national enemy. One might indeed argue that he is telling the truth now and was lying before, but the question is settled by Judges xiv. 4:

> But his father and his mother knew not that it was of the Lord, that he sought an occasion against the Philistines; for at that time the Philistines had dominion over Israel.

Milton's echo of this makes Samson rather more conscious and determined; he had argued about it with Manoah:

MAN. *I cannot praise thy marriage choices, Son,*
Rather approved them not; but thou didst plead
Divine impulsion prompting how thou might'st
Find some occasion to infest our foes. (420)

Samson himself rapidly abandons the claim that the Philistines hit him first. He next points out that, as their government had been established by force, the conquered might rightly use force to oppose it; 'but', he goes on, as there was no such war, he acted alone:

But I a private person, whom my country
As a league-breaker gave up bound, presum'd
Single Rebellion and did hostile acts.
I was no private but a person rais'd
With strength sufficient and command from Heav'n
To free my Country; if their servile minds
Me their Deliverer sent would not receive,
But to their Masters gave me up for nought,
Th'unworthier they; whence to this day they serve. (1210)

The poem was calculated to strike the first readers as about Milton himself, and *a fortiori* about current politics; and it drives home its political point very firmly. The rebel doctrine of the Inner Light, as they already knew, gave a dangerous amount of encouragement to any self-righteous fanatic; indeed the licensers deserve some credit for letting the play be printed. It seems odd that critics in our very political age regard the matter so religiously.

Samson regularly gambles on knowing the purposes of God, and this is held to be justified because they are inscrutable. But Eve also broke a literal commandment on the prompting of her Inner Light; why did she too not turn out lucky? The answer has to be that she allowed her conscience to actuate her, and did what she thought right. Samson only wants to do what God wants, and does not even consider whether it is wicked, except that it will be more fun for him if it is rude. The distinction is inherently unreal if God and goodness are mysteriously one, but not as regards the ideas of God held among mankind; and we can at least observe a practical difference in the mode of knowledge. Samson just gets occasional flashes of certainty that he must do some wild thing, much as if he had dreamed which horse would win the Derby; he is quite clear whether this has happened or not, as we realise when he says God told him to marry his first wife but not his second. As to marrying Delilah, he says,

> *I thought it lawful from my former act,*
> *And the same end; still watching to oppress*
> *Israel's oppressors.* (230)

He wants here to bewail his marriage to Delilah, and is struggling not to blame God; also no doubt Milton wanted the point mentioned because the marriage to Delilah is not in the Bible. A reader may reflect that the first marriage was a total failure from the start, not even needed to make Samson hate the Philistines, whereas the second marriage at least leads him to his lethal triumph; so it is doubtful whether the distinction is to the credit of God, or of Samson's intuitions about God.

Some previous theologians had presumed that Samson married Delilah, but one might suspect that Milton was trying rather absurdly to give the hero of the Gaza brothel enough respectability for tragedy. So far from that, the marriage is essential to the poem, because it yields a peculiarly shocking moral paradox. I left out a bit of the quotation from his refutation of Delilah:

Why then
Didst thou at first receive me for thy husband?
Then, as since then, thy country's foe profest:
Being once a wife, for me thou wast to leave
Parents and country; nor was I their subject,
Nor under their protection but my own,
Thou mine, not theirs; if aught against my life . . .

He goes on to say that the Philistines went against the Law of Nature 'if' they tried to make her kill him (they did not). Now, please consider how this argument would sound in the newspaper report of a current trial. The aristocratic girl, we gather, married the nihilist in the belief that she could quiet him and save him from crime; but as soon as they were married he said, 'Now you must help me to murder all your relations; that's the only thing I married you for, you fool. Don't you know it's your duty to do anything I tell you, now that we're married?' We do not hear of any political use that he made of his wife, but that he could do so is his defence for having married her; it is the moral point of her part of the story.

Therefore God's universal law
Gave to the man despotic power
Over his female in due awe,
Nor from that right to part an hour,
Smile she or lour:
So shall he least confusion draw
On his whole life, not swayed
By female usurpation, nor dismayed.

Least implies that a man must expect some degree of confusion if he has anything to do with a woman. The poem has been called narrow, but it is a remarkable range which can say this with cool assurance and yet write the speeches of Delilah.

They are greatly to her credit. It would be wilful to doubt that she still loves him and wants to help him, because we are given no other reason for her visit. She might indeed have a general political intention, to try to heal even now the divisions threatening civil war, as she seems to have intended by her marriage; but she cannot be trying to trap Samson, because she thinks him no longer a danger. It is entirely credible that she betrayed him to her relations to save him for her love from the monstrous folly of his political programme, and that she was shocked and astonished when they blinded him. We are rather hampered in plumbing her mind because, from her point of view, most of her talk to Samson is an attempt to cure a lunatic; it would be useless for her to tell him how outrageous his behaviour towards her must appear to any civilized person. Her lines convey a cool though generous-minded assurance of being in the right; as Milton would intend them to do, because he could not present his moral paradox unless he made her an impressive representative of 'the world'. We hear most of her mind when she realizes that the attempt to recover his love is hopeless; she begs to touch his hand, and the blind man warns her not to do it lest he tear her in pieces. Then she does speak up for herself a little; she can at least save her pride. But even then she does it with such large-mindedness, such inability merely to call the kettle black, that she gives us no excuse for calling her earlier professions of love insincere.

To mix with thy concernments I desist
Henceforth, nor too much disapprove my own. (970)

Such is the firm moral delicacy with which she introduces her final speech, explaining that, rather against her will, she has won eternal fame. Fame, she is far from denying, is double-mouthed:

But in my country where I most desire
In Ecron, Gaza, Asdod, and in Gath
I shall be named among the famousest
Of women, sung at solemn festivals,
Living and dead recorded, who to save
Her country from a fierce destroyer, chose
Above the faith of wedlock-bands, my tomb
With odours visited and annual flowers.
Not less renowned than in Mount Ephraim
Jael, who with inhospitable guile
Smote Sisera sleeping through the temples nail'd.
Nor shall I count it heinous to enjoy
The public marks of honour and reward . . . (980)

To recall the Israelite Jael is a telling stroke; Shelley could have said here too that the decisive proof of Milton's genius is that he alleged no moral superiority for Jehovah's religion over Dagon's. But she has no impulse to rub it home; she continues sadly and peacefully to say that, knowing she has done her best to reconcile the quarrelling factions, and has now made certain that the division is beyond healing, she will not count it heinous to receive eternal public honour from one side only, nor too much disapprove of herself for becoming a national heroine, imagined by the people to have been as savage as the Israelite Jael. It is one of the noblest speeches in Milton. A similar attempt to prevent the division of India single-handed would perhaps be the nearest modern parallel. I grant that she arrives at this tone of self-abnegation because she has strong personal grounds for regret, or what she may regard as guilt; her own people blinded Samson after they had promised her not to hurt him (800); the fanaticism on both sides turned out too strong for her, and she must at least feel she misjudged. And I grant, of course, that she does not express the aim of reconciling the two parties; that would exasperate Samson and at best sound a useless excuse to other people. However, she does say earnestly that her betrayal of Samson was actuated solely by public spirit:

at length that grounded maxim
So rife and celebrated in the mouths
Of wisest men; that to the public good
Private respects must yield; with grave authority
Took full possession of me and prevail'd;
Virtue, as I thought, truth, duty so enjoining. (865)

We should remember that this maxim, whether viewed ironically here or not, was the sole ground C. S. Lewis could find when he rebuked Adam for joining Eve in her fall. Even if she meant only Philistine nationalism by the public good, which is too small for the way she talks, that would leave her no worse than her husband.

An opponent might answer that Milton intended her as a smooth-tongued hypocrite who is exposed at the end of the scene. She is only present for 270 lines, and the author could hardly intend to delude us (I may be told) by the words of the Chorus at her exit:

She's gone, a manifest Serpent by her sting,
Discover'd in the end, till now conceal'd. (1000)

But the Chorus are Israelite patriots, and she has just said, at last, that she too had been actuated by public spirit; the comment does not need to be viewed as 'dramatic irony', which I agree would feel irrelevant if at all pointed. The Chorus is merely giving firm support to Samson, who feels greatly revived by the whole incident. A niggling reader, indeed, might think that by 'the end' they mean her last four words, which perhaps have been said with defiant triumph. Certainly a reader should try to imagine a performance, even though the preface claims that nothing so unpuritan was intended; and an actress, or even the boy actors Milton could recall, would prefer to get a bit of punch into the exit line. But this interpretation would have to fight all along against the cool sad dignity of the words, and in a play so genuinely not meant to be acted they deserve even more priority than usual. She ends by saying that, if anyone envies or repines at her being a public heroine,

I leave him to his lot, and like my own.

This is a rebuff, to be sure, but we should remember that the police are on her side; if she feels revengeful, she need not confine herself to an insinuating cadence. Though in a situation of mounting civil war, she takes liberty of conscience for granted and gives an assurance that she will take no reprisal against her implacable foes. To anyone who understands the politics of the thing, the quiet last line only makes ring on in the mind the generous disillusionment with which she has said she will make the best of it. The whole speech of course does carry a dramatic irony, because she will be remembered for a disaster to the Philistines and not as she now thinks for having saved them from one. This may give an air of insinuation, but from the mind of Milton or perhaps of his God, not of Delilah. And I need not deny that on her own account she has sounded at times a bit insinuating; so would most of us when trying to make contact with a dangerous lunatic, and it is fairly creditable to get through, as she did so far as we learn, without telling him any lies.

This picture of her as a hospital nurse will no doubt be resisted, especially by the argument so often used in the case of Satan; as Milton intended Delilah to be a liar, it is only simple-minded to believe what he makes her say. The answer seems to me decisive; he must have wanted the character to be intelligible somehow, and what ambitious or deceitful purpose could she have in offering to spend the rest of her life as nurse to a blind and (from her point of view) totally discredited husband? One can imagine the corrupt Delilah doing it 'for a whim', as the phrase goes, but even so the whim would not be a bad impulse. The belief that she is a Vamp, I think, comes from supposing that the old puritan must have wanted to make her one but did not know how, so that it is a kindness to let our fancy help him out. So far from that, he has laboured to describe her as a high-minded great lady, wholly committed to the values of 'the world'. The author of *Comus* was not ignorant of such characters; indeed the importance of appreciating the merits of an aristocratic patron, even if her morals were rather dubious perhaps, would not be beyond his imaginative range even in the days when M. Morand counts him yet unsmirched by domesticity and patriotic propaganda. In a way, great people were all his life the only types he cared to lavish his imagination upon. This of course was another reason why he married her to Samson; he wanted to save the lady's dignity, not the hero's.

It might now seem tidy to maintain that Milton never allowed one of his characters to fall except through a temptation so subtle as to be almost a justification; but Samson is the grand exception to this rule. His shame at having fallen to an inferior temptation is so crippling

(370 on) that we feel he is starting to recover his nerve when he blames God instead (630 on). The Chorus also complains how cruelly God treats his heroes in later life, and various critics have thought that Milton is blaming God at this point for his gout (700), not being able to claim that Charles II had martyred him; but Rose Macaulay in her too brief book on Milton said that he was grizzling over the executions of regicides he had known, which were carried out with the traditional barbarism. The sense of public shame and the baffled hunger to argue that it is undeserved are presented to the reader much more intimately here than in Satan or Adam, and the parallel to Milton's own life is so direct that he must have wanted it to be intriguing. One is tempted to ask whether he too had blabbed to a woman; but there is no hint of it among the anti-Milton gossip. The thought is perhaps only a failure to carry the parallel far enough; in such a case, the author would have been too crippled by guilt to write the poem. So far from that, I think, he found it rather a comfort to transfer his troubles to the ancient huge half-comic figure whose tragedy had been so unlike his own. He realizes that Samson is not an intellectual type, so that the subtle arguments about his case have to be said by minor characters; and this made the poem more like a play. Even so, it had to be a 'classical' play, in which the fatal bit of garrulity is only recalled, because Milton did not care to come nearer to a crude conflict between lust and principle, or to the self-delusion of a hearty boaster; we do not learn how and why the Fall of Samson occurred, as he is not self-analytical enough to describe it. But at least he is a dedicated man; Milton is only interested in the problems of such persons, being one himself; and the story itself provides a justification, though of a somewhat weird kind. After

Samson had felt shame for his folly sufficiently deeply, even his folly could turn out to be part of the deep purpose of God; his Fall is thus Fortunate in exactly the same sense as the Fall of Man. Some such mystery was much needed to explain the disastrous end of the Commonwealth; and one can see that, coming at the story from this angle, Milton would feel no eagerness to make Delilah contemptible.

Many critics have recognized that his theology in *Samson* has been beaten down a further stage since *Paradise Lost*. Sewell, who I think understands it best, puts it on the rather dreadful ground that he had lost the pride of reason: 'he turns to the idea of obedience, away perhaps from the idea of rational co-operation' (p. 213). The individual conscience is still decisive, in a way, but Milton no longer thinks of it as digesting a man's experience of life so as to make that readily available for a practical decision; instead, a man should purify himself from his experience, and wait for an illumination from God. I must not deny that the human mind can perform unconscious processes of digestion; not only an illumination, but also a failure to get a desired one, may proceed from a total appraisal of a man's situation, or at least quite as much of it as he could get by arguing. The trouble is that you may get very bad results, and that they are not open to scrutiny; but this is hardly more than the difference between the written arithmetic we are taught and the older technique of the abacus; the abacus is actually quicker (as I could observe in the Far East), and the decisive objection to it has merely been that another man can't check the figures afterwards. Seeing how personal the poem is, we may expect that Milton was trying the technique, and if so his failure with it is to the credit of his sanity. He is not feeling 'I do wish I wasn't too much of a coward to kill Charles II and Rochester and all the rest of them, blind as I am,' but 'I do wish God would only tell me to; I have tried to get him to, and he won't; but if he did I would get it done somehow, blind as I am.' It makes the final Milton and the unintellectual Samson peculiarly sublime examples of the Independent Conscience; and we need not be surprised if a certain amount of sympathy may also be felt for Delilah.

It has been said that Milton showed historical understanding or conscious artistry in *Samson* by making no mention of a future life; he was unusual for his time in realizing that Samson would not have expected one. On the other hand, the always reverent-sounding Sewell lets drop a belief that Milton did not expect one himself:

> Men are known by God, either as good or evil, persevering or backsliding. I think that Milton must have held that to be their immortality. (p. 185)

Thus in effect he agrees here with Shelley. This seems to me to show how hard it is for modern piety to understand the practicality of the earlier kind; Milton would not have taken care to avoid disturbing the simple but ennobling thoughts about Heaven of the children by the evening fireside after their bath, as is so much the modern attitude, because he would think of these kids as certain of Hell unless they fought like cats to keep out of it. If he had decided that there was no real danger of Hell his whole tone would have been quite different, and he would have thought passing on the good news an immediate duty, though an inspiritingly dangerous one.

All the same, I think these views can be reconciled in terms of the mood of an artist; Milton would choose a theme which suited his feelings in more than one way. Knowing he was not far from death, and realizing the complexity of the doctrinal position about the future life, even he would prefer, because the belief that boasting is bad luck lies deeper than good taste, a theme which required no mention of a hero's prospects of Heaven. This is much more agreeable, surely, than when the young Milton in *Lycidas* expected God to pat him on the head in Heaven, as a first-class author, even for the books he had failed to get written. Hell he would feel safe from, but he would not care to make specific claims. Living now on his pride in his past, and yet in a way free to be critical of it, he would feel himself (though of course quite ready to toss the printers a Latin Grammar or what not) much less unlike the unintellectual Samson than before, or at least that he could throw himself into that theme without the danger of suddenly finding it painful. The opportunity to treat Delilah with breadth would strike him as a salty, though very minor, part of the project.

It may be objected with sad truth that the mind has a rather dreadful power to retain a resentment while losing almost everything else, including its affections; so that the old man was probably getting his knife into Delilah. But the human brain at least continues to delight in its strength, as long as the strength is there. Milton's power was evidently not failing, and he would keep his love of moral paradox, or rather of adjudicating high and subtle points of conscience. He could not get under the skin of a character unless he felt he was behaving like a defending counsel, and he need not dirty his hands with inferior clients ever again. He would be sure to work up an interesting case for Delilah. Such at least is the thesis I want to put forward; it seems to me that critics of Milton become cross and puzzled each time they do not realize that the temptations are meant to be pitched staggeringly high.

Chapter 7

CHRISTIANITY

I HAVE now tried to state my position about *Paradise Lost*, but I need also to try to state my position about its topic; because, to a reader who starts with different presumptions about that, the literary argument must often seem to pick unnecessary holes. It is only if you realize what a difficult and unpleasant thing Milton was trying to handle that you can give him his due for the way he handled it, let alone appreciate the adventurous and entertaining quality of the huge poem. When I was young it was considered rather bad taste to make points against Christianity in the course of discussing something else, as being painful to many good persons and also unnecessary because the moral objections to the religion were well enough known. It strikes me that the younger present-day Christians have been brought up so genuinely ignorant of them, and are so likely to do harm in consequence, that this attitude needs to be abandoned. Hence I would think it proper enough to make a digression on the subject, but I am not really doing that here; because anybody brought up on our current neo-Christian principles of literary criticism is bound to find my account of the poem wrong, unless I can influence his judgement by a brief statement of the case as a whole.

'Neo-Christian' seems the right way to describe those recent literary critics, some of whom believe in Christianity and some not, who interpret any literary work they admire by finding in it a supposed Christian tradition. Christianity has been so various that very different traditions might be meant, and the critics themselves often say that the author they have in hand was unconscious or only half-conscious of the tradition they have in view. Their claim is to be bringing back to notice something which has remained inherent among good (European) authors and readers, so that the 'neo-' need only mean the recovery; clearly, the term when used with this definition is not insulting. I do not know who invented it. However, neo-Christians agree a good deal on the tradition in view, so that the class described by the term has more attributes than the defining one; and I think they are chiefly wrong in not realizing that Christianity has always had to be kept at bay, by people with civilized consciences. Gallantly determined to fight 'materialism', neo-Christians tend to appear quaintly savage; they boast of the morally disgusting aspects of the religion, which more traditional Christian writers have commonly been anxious to hide or explain away. Such a critic will often impute to an author a meaning too nasty-minded for the author to have intended, and he does this with a pathetic pride, suggesting a gun-dog fetching out of the covert a dead bird which it was illegal to shoot; because he has been taught to regard this nasty-mindedness as high-minded or other-worldly.

The trend is by no means only a literary one, whether or not it started among critics. During my return from Communist China in 1952 it struck me as widespread. I first noticed something like it on the boat in an informative book by Mr Alan Moorehead about The Traitors, the scientists who had been convicted of telling Russia about the atom bombs; he did not often moralize, but when he did he specifically denounced them for having had the impudence to obey their own consciences. He would describe with sympathetic understanding a case which presented difficult problems of loyalty, and then take for granted, in a general remark, that a man ought to concur with any herd in which he happens to find himself. The old Protestant in me stirred, and I reflected that this was just the way the Communists would talk about such a case in the reverse direction. A year or two later Parliament decided to exclude from England the American Horror Comics for children, and a leading Church of England scholar remarked jovially that the kids could get quite enough sadism from Christianity anyway. What struck me was that he would not have dared to say it thirty years before; something queer was going on with this side of modern Christianity. From the literary critics, a few plain examples are all that are needed.

To begin with a slight one, there was a controversy in *The Times Literary Supplement* a few years ago on what Gerard Manley Hopkins meant by 'The Windhover'. The poem is obviously very good, but it is so telegraphic that various opinions have been held about its connections of thought. After we local literary characters had aired our views for a few weeks, letters began to come in from Roman Catholic experts all over the world, and the correspondence was closed. They were all convinced that the poet had seen the hawk catch its prey (conceivably the word 'Buckle', but probably only 'AND' in capitals, can be taken to mean the swoop and kill) and that this symbolized the way Christ treats a worshipper. The octet describes the bird's movement in surveying its territory; and my view is that the poet regards this skill as due to continual practice. Praise of the beauty of a skill learned through a daily grind (an unexpected but very penetrating way to look at a hawk) is the only thought I can find which connects the aristocratic bird to the ploughman in the sestet; and then it can make a unity of the whole poem by another leap to the final embers. Hopkins might well be thinking about training, as the poem was written in the year of his ordination; indeed, the basic complaint of the later 'terrible' sonnets is that the severe Jesuit training doesn't seem to have made him any better. He would of course know that a hawk learns its skill in order to catch its prey, and one can readily believe that he accepted the hawk as a traditional symbol of Christ. But though highly conscious of the fierceness of his religion he was an excessively sensitive person; if he had actually seen the bird catch a rabbit he would be more likely to vomit than to write a poem. And the two examples of the theme in the sestet gain nothing by your forcing this brutal picture upon the octet. The plan is 'neo-Christian' merely in that it is proud of making the religion look nastier than the author would have intended.

When Joyce's *Ulysses* came out, gradually leaking through censorship, nearly all critics denounced it as a cynical book which expressed contempt for the basic human impulses and affections. This position was summed up by E. M. Forster in *Aspects of the Novel* (1929); but later he decided that he had been mistaken about the intentions of the author, and this gave an important lead to general opinion. It has become clear enough now, I think, that the book is meant to be gay and humane about the family life of Bloom, and triumphant about the eventual escape of Stephen from his throttling troubles; but the evidence that made E. M. Forster change his mind must have been rather subtle, in fact largely what a theoretical critic would call gossip. A reader properly absorbed in arriving at his own judgement of this novel does not easily realize that several independent factors are at work in the way a person is expected to react to it, planned as it was with 'silence, exile and cunning'. Recently the American Roman Catholic critic Mr Hugh Kenner, in a highly appreciative survey of Joyce's work (*Dublin's Joyce*, 1955), has praised him for doing exactly what his first critics execrated him for doing. Joyce, we are told, felt nothing but contempt for Stephen Dedalus—"There is no question whatever of his regeneration" (p. 112); though Joyce was rightly enough a self-important man, and had told the world by the book-title *Portrait of the Artist* that this character is himself when young. The 'liberalism' of Bloom now has to stand for the ridiculous eighteenth century as well as for H. G. Wells; Joyce has to be presented as bemoaning the entire development of European thought since Aquinas. But Mr Ellmann's biography (1959) has shown that Joyce considered himself politically on H. G. Wells's side, and was so fiercely anti-Christian that the baptism of his grandson had to be kept secret from him; it was thought fortunate that, when the baptism was carelessly mentioned, he assumed the idea could only be a coarse joke. With firm consistency, Mr Kenner goes on to argue that the generous-minded and expansive close built into the whole structure of *The Portrait*, *Exiles*, *Ulysses* and *Finnegans Wake* is intended by Joyce in each case, though the effort sometimes makes 'painful reading', to be greeted with sickened contempt by the fit reader. Necessarily, then, Joyce means us to jeer at Bloom for wishing he had a son, because to be a real father, as apart from a priest, is quite shocking: "The panther-theme exfoliates into an image of paternity *secundum carnem*, laying its curse on all the inhabitants of this animal hell" (p. 246); as for mother-love, it is "rank nursery sentimentality" (p. 306). Obviously there can be no interesting ideas in the book, because "It is precisely the pathetic absurdity of Bloom's and Stephen's bits and pieces of speculation that is being exposed" (p. 209); and Mr Kenner implies with complacent approval (p. 157) that the happiness felt by the reader in watching this exposure is like that ascribed to the blessed in the *Summa Theologica* from the punishment of the damned. I could go on about other critics of Joyce, but we only want an extreme case here. The interesting and alarming point, I think, is the rapidity of the change; as little as twenty years ago, Mr Kenner would hardly have dared to print these unnatural sentiments, and thirty years ago he would probably have joined in denouncing the book for having supposedly expressed them.

An interesting survey of British political novel-writing by Mr Gerber, in the *Critical Quarterly* for Spring 1959, discussed briefly among others the horrible book *1984* which George Orwell wrote while dying. The critic presumed that it was merely another attack on Communism, but found in it a more interesting aspect:

> the individualistic, rational, liberal and humanist conception of man is opposed, not only to party collectives, but also to the complete unconditional surrender to the transcendental, paradoxical nature of God. It almost seems as if Orwell, being gradually broken down bodily and on the point of death, had filled his political satire with unconscious or half-conscious meanings of another kind.

An excellent selection of details from the book was then given to prove that its satire

> has the age-old symbolic structure, and even phraseology, of resistant man's breakdown to some power which we generally call by the name of God.

I heard nothing from George Orwell after leaving England early in 1947, but I well remember how dreadful he could make you feel if he considered your political understanding of a question inadequate. Passionately indignant with Stalin's betrayal of the Left, he considered that one of the most shocking things about it was that Communism had nearly got back to being as bad as Christianity. Communism had no need to do this, not being a system of torture-worship; so its development had somehow proved that the human mind is pre-determined to behave badly. The political forecast of *1984* is that the two warring sides will become indistinguishable; that is why the author refuses to mention whether the London in view is a post-Communist or post-Christian one, and why nobody can find out whether Big Brother is a live man, a dead man, or a god. A Ministry of Love whose towering office hag-rides the city because each citizen believes it has calculated for him the torture he would find most unbearable is traditional for Christians, or assumed to be, but hard to relate to the ideals of Communism. The book was at once sent to me in Communist Peking, and one of my Chinese colleagues who was being recalcitrant at the time felt much cheered up by it; tiresome though the committees were being, the comment was, at least one knew that that kind of stuff was nonsense. The story (I still agree) becomes tiresomely incredible; but only because the author is determined to make his allegory apply to both Communism and Christianity at once. All the details of likeness found by the critic in the magazine article were correct; he was only wrong in presuming that the author must have been partially unconscious of them, in that they necessarily excite a reverence which he was unlikely to intend. But George Orwell very positively thought it the ultimate shame for a man to yield his conscience to an authority which craves to torture him and can only be restrained by a renunciation of thought, whether the authority is Stalin or God the Father. To be fair to this critic, poor George Orwell used to speak with great gloom of the certainty that even *Animal Farm* would be used for evil; but this was because he realized the state of mind in the reading public which I am trying to describe. Critics who write about *1984* like this are doing precisely what the book prophesied that they would do, without having any idea that that is what the book means. The book as a whole I have always thought a silly prophecy, but to this extent it has already come true. It is interesting to deduce that a neo-Christian critic could easily be toppled over and turned into a Communist one.

I hope these examples are enough to show that the literary critics of our present dominant school are unlikely to understand the forces at work behind *Paradise Lost*, because they completely misunderstand authors who lived under more familiar circumstances and left more documents. I am next to consider the tradition that Milton was trying to sum up, and will use the information now generally available, as he above all men would expect a fit reader to do. The cave artworks give bits of what may be evidence of human sacrifice among Paleolithic hunters, but such men would probably only fall back on the last extreme of magic at very bad times. A yearly ritual of human sacrifice is likely to begin with the Neolithic, at the start of farming; the technique of growing a crop involves such a nerve-racking delay after apparent waste of food, and is so liable to go wrong for reasons nobody understands, that the first groups who were induced to carry it through may well have required a startling mental comfort. The administrators of the first towns, as I have already remarked while peering into the depths of the operative speech of Satan, had to put extra weight on the existing tradition of ritual sacrifice so as to induce the neighbouring farmers to send food to the town. Once the routine had been established, such heavy ideological pressure was no longer needed; a town is in a strong position, if the neighbouring farmers have planted crops which can only be sent to that market. But the minds of city officials became so sunk in ritual sacrifice that they might never have emerged from it, and in Mexico never did. In the more open field of Europe and Asia, conquest by nomads is thought to have made a crucial difference; when they captured a town for loot, and suppressed the ritual which had been supposed to make the crops grow, the town survived because the peasants continued to send it food for barter. To go on behaving sensibly after loss of religious faith is an important capacity of the human mind; and no doubt a good deal of rough knock-about teaching had to go on before the next major step could be taken.

This was done right across the land mass. We do not easily realize how impressive it is to have the Second Isaiah and Pythagoras and the Buddha and Confucius all alive at the same time, because we think of that time, rightly enough, as the start of history; but the town civilizations had been going on for thousands of years. The Hebrews do seem to hold a slight priority, but it need not make them a world source. None of these thinkers invented his whole position for himself; he was a centre of crystallization for a frame of mind which had been growing up for a generation or two. This must have depended upon some idea which was portable. Rather few ideas could cross the land mass, and no early thinker travelled much; probably none of these four heard of the existence of any other. But a man who had done such a trip would be likely to jeer at the provinciality of the beliefs and ritual he found at the other terminus, and perhaps even at home when he got back; and he would be listened to with curiosity. What could cross the trade routes was a practical suspicion, very welcome to all decent persons, that the technique of obtaining benefits by human sacrifice was not really efficient. The wastefulness and nuisance of other ritual sacrifice would also come up, but the surviving records are likely to have been censored later to hide how much human sacrifice was then going on, and a revolt against that is what would make the decisive mental change. Granting that a lightening of the burden had already come locally from nomad conquests, the reason why these four thinkers were alive together needs to be considered in terms of trade routes.

Thinkers began to talk about what is good or right or just for all men, instead of about the correct procedure for sacrifice to the local god or king. Even the Romans, though not otherwise enlightened one would think, were ready to make propaganda out of the human sacrifices of Carthage and to suppress the human sacrifices of the Druids. Greek tragedy is the reverberation after the fall of human sacrifice; no wonder its theology is adventurous and rather confused. To make the chief god male instead of female, as in the fascinating accounts of Mr Robert Graves, no doubt also often happened during this process; but the sexual change is unimportant compared to stopping the custom of predated ritual murder, a change which inherently sets the mind free to consider the good life as such. I grant that the evidence about yearly sacrifice of the king is very shaky, and indeed that it is hard to imagine any viable human society which carried out the ideal at full blast; on the other hand, the overall evidence that an escape from the partial application of this ideal became an urgent need does seem very strong.

I must give some references to fill in the picture for

India and China. Ancient India is a problem for the historian because it did not believe in history, but the great Sir Charles Eliot, if I may go back to the book I learned from (*Hinduism and Buddhism*, 1921), sums up the position as:

> To the age of the Vedas succeeds that of the Brahmanas or sacrificial treatises. . . . To read them one would suppose that the whole occupation of India was the offering of sacrifices. . . . A great blow was struck at the sacrificial system by Buddhism. (Vol. I, p. 64)

However, he also finds evidence that there had been movements of resistance against sacrifice a generation or two before the Buddha (pp. 122, 133). The Brahmanas are given as about seventh century and Buddhism as sixth or fifth.

> Vedic ritual includes the sacrifice of animals and there are indications of the former prevalence of human sacrifice. At the time when the Brahmanas were composed, the human victims were released alive, but afterwards the practice of real sacrifice was revived (p. 68)

Sir Charles was a very high-minded man, ready to believe the best he could from his sources; it is not cynical to reflect that other men with similar moral feelings may long ago have made these sources more edifying. In any case, India developed in parallel to the Mediterranean basin, though because Hinduism never accepted a complete purge it retained a capacity to revive the practices of Ancient Night. The same social and intellectual advance is recorded by the historical-minded Chinese as of the sixth century, that is, not started by Confucius, who greatly helped it forward, but beginning a generation or two before him. Thus in 531 B.C. a local ruler captured the dukedom of his neighbour, presumably killing him in battle, and then sacrificed his eldest son. Shên Wu-yu said:

> This is inauspicious. The five animals used as victims cannot be employed for one another; how much less then can the ruler of a State be used as a victim!
>
> (H. C. Creel, *The Birth of China*, 1936; p. 207)

The idea that he would be inferior to a ritual pig seems to us a joke, and probably felt so within a century or two of being recorded; but probably Shên just saw how to twist the rules so as to forbid a thing he disapproved. Mr Creel follows this with another example from just after the time of Confucius, which has more clearly the tone of militant comic primness which we find so typical of the scholars of old China. A disciple of Confucius called Chên Tzu-kang was younger brother of a grandee, at whose funeral the wife and the major-domo wished to sacrifice a number of attendants. The brother said:

> If the nature of his disease makes it necessary for him to have attendants in the grave, who could fill that place so well as his wife and his major-domo?

so they called the plan off. Somehow, in fact, the Chinese intellectuals found that scholarly ridicule was enough to get rid of the beastly thing; but we need not doubt that they thought this an urgent bit of work, and indeed felt much the same about it as their contemporaries at the other end of the land mass. According to the masterly Penguin of Mr William Willetts (*Chinese Art*, 1958), the date fits a decisive change in the surviving artworks, which enter the urbane 'Third Phase' or 'Later Chou

Style' and no longer remind us of the sculptures for Aztec human sacrifice.

Thus around 600-500 B.C. China, India and the Mediterranean basin behave like three great trees in a park in the springtime, doing the same things in parallel without apparent contact; and a mood of doubting the practical claims of murderous and expensive priests is about the only thing we can imagine them to catch from one another. The effect of giving up human sacrifice was that thinkers felt free to consider what was just and good for all men. The effect of this again, in various cases, was to make them conceive a God of all mankind, transcendent and metaphysically one with Goodness; though both India and China tended to conceive an Absolute rather than a Person. The belief in progress may sometimes be delusory, but this rapid simultaneous development is the most impressive case of progress on record; that is, of the kind of thing a theorist has in mind when he speaks of progress as if it could be expected to be quasi-automatic.

Among the various universal religions which were formed as a result of this change and still survive, Christianity is the only one which ratted on the progress, the only one which dragged back the Neolithic craving for human sacrifice into its basic structure. This is what is the matter with it; people recognized at once that the thrilling piece of religious engineering carried excessive strain at this crucial point. Public opinion would no longer allow regular performances of human sacrifice; the Roman officials, indeed, suspected that the early Christians were secretly doing what they were always talking about, and tried to catch them at it. They revived it only in the sense that they said nothing had ever been more important than doing one human sacrifice once for all, and nothing would ever be so important again as to excite oneself by representations of it. The trouble was that, as soon as you transferred your ancient savage custom to your new metaphysical universal God, people said: "But why did God want this sacrifice? Mustn't it be because God is very wicked?" Hence the Gnostics maintained, in one form or another, that the Creator must be the Devil, as learned Christians like Milton always knew from the refutations of Gnostics in the Fathers, and as Blake and Shelley would know from their Gibbon before they read further. The Christian God has never lived down this problem, for anybody who has thought about him seriously; Milton was right to feel that, in undertaking to defend the Christian God, he had accepted a peculiarly difficult client. Modern Christian apologists are fond of saying that their religion is the most profound one because it gratifies such ancient impulses and includes all the paradoxes about the nature of God; I am ready to believe that what goes on in their own minds is innocent, but what they are playing with has done great harm in other hands, and they should not expect an informed Asian or indeed African to feel much reverence for their interesting God.

Thus we are often told that the ancient belief in the need for sacrifice corresponds to a profound spiritual truth, though one which was never expressed in its full purity and splendour until fulfilled by Christianity. I agree at once that no good mode of life is secure unless its participants are ready to make sacrifices for it. For example, I ought to let the Christians burn me alive rather than pretend to accept their evil belief, which if powerful enough will do grave public harm. And no doubt a Neolithic chieftain would often be actuated by motives which were both practical and genuinely public-spirited when he decided to sacrifice his son. But he was assumed to be giving up what was most valuable to him, very unwillingly, for the good of his people. The moral interest is in the sacrificer and the sacrificed, not in the deity who is gratified; indeed, the technique might be regarded as only a magical one. When the Christian God sacrifices his Son, he can hardly be envisaged as acting under necessity because it appears that the Son can bribe him by the offer; that is why the Father is a very bad example to imitate. Besides, even if you protest that this is not really a perversion of the ancient tradition, because the god was always dimly presumed to take an evil pleasure in the sacrifice, the argument still cuts both ways; our minds may be too hag-ridden by the tradition of human sacrifice already, instead of needing to have more of it incessantly inculcated. Most societies, even if not most people, are rather alarmingly ready for heroic behaviour to defend their way of life, so that it does not need to be presented as the supreme virtue; we need not be trained to do it by having the reek of the torture-chamber pumped into every room of the house, a thing which is bad for us in other ways.

A Christian reader will be feeling that there is an obvious and decisive answer to such talk in the doctrine of the Trinity. The Father is in some sense identical with the Son, therefore the story means that God mysteriously sacrificed himself on behalf of mankind; because he so loved the world. He is thus infinitely above these stupid accusations. This doctrine, one can readily believe, was of crucial importance in shoring up the structure enough to make intelligent men with good feelings trust it. For the followers of Jesus to start murdering and torturing soon after they got power (e.g. Gibbon, Chap. 21 at n. 157) was ludicrous, but at least they needed to settle the Arian controversy as they did. Perhaps then the trouble with Milton's God in *Paradise Lost* is simply Milton's Arianism; his God is patently sacrificing someone else for a political programme, whether his own Son or ourselves. But it seems to me that Milton was merely being honest there, because Christians can seldom avoid regarding the Son and the Father as he presents them. When the Church had sufficient power, it would regularly happen that a man was promoted to high place in it through a widespread recognition that he was genuinely imitating Jesus Christ; and then he would say to himself 'Come now; a man with my responsibilities has a duty not to go on imitating Jesus Christ; it is time to imitate God the Father'; and immediately he would start behaving with monstrous cruelty, apparently without any psychic shock. The other side of his nature had long been growing underneath; he had been reconstructing himself in the image of the Trinity.

I grant that in some walks of life you actually want a metamorphosis at the initiation ceremony; the obvious case is the medical student, who traditionally keeps up his courage against the taboos he must violate until he suddenly becomes the reticent and trusted doctor; but, even so, you do not want to exaggerate this human change into the emergence of a gadfly from its pupa. The persecuting bishop would fiercely and sincerely deny that he had failed to believe in the identity of the Son and the Father, but his behaviour had interpreted them as directly opposite characters. This mental trick is more usual or even standard than we can be brought up to appreciate; our minds have a wonderful readiness to satisfy themselves with admittedly false identities, but any orderly schooling needs to drive the process into the background of its area of practical work. I tried in my book *Complex*

Words to show how very fundamental it is; the baby could not learn to talk without it, and the learned man still needs to fall back upon it whenever he gets an obscure feeling that his work has been missing some essential point. Regarded simply as a bit of our mental equipment, it carries within itself a kind of recognition that the matter would bear looking into, or an impulse to do that later, though enough is settled for the immediate decision. Thus we should make terms with the process rather than struggle to renounce it; but educated people rightly suspect it, so that they recognize a familiar type of error, systematically misused, when they read an anthropologist's account of 'primitive thought'. The most staggering misuse of it is the Doctrine of the Trinity. One can hardly discuss whether a man believes this doctrine, because it is merely a thing which his mind can be induced to do. To be sure, many good men have passed on from accepting the process here, feeling it as deeply subtle and noble, to the natural next step of forming some intellectual construct about the matter; and they have often been burned alive for it. But even without this result any such construct is precarious, because the mind so easily falls back on the primitive assurance that the Father and the Son both are and are not identical. The machine is best described in the terrible book *1984*, where it produces a number of horror-slogans such as 'War is Peace'. I have thus to conclude that the Doctrine of the Trinity is a means of deceiving good men into accepting evil; it is the double-talk by which Christians hide from themselves the insane wickedness of their God. But it lies on their minds so very lightly, merely as the protection from an unwanted recognition (which is how the primitive device is often used in other cases), that Milton could leave it out of his epic without even attracting unwelcome attention for about a hundred years. One must deduce that he was giving a truthful picture of the minds of most Christians.

To say this does not mean that they ignore the doctrine. The Creed of St Athanasius (my mother told me as a boy that my father had threatened the Vicar to walk out if it was read, but unfortunately happened to be asleep when the occasion arose) amounts to saying that the Father and the Son both are and are not identical, and that you will go to Hell unless you believe both. Christians have always been encouraged to recognize the negative half of this paradox by the insistent metaphors about money, which led them through their natural exasperation into persecution of the Jews. Terms such as 'redemption', deep into human experience though they undoubtedly plunge, are metaphors drawn from the slave-market. It is hard to call up the identity of Father and Son at such points, and envisage God as driving a hard money bargain with himself before he agrees to torture himself to death out of love for mankind. No wonder Milton found the clause 'By payment of the required price' enough reason for rejecting the Trinity altogether. And yet, as soon as we let slip the veil of identity enough to allow any sense to the money metaphors, the Christian God becomes nakedly bad. The only intelligible motive for him is a sadistic one, so horrible that the worshipper would be risking damnation, as he used in effect to be warned (p. 192), if he even allowed it to enter his conscious mind. Only if this God had a craving to torture his Son could the Son bargain with him about it. In return for those three hours of ecstasy, the Father would give up the pleasure of torturing for all eternity a small proportion of mankind; though such a tiny proportion, it has usually been agreed, that his eternal pleasure can scarcely be diminished. God's justice has regularly been said to be what required this peculiar satisfaction, but no man who was himself accustomed to administer justice, and to come away from the work feeling himself recognized to have done it decently, can ever have felt the picture of God's justice to be literally true. Such is the extremely basic objection to the Christian God which Milton tried to handle by making him hint at his eventual abdication. The origin of the problem is obvious enough, given a knowledge of history which anybody can find in a public library; it came from trying to patch the ancient Neolithic craving for human sacrifice on to the new transcendental God of all mankind. Because this could never be admitted, the horrible doctrine has gone on doing great harm for two thousand years, with brave and intelligent men incessantly struggling either to stave it off or to drive themselves into facing its logical consequences.

Men always try to imitate their gods, so that to worship a wicked one is sure to make them behave badly. But no god had ever known before how to be so eerily and profoundly wicked. The new God is somehow one with Goodness itself, so that men must struggle to prove they are good by learning to enjoy his especial pleasure. And to learn this disgusting trick is not merely needed for life on earth, which we expect to be rather rough; it is also essential before we can enjoy Heaven. The extra doctrine seems already to have been invented by Tertullian (c. 155-220 AD), in an ecstasy of spite against people who still enjoyed the pleasures he had renounced (Gibbon, Chapter 15, n. 73); and I suppose that most present-day Christians of all sects feel sure that they may reject it, so that they would feel as much shocked as I do by a spanking neo-Christian such as Mr Hugh Kenner. But Aquinas himself, though leaving the impression of being a man of decent feelings, was held to have laid down as a matter of logic that all the blessed will have to enjoy the tortures of the damned, like God and Tertullian. The only easy reference to find is *Summa Theologica* Question 94; on going back to the text of Mr Hugh Kenner, I found he had already given it, but had added that the passage was written by one of Aquinas's pupils. I greatly hope so, but the scholarly reservation does not affect the ancient and continued authority of the book. The author of this Question denies that the blessed will rejoice "directly" in the tortures of the damned, but says they will do it indirectly "by considering therein the order of Divine Justice and their own deliverance, which will fill them with joy". "By their fruits ye shall know them," said Jesus very searchingly; thus I cannot be wrong in translating these doctrines into their effect upon human behaviour, seeing the inquisitor in an ecstasy of diseased pleasure buttoning his lips and decorously reassuring himself that his pleasure is still only an 'indirect' one. In any case, the text goes on, "the blessed in glory will have no pity on the damned", since they could not according to right reason. We gather indeed that they can never even wince away from the spectacle:

> Nothing should be denied the blessed that belongs to the perfection of their beatitude. . . . Wherefore in order that the happiness of the saints may be more delightful to them and that they may render more copious thanks to God for it, they are allowed to see perfectly the sufferings of the damned.

We are not actually told that they are forbidden to stop, but we cannot suppose a temporary slackening in any part of the perfection of their beatitude. It is interesting to pursue the main Bible text given to prove the doctrine. Of course, plenty of Old Testament texts approving a temporary desire for revenge could be found and were used, but the crucial text is the last verse of the Book of Isaiah, where the intentions of the Second Isaiah seem to have been unexpectedly generous-minded ones. What he is trying to say is that Jehovah will eventually offer salvation to the deserving among all mankind. After the Lord has come with fire "shall all flesh come to worship before me, saith the Lord", and the book ends with a picture of them rejoicing over their wisdom in having behaved well though not born as Jews:

> And they shall go forth, and look upon the carcases of the men that have transgressed against me; for their worm shall not die, neither shall their fire be quenched; and they shall be an abhorring unto all flesh.

These 'carcases' are presumably not envisaged as in pain, let alone eternal pain, but merely as exhibits not allowed the standard ritual burial. A footnote to the translation by the Dominican Fathers, which was what I looked up (Question 99), explains that the Latin text for 'an abhorring' is "*ad satietatem visionis*, which St Thomas takes to mean being satiated with joy"; by the way, this implies no doubt of his authorship. The whole case illustrates how you may reach a point of ecstasy by teaching yourself to enjoy what your unspoiled taste thought loathsome; rather like the kids who struggle to prove they are manly by learning to enjoy the initially disgusting cigarettes which will in the end kill them of cancer. No wonder Aquinas refused to write any more after he had achieved a direct vision of God, and we are free to reflect to his credit that perhaps he would have been burned alive if he had written another paragraph. As these offensive parts are presented as a necessary deduction from the system as a whole, which they certainly appear to be, and as the treatise has been much praised for its logical grasp and power, it is hard to see the relevance of a reservation about whether Aquinas wrote them.

Survivors of the Nazi concentration camps agree that the most powerful technique used there for the destruction of human conscience and personality was a more subtle one than might be expected in so brutal a setting; each of the starving and tormented prisoners was tempted, by the offer of very small alleviations, to take a share in torturing his fellows. Except that the blessed are offered no activity, this is what Christians have to regard as Heaven; if they take the vaunted 'logic' of their system seriously. They must sit beside God for all eternity and watch almost all the people they have loved on earth being tortured by God (with eternally increasing torture, Buckle reports from the seventeenth-century Scotch) and they must incessantly praise God for his mercy. To guard against being tricked into accepting such a doctrine, and then gradually corrupted by it, one needs not to be prevented by fear from realizing it in terms of human experience. Consider the type of man who would like arriving in Heaven; still half afraid to let God see his cravings and half incredulous that God can share them ('By God, sir, it is a bit embarrassing, isn't it?'), and then settling down to hold kind God's hand for all eternity and watch old mother being ripped up so much more satisfyingly than he could ever have imagined. This was never stated as anybody's ideal of Heaven, but there is no stopping short of it once the logic runs in that direction. Shelley remarked that no man of honour could go to Heaven, because the more he reverenced the Son who endured the more he must execrate the Father who was satisfied by his pain. But this is only the basic moral objection to the religion, which had been found obvious since its beginning; the ground for an even more severe one had been added during the first centuries. With the additional doctrine, which at least appears to be logically necessary and, as we have seen, is at least not always rejected by modern Christians, the objection becomes hard to express sufficiently strongly. The Christian God the Father, the God of Tertullian, Augustine and Aquinas, is the wickedest thing yet invented by the black heart of man.

The conception could not have been imposed without the sex-horror of the early Christians, which is no part of Jewish tradition but seems to have reached the Essenes beforehand. Mucking about with people's sex, always a disgusting business of course, is the epidemic or grass-roots way for Christians to gratify their God, when prevented by public opinion from having an epidemic or orgy of torture. The phrase 'mucking about' may seem to lack precision and dignity, but I do not know what else would cover what it is needed to describe. Apart from what goes on among believers, it is a regular demand of Christians to alter the public law, so that people who are not even supposed to be Christians can be tormented under rules invented for the edification of believers. To understand why this is done one must recognize the basic psychological impulses at work, which in one way are flaunted rather than hidden; the symbol of the Religion of Love is a torture. Worship of torture is itself a sexual perversion, oddly and shockingly at home in the human psyche but rather hard to teach without interference with normal sex. Of course, to accuse the clergy of doing this seems to them absurdly remote from their feelings and activities; they seldom even approve of punishing heretics, except at times when the secular arm permits it. Once permitted, it comes to be recognized as a grim duty. The confusion of our sexual nature is even more deeply buried. A demand for total chastity already makes normal people feel ashamed, determined not to tell the truth if they can avoid it, and secretly afraid that they themselves have already incurred Hell; it thus gives impulses towards cruelty before an actual perverse craving for cruelty has been acquired. The fires of unsatisfied sex can be relied upon to stoke the fires of Hell, that is, give a psychological reason for believing in it and brooding over it; and then the fires of Hell stoke the fires of Smithfield. There can be no deterrence from unaided reason or normal sentiment, which is in any case viewed with contempt; because it is a logical kindness to the heretic, or at any rate to those whom he might otherwise seduce, to kill him by slow fire rather than leave him to the eternal fire of Hell. An eerie class sentiment then reinforces the thing. All normal and all genuinely civilized pleasures are low-class; the only high-class pleasure is God's pleasure, the satisfaction of inflicting punishment; and if you do not enjoy this spontaneously you must torture yourself till you do, as in learning to crave for tobacco. Also a distinction can be drawn between the Christian attitude to sex and those of other world religions, even apart from the invention of a crown for male virginity. Ascetics of all the universal religions have recommended chastity for those who wish to approach the divine; although Blake was in a firm Hindu tradition if he meant to claim, or meant to claim in his younger poems, that he approached it by loving his wife. But these other religions do not at the same time make the demand exasperating by putting a unique value upon love; as is hard to avoid for a reader of the Gospels and prominent in later Christian tradition. Much has been said in recent times of the marvellous intellectual completeness of the religion, securely based upon its profound paradoxes; but they are a matter of jamming together all available contradictions with the standard solution "Heads I win, tails I burn you alive." Trying to connive reverently at any 'Christian paradox' met with in reading therefore does harm to the judgement of neo-Christians. The paradoxes are directed at heightening the tension, thus making the system liable to work itself up like a typhoon so as to create greater and greater horror. Voltaire was not much at leisure to sympathize with the moral difficulties of his opponents, but this power to make good men behave badly seems to be at the root when he calls the religion The Infamy, the most insinuating of all organized evils.

My attitude to Christianity will seem out of date, but that I think is chiefly because Christians have been kept under a fair amount of restraint for about two hundred years. A decisive swing of public opinion against the Christian use of torture heaved its way through Western Europe from the sixteenth to the eighteenth centuries, so that Milton though brave on the subject was by no means alone there. A man like Voltaire, who was energetically helping to push the change forward, naturally thought Christianity very wicked; but the sheer success of the effort made his attitude come to seem out of date. Buckle's *History of Civilisation* (1857-61) contains so far as I know the best examination of how the change occurred, and gives much evidence that it was due to a growth of tacit scepticism, so widespread in 'the spirit of the age' that it affected Queen Elizabeth I in much the same way as it did Cromwell's Independents. Towards the end of the eighteenth century even the devoted Spaniards were almost deprived of the pleasure of burning people alive, though Buckle reports a reprieve at an *auto-da-fe* after which the slavering crowd tore down the barriers and burned the accused with its own hands; the moral advance was a difficult one. I read the book as an undergraduate because it was praised by a character in a novel of Aldous Huxley, and was much impressed by the ample detail; it excites a sickened loathing for Christians when they are let loose which I have continued to feel. So I was interested recently to come across a scholarly re-edition by J. M. Robertson, who had checked the references of Buckle (1904). He scolds the author a good deal in footnotes for errors of theory, but decides the facts are correct, and he was well competent to check them. He calls Buckle in the introduction "a strenuous path-breaker", and says "after we have appreciatively read him, hardly any history satisfies us, so poorly does the average narrative feed the curiosity he aroused". It so happened that this bit of casual reading put me a month or two ahead of the Centenary of Buckle, which was celebrated by two Lives reviewed in all the weeklies. The reviewers were professional historians, quite certain that history teaches nothing whatever; they treated him with contempt for having any theories about history at all. It felt to me as if night had descended; only a hundred years, and the historians genuinely no longer had any idea even of what the question was that he had been discussing. And yet it is still a practical question. Many good people still believe that support for Christianity is a public duty, however absurd it feels, because other people (though not themselves) cannot be made good without it. A great deal of whitewashing still hides from them that, until there were enough influential and well-intentioned sceptics about, the Christians could not be prevented from behaving with monstrous wickedness. It remains a tribute to the stamina of European civilization that the religion could not corrupt us even more than it did, and by this time we seem pretty well inoculated against its more virulent forms. But it is not sensible to talk about Christianity so cosily as is now usual, ignoring its theoretical evil, ignoring its consequent use of rack, boot, thumbscrew and slow fire.

I realize that these remarks about Christianity will seem rather like the treatises of Miss Hannah Arendt against Communism, although so much slighter; logically interesting perhaps, a reader may reflect, but not smacking much of day-to-day experience of the system when in its more placid moods. Indeed, I think that her analysis applies word for word to Christianity; what is peculiar is that that does not occur to her. All the current accusations against the Totalitarian State are simply inherited from anti-Christian polemic; 'brain-washing' is not a new scientific invention, and Hitler had no opportunity to use 'the technique of the biggest lie' as grandly as the Christians—since they worship as the source of all goodness a God who, as soon as you are told the basic story about him, is evidently the Devil. And it is not only the accusations that are alike. Happening to cross the fighting lines by an unauthorized route during the siege of Peking, I was greatly struck by the beautiful evangelistic feelings of the troops who captured me, all consciously and confidently redeeming and redeemed; and I admired the feelings of many other Chinese during the following two years. Christianity has always smelt bad to me, though of course I have admired individuals for contriving to build a good character within it; but I recognize that anybody who has experienced either system working well is bound to retain an affection for it, even after coming to realize that it is liable to behave badly.

Still, one needs the realization; and that is what I think people have lost, quite recently, about Christianity, so that I keep meeting pronouncements which feel somehow alarming; after all, the ill-effects of worshipping a wicked God are bound to ooze out somewhere, and devotees who are kept in a state of artificial ignorance cannot guard against them. During the big London Aztec Exhibition (1958) somebody wrote in the weeklies that perhaps we got a wrong impression from those grindingly horrible though superb artworks; perhaps they really meant something nice, like the Crucifixion. There is indeed evidence for a certain brotherhood; the Aztec priests, earnestly devoted to torture but not mechanically inventive, started crucifying people as soon as the Spaniards had given them representations of the process. Soon afterwards I was reading an excellent work *The Rise and Fall of Maya Civilisation* (1956), by J. E. S. Thompson, who had given years to a scholarly and sympathetic interpretation of its ruins. He remarks in the Preface that "study of the breakdown of Maya culture led me, after many years in the wilderness of agnosticism, back to the Anglican Communion". The lesson was learned, one gathers in the book, from the acquisition of power by the Aztecs, who did too much human sacrifice; evidently this moral is not in favour of human sacrifice, but he has an affectionate admiration for the previous Maya. "Human sacrifice was certainly practised . . . in all periods of their history" (p. 245):

> The sacrifice of one's own blood was very common. Usually a cord set with thorns was passed through the tongue. . . . The stings of sting-rays were used by the priests in drawing blood. . . . Blades of a reedy grass were passed through the holes. . . . The usual sources of blood were tongue, ears, elbows, and the penis. (p. 252)

Reading the book, I did not get any impression that his

feelings were at all sadistic; but I did not see how he could admire such a society for its wisdom.

I got the same uneasy feeling, though she would be even further from intending it, in a footnote to Dorothy Sayers' translation of the *Purgatorio* (p. 57):

> All unmerited suffering (including that of children and animals) is the participation of the creature in the sinless offering of Christ, and is offered in Him and by Him for the sins of the whole world.

She appears to report this as a settled doctrine, though its tenderness for the sufferings of animals makes it evidently a new one. Her feelings in accepting it would be entirely good, including a certain pride at finding yet another device to justify the ways of God. The children and the animals are held to be in some degree identical with the Son, and hence (we may presume) with the Father, who thus also participates in their suffering. The subtle palliation has been carried a further step. But consider how this new doctrine would have to be implemented, if a practical administrator took it seriously. However refined the theological explanation may be, the agreed fact is that God can be satisfied by an 'offering' of pain, and we now learn that he can get a certain amount of satisfaction out of the pains of animals too. In particularly bad times, it would become the plain duty of a ruler to try to dissuade God from further torture of the people by glutting him with the tortures of animals. Crucifying relays of cats day and night in the cathedral, for example, might be found an efficient technique. To try to justify such a God is positively dangerous, and we may be thankful that Milton took the process no further.

It is thus always a puzzle, in trying to follow the mind of a Christian, to estimate how near the surface of his mind or his judgement is the basic evil of the system he has submitted to. An outsider cannot help feeling that it is still in a way present in his character even when the unconsciousness seems complete and the results have been good. When the silver-haired parson raises his eyes to the groining to sing "Blessed be he that taketh their children, and dasheth them against the stones" (perhaps he no longer does; he was still doing it when I was young) the first thing you feel is how wonderfully remote it is from him; and then you reflect that the spiritual strength he has won by renunciation cannot come from renouncing the pleasures of the world, since they would be too coarse to tempt him; presumably then from renouncing the pleasures of the torture-chamber. He clearly has some unformulated awareness that Hell is one of his great allies. Very likely he feels that this is what prevents the Religion of Love from becoming mawkish, also perhaps that it allows him not to call in the police, while wrestling for the soul of a criminal, anywhere short of the point where he legally must. His mind has resolved the paradox in some way which he finds by experience to be morally good and practically useful. But his flock have not all followed this turn of mind, and many of them simply feel what a Victorian girl did about her tight-lacing; it was a duty to be endured, but she could feel it all the time to be intimately and disgustingly bad for her. For a very long time, the best characters of Europe were all Christians; a man is not tempted to deny this in thinking it a tragedy that Europe got saddled with such a very corrupting religion. Its greatest appeal is for the noblest because it seems so very good, and then, as its darker side happens to get prominence, it is liable to contort them into being very bad. As it is beyond reason, there can be no control over it from a rational ethic; so that at any time, especially in parts of the world where an endemic tolerance has not been acquired, allowing a traditional influence from a rational ethic, worthy Christians may again feel it their evident duty to plunge headlong into great wickedness.

I need then to try to say what a rational ethic may be; a grave undertaking, except that I would claim to feel much like anybody else who hasn't been specially perverted. It is the opponent who makes the positive claim, that there cannot be ethics without a supernatural sanction for them. But it would be better to have principles, and I am still inclined to the theory of Bentham which was in favour when I was a student at Cambridge; that the satisfaction of any impulse is in itself an elementary good, and that the practical ethical question is merely how to satisfy the greatest number. The doctrine has always been accused of selfishness, but the generalizing mind of Bentham was inherently interested in anybody's satisfaction at any time, and could see little need to find a reason why we ought to help forward one another's satisfactions. Hazlitt remarked in his sensible journalism that this theorist must enjoy being approved more than we common chaps do, because he had made it a plank in his system; meanwhile Bentham was answering letters from South America asking for advice about new laws, and the chief reason why he was asked was that his mind was so evidently above the hunger for immediate approval which rightly enough actuates a journalist. The Bentham theory feels healthier than any holy one and actually did make a number of laws better; modern theorists tend to call it soft or weak, but it was a great bull-dozer through the legal jungles. It has the same kind of claim in aesthetics. I feel now, even more than I did at the time, that Dr Leavis brought moral confusion upon his many followers by the denunciations in *Scrutiny* of

Professor I. A. Richards' treatment of Benthamism as fundamental; which had mainly come in *The Principles of Literary Criticism* (1924). All the same, there is a basic objection to the theory; unless some special gadget can be fitted in, the satisfaction of an impulse to inflict pain on another person must have its equal democratic right. Bertrand Russell wrote some brave pages trying to defend this belief, but has now as I understand given it up. I am much inclined to agree with the later Russell that this satisfaction is an elementary evil; and this makes it a remarkable object, carrying the only inherent or metaphysical evil in the world. The definition needs to be narrow; a cat is unlikely to imagine the feelings of a mouse, when it plays with a mouse, and any sensible father wants his son to have enough aggressiveness to hold down a pay-packet, or in simpler times defend the cave. Sadism means an imaginative experience of the other party's suffering, which is then enjoyed; a peculiar thing to find the human make-up so prone to, especially if you imagine trying to build the tendency into a robot. No doubt, like other vices, it comes in the end to cripple the normal satisfactions; but some people are clever at making adjustments to their vices, and this one does not seem to punish itself enough. Still, a planner need not regard it as uncontrollable, because it only reaches its high points after being allowed considerable real or imaginary practice. The basic trouble about Christianity is that it provides a great deal of such training, after apparently setting out to do the opposite. I recognize that my own position about ethics is too indefinite, but I am left in no doubt that such training is bad. The chief thing I felt I had learned, after trying to consider ethics in a fundamental manner, is that what Christians are worshipping, with their incessant advertisements for torture, is literally the Devil.

A Christian is likely to find this idea evidently wrong, by definition; because it is a basic belief of Christians that their God is the origin and sanction of all goodness. There is no harm in the dogma itself, so long as we are allowed to recognize that our own consciences must decide whether what other people tell us about God is really good. Our own consciences are therefore the final judges even of truths vouchsafed to us by Revelation; there are seventeenth-century Anglicans who use this important doctrine, but it was not standard and I do not know its earlier history. The curious moral impudence of the neo-Christian literary critic comes from presuming that he has already been told the only correct moral answers. Maybe this is a fair enough reaction when confronted with much of our current literary output, but it is professionally bad for him, because the central function of imaginative literature is to make you realize that other people act on moral convictions different from your own. This indeed is why I think it makes an important difference to one's reading of Milton if he can be found good at such acts of imagination. What is more, it has been thought from Aeschylus to Ibsen that a literary work may present a current moral problem, and to some extent alter the judgement of those who appreciate it by making them see the case as a whole. I was startled to realize that Professor W. K. Wimsatt, in his essay 'Poetry and Morals' (*The Verbal Icon*, 1954), in effect rejects this whole conception as romantic, since he already knows moral truth from a better source than the records of human experience. How about Huck Finn saying "All right, I'll go to Hell then" rather than betray Jim? Surely a lot of characters in fiction, not only Milton's Satan, must become pretty dull if the orthodoxy is always right. I do not mean to deny, of course, that the critic ought to express what moral convictions he has, and ought often to say that the author is wrong; but the idea that there actually couldn't be a moral debate in a literary work amounts to a collapse of the Western mind, quite unforeseen when I was young. For one thing, it means that an essay like Professor Wimsatt's does not even recall the examples which would be found interesting in the subject he is discussing.

The belief that the Christian God is the only source of goodness also causes the despair so often expressed by authors who have lost their faith; at least, I cannot feel that they deserve much respect otherwise. To say 'Oh, why isn't there a Hell? I am so bored without Hell' is entertaining enough as a kind of epigram, but if taken seriously, with the actual doctrines in view, the supposedly high sentiment becomes about the lowest on record. Perhaps I have not a deep enough understanding of the anti-humanist position, which has been strong among most of the great writers in English earlier in this century, but I seem to have appreciated its products without feeling a need to worry about its theory. So far as it meant seeing the merit of Byzantine mosaics, for example, there was no occasion for worry; but even an admirer could notice that the position was a hard one for its exponents to hold with grace. A humanist, as I understand the term, says "This world is good enough for me, if only I can be good enough for it"; an anti-humanist, however noble in personal character, at least appears to be committed to saying "Nothing but Heaven is good enough for me; I ought to be there already"—nobody but God is aristocratic enough for him. The attitude is not always combined with interest in Hell, but that seems to fit on to it very easily, as one of the aristocratic pleasures of Heaven. A political-minded reader is inclined to reflect how easily this spiritual-minded author might instead have become a frustrated revolutionary, saying: 'If I had my rights, I'd be sitting in that police-station already, pulling out people's finger-nails.' I am glad to be able to add at once a less sordid reflection; it really does argue great sweetness of character in other readers that they so readily view the anti-humanist line of talk with so much respect. But there is another aspect of it which does at least deserve patient sympathy, and is probably what keeps the good-will of the audience. How a child is brought up to be a good character is hard to say, but the thing is often done, and fear of Hell is far from being an essential ingredient. But if a child is brought up to believe that without the Christian God there is no difference between good and evil, and later ceases to believe in that God (through having an intelligent conscience perhaps), he is liable to become like a dog with its back broken on the road by a motor-car, which one feels ought to be put out of its misery. This happens most often in Ireland, where religious education is particularly fierce; it is the whole theme of *Waiting for Godot*, which English audiences found somehow familiar and yet excitingly mysterious. I know a little about what the audience thought, because I was kindly invited to speak on the stage, as one of the two Devil's Advocates in the initial debate, when a packed house of enthusiasts for *Waiting for Godot* discussed in the theatre what they thought the play meant. No two of them agreed, and I came away strengthened in my own belief that this kind of religious education is a very unfair trick to play on a child.

When I was emerging from Communist China in 1952 there was a midnight eve-of-sailing removal of my passport, never explained, which gave me an interesting peep for two weeks at the nerve-racked foreign business community of Tientsin and its weeping but heroic bank managers; a scene which might have prepared me to salute the Western freedom for the individual. The first newspaper I saw in Hongkong described the latest sex case in the homeland. A man had met a girl in Epping Forest and, after talking to her for half an hour, had offered to kiss her; four sweating policemen had bounded out of the bushes and arrested him, because she was a policewoman dressed up to seduce him. The magistrate dismissed the case, but as the culprit was a teacher like myself he would probably lose his job all the same. 'Good God,' I said, with an involuntary cry, 'it takes a bit of nerve to go and live in that country.' I was coming back under the power of Christianity, and the smell already hit me at the other end of the world. The papers do not force you in the same way, for example, to notice the insistence upon keeping alive children known at birth to be imbecile or crippled, when the parents will only pay for two children and would prefer to have two healthy ones, as would be better for all concerned. They make you notice the trials, and the next thing was a big homosexuality trial, with the lawyers competing against each other for which could give the best imitation of Sergeant Buzfuz, bewailing the duty of acquainting themselves with the evidence, and begging the public to protect its innocence by withdrawal before some warm-hearted love-letter was read out. Both the judge and the prosecuting counsel in such cases must know that they are talking nonsense; to suppose that they don't is hardly even charitable. It is not their fault that they have to administer a wicked law, but when they enjoy it so much I think they ought to be penalized themselves for bringing justice into contempt. I realize that the British law here is accidental and almost unique, and not supported by the Churches; but it must surely be regarded as part of our Christian heritage. The

Religion of Love (e.g. Gibbon, Chap. 44 at n. 203) was torturing men to death for loving each other, as well as for subtle points of theology, soon after it got power. It would be off the point here to try to discuss the rather confusing subject of homosexuality, apart from testifying that I too think the law wrong; but the question has one direct bearing upon this argument. The term 'sexual perversion' is used rather trickily; psychologists of all schools, I think, would agree that some emotional attachment upon others than the sexual mate is a basic requirement for a social animal, built into it by its evolution. If the term means altering the impulse into something inherently evil, only one of the things commonly so called deserves the name; the craving to gloat over torture, which Christians are kept upon the edge of worshipping, and contrive to indulge themselves in by their wicked laws.

We are fortunate at present in England compared to some other parts of Christendom. But in any case the harm done by the religion now is trivial compared to what it threatens in the future. To have whole continents brought up thinking Christianity the only alternative to Communism might seem alarming in itself, especially as Asia and Africa are so unlikely to be in sympathy. But most people realize that they do not want an atomic crusade, even if they feel they should. They do not realize in the same way the world need for birth control. That the Chinese also refuse to recognize it (at the time of my writing this) is of course also bad, but that is a matter of policy, not of principle, and the Government could change the policy overnight. The Moslem position, as I understand, is confused. The Roman Catholics are the only major group standing out on principle, though with a concession which makes the principle hard to take seriously. It would be consistent, even in a world breeding headlong towards famine, to condemn any act of sex not performed with the intention of producing a child. But they allow it in a supposedly safe period, confessedly chosen to avoid producing a child; while describing as 'murder' any other procedure with the same purpose, except celibacy. (I have not noticed them calling masturbation murder.) The calculation of the date is likely to be very disruptive of normal affection, especially as it is exasperatingly well known to be unreliable; and even if it were not it could hardly deserve reverence. Here as so often one has to ask what motives the pious can ascribe to their God, other than very bad ones, for making both the biological quirk and the moral rule which gears in with it. Considering the issues at stake, and the moral triviality of the point of difference, the stubbornness of the high officials who cling to it is hard to regard charitably; it is hard not to suspect at the back of their own minds, as of their God's, the sentiment which Milton would only allow his God to express through the voice of his Chaos:

Havoc and spoil and ruin are my gain.

Compared to this, a prospect of the destruction of all life on the planet, including the fish at the bottom of the sea, by atomic war induced by famine induced by religion, it may seem trivial to grumble about neo-Christian literary critics; however much they lecture us upon morality without having any idea what the word means, since they think it means licking the boots of some earthly or heavenly policeman. But, as a matter of ethical theory, the two processes are the same. I see no hope before Christians until they renounce the Devil and all his works; that is, stop worshipping a God who is satisfied by torture, and confess in public that they have done so.

Such is the kind of background, I consider, which a present-day reader needs if he is to appreciate what Milton was getting at in *Paradise Lost*; and there is a historical reason why he needs it. A modern Christian has only philosophical and ethical grounds for his belief, so an Anglican, at least, feels he can resist the more appalling deductions from it, unless indeed he doesn't want to. This sense of freedom is likely to be mistaken if he has been treating the religion seriously, because his genuine moral feelings will have been mangled by it, but only through a gradual process which he does not remember. So far from this, a seventeenth-century intellectual felt himself surrounded by what seemed unbreakable proofs, of a very external kind, for morally unwelcome conclusions, such as 'Thou shalt not suffer a witch to live'. The proofs were largely historical, especially the Argument from Prophecy; and the labour of generations of courageous scholars had to go on before such proofs were tacitly dropped. Learned and responsible characters like Donne and Milton could therefore become hag-ridden by the moral objections to the religion without giving it up; they regarded it as an unescapable fact, and wrestled with it enormously, as if they were monsters of the deep. This was usual behaviour for theologians, but I think one can gather that the two poets though extremely different in thought both produced fairly good later moral effects, as the inherent power of sympathy which made them poets made them deserve to do. A modern critic who assumes them to accept Christianity in the same way as he does, and appears to boast of not being troubled by the moral problems which engaged their main intellectual attention, is unlikely to be able to follow their minds even at the points which are agreed to be of literary interest.

All the same, there is a great deal of agreement about

Paradise Lost already. Thus Dr Tillyard (*Studies in Milton*) concludes that Milton does not enjoy the Doctrine of Atonement; the announcement of the angel Michael at XII. 385, he says in his flat central truthful way, has 'notably little energy or passion':

> As passionate writing, the lines on Christian liberty a little before and the lines on the world's decay a little after quite overshadow the account of Redemption. On the other hand Milton insists, with an emphasis he could have avoided had he wished, on the legalism of the transaction. Had not Milton written more passionately in nearby places, it could be argued that he was for some reason tired. Ingenuity could find many explanations, but a possible one is that Milton was powerless either to free himself from, or to impassion, the legalism that then for all Christians, but especially for the Puritans, was inseparable from the doctrine of the Redemption.

The only appropriate passion, it seems to me, is that of cold horror at the 'justice' of God, as at a commandant of Belsen; and Milton expresses this well enough, with a feeling of grim endurance. It is rather hard to pick one's way between the two assertions that all Christians were then legalistic and that Milton could have avoided emphasizing it had he wished. The Cambridge Platonists were not; and I have offered evidence for a possible way out of the dilemma—Milton decided that they were wincing away from the evidence, but that their graceful picture would be true of an eventual better world. The historical mistake, I think, in this otherwise very understanding treatment by Dr Tillyard is the civilized presumption of modern Anglicanism that a man need only believe what his conscience prefers; whereas Milton considered himself driven by the findings of hard study, even though they happened to be confusing enough to give him a decent amount of moral freedom. I could never see that any belief except 'legalism' is possible to a Christian at any date who attends to the doctrines laid down for him; indeed this 'legalism' (which really means something much more horrible) is bound to go on working at the back of his mind whatever struggles he has made to purge himself of it. I thus find it cool of Dr Tillyard to remark that the thought of the poem, as now cleared up, is good as a whole:

> There may be this or that detail which the reader dislikes; the presentation of God the Father, for instance. But this is still but a detail which counts for little compared to weakness in the part of the poem where strength is most needed.

The Father himself, from what we are told of him, would consider himself rather more than a detail in a poem written to justify his ways.

A person in the secular tradition does not go through the same process of mind as Dr Tillyard. While he is first getting hold of the poem he feels spontaneously, though he naturally dislikes Milton's God, that the familiar bad smell of Christianity is somehow surprisingly absent. This must explain why the poets backed Milton solidly all through the eighteenth century, and why they continued to back him in the nineteenth century after deciding to call Satan his hero. No wonder they felt they ought to support the poem unflinchingly, because it is so startlingly innocent compared to the religion it claims to describe. Milton has cut out of Christianity both the torture-horror and the sex-horror, and after that the monster seems almost decent. This book has already considered

Milton's treatment of sex and his refusal to remark that the Crucifixion was painful or let the rebel angels yield in any degree to their pains; it still needs to consider, while trying to sum the matter up, his treatment of Hell as a danger confronting the reader. One might naturally deduce from the Debate in Heaven that God intends most of us to be saved, if only to spite the Devil; but towards the end of the poem Milton seems in no doubt that the blessed will only be a tiny proportion of mankind. It would be of great interest to know whether the Restoration had happened in between, but anyway (though the last two Books are dismal) the poem does not feel as if he changed his mind in the middle. After 'great numbers of each nation' have been converted to Christianity, Michael tells Adam:

> *heavy persecution shall arise*
> *On all who in the worship persevere*
> *Of Spirit and Truth; the rest, far greater part,*
> *Will deem in outward Rites and specious forms*
> *Religion satisfi'd; Truth shall retire*
> *Bestuck with slanderous darts, and works of Faith*
> *Rarely be found: so shall the World go on,*
> *To good malignant, to bad men benign . . .* (XII. 535)

One might think that the formal persons need not all be among the damned, but Milton regarded salvation as through Faith alone. The prospects before the reader are thus not at all bright, but even Michael, though almost spitefully severe about affairs on earth, has nothing specific to say about the pains of Hell. Milton in the *De Doctrina* (Chapter XXXIII) admits "eternal torment, which is called the punishment of sense" but adds "The intensity and duration of these punishments are variously estimated" and "Punishment, however, varies according to the degree of guilt". He turns with an air of relief to speak of the perfect glorification of the righteous. This leaves an impression that his moral feelings had made him try to break the evidence about Hell, but that it had stood firm; he could thus allow his Old Adam a minor amount of pleasure in the poem from revenge on his enemies, and we are not to deduce hope merely from his reticence. What does I think affect a reader of the poem is the suggestion, whenever Hell is mentioned, that he is one of the saved because otherwise Milton would not be talking to him; Milton only cares to address dedicated persons, and does not bother about the others, any more than his God does. It is particularly noticeable in God's forecast of the Last Judgement:

> *Then all thy Saints assembled, thou shalt judge*
> *Bad men and Angels, they arraigned shall sink*
> *Beneath thy Sentence; Hell, her numbers full,*
> *Thenceforth shall be for ever shut. Meanwhile*
> *The World shall burn, and from her ashes spring*
> *New Heav'n and Earth, wherein the just shall dwell*
> *And after all their tribulations long*
> *See golden days, fruitful of golden deeds . . .* (III. 330)

"How tidy," one feels, "to get rid of them like that"; God is like a cat shaking a drop of milk from his paw. The reader is somehow encouraged to feel sure that he won't get caught in this trap; perhaps because the only sympathy expressed is for the earlier tribulations of the saints in the world. The tone here, though there is no direct challenge in the meaning, rejects the doctrine that God and his Saints will eternally enjoy the spectacle of the sufferings of Hell. There is a more decisive bit of evidence, though it is put in an unchallenging position. Milton reports that some of the loyal angels, the more political-minded types, had waited around the Throne to hear what happened next after the creation of mankind, instead of becoming remote in the bowers of blissful interpenetration, and these ones met the angelic guard returning from Eden after the Fall of Man:

> *Soon as th' unwelcome news*
> *From Earth arriv'd at Heaven Gate, displeas'd*
> *All were who heard, dim sadness did not spare*
> *That time Celestial visages, yet mixt*
> *With pity, violated not their bliss.* (x. 25)

It was actually because they felt pity that their displeasure did not violate their bliss. Milton is always well-read, so one must expect he put this in, giving more credit to the loyalist angels than he allows anywhere else, as a specific rebuttal, carrying a good deal of psychological truth, of the disgusting picture of Heaven considered logically necessary in the *Summa Theologica*. And Milton's God too, since he intends at the proper time to turn himself into the Absolute, will patently not gloat eternally over his revenge, let alone force the blessed to join him in it. Here Milton's God is morally very much better than the traditional God of Christianity, not worse as has so often been said in recent times. Some of those who said it did not realize how bad the Christian God is; others, one would gather, were complaining at the lack of their familiar Horror-Comic or drug-like thrill.

A reader may agree that Milton intended to reject this louche detail of standard theology but deny that his God is otherwise better than the Christian one. I had better try to sum up the considerations on the two sides. Milton's God, except in formal assurances such as at v. 220, where he is said to pity mankind before taking a legal precaution to secure man's condemnation, seems indifferent to the mass of suffering he causes by his sustained trickery. But his tricks are a high political manœuvre, designed to produce good enough characters to allow him to retire and dissolve into the Absolute, thus greatly improving his own character too. But this is not a novelty; most Christians have believed that God wants to produce good characters, and is operating some large plan to do it. But Milton's God is not interested in torture, and never suggests that he uses it to improve people's characters; here we reach the point of difference, however it is interpreted. What is morally corrupting about Christianity is that the extreme difficulty of imagining the plan of its God, together with its ritual insistence upon torture, drive the worshipper at the back of his mind into treating God's motive as a sadistic one. Viewed against this background, the apparently slight change made by Milton questions the psychological basis of the religion, and can be felt in the poem nearly all the time.

This firm rejection by Milton of interest in torture is the more remarkable because, just before composing at least most of the poem, he had spent several months in hiding waiting to be disembowelled and castrated after being half throttled. Masson's *Life of Milton* (Volume VI, 1880) is still so far as I know the fullest account of how very touch-and-go the affair was; he decides that it cannot have been only a matter of (say) Marvell whispering an influential word in high quarters, but of many informed people choosing to hold their tongues, towards the end of the prolonged and confused negotiations, when it became evident that Parliament was forgetting to reconsider this one of the various cases which it had decided earlier to shelve. If you follow the mass of detail you come to regard the sparing of Milton as an obscure but public moral victory, and he would feel this, after the calculated defiance of the enlarged second edition of the *Ready and Easy Way*, to be what is really meant by saying that a man's life was saved by miracle. The political breadth of the process, instead of making him feel it was just a toss-up, would make him honour it as an act of God.

The prologue to Book VII claims that he is inspired, and shows that he does not mean it as a literary convention. In form this prologue is merely a prayer for inspiration to the Holy Spirit, like the prologue to Book I. There he asks to be inspired as Moses was when God enabled him to tell the truth about the Creation, in the first chapters of Genesis, though Moses had not seen it; this means that Milton was trying to imagine the truth about how Satan came to fall. Halfway through the epic, he again prays that he may tell the truth in the next half; what is startling is that he assumes his prayer about the first half has been answered. "Up led by thee / Into the Heav'n of Heav'ns . . . With like safety guided down / Return me." She visits his slumbers "nightly". But perhaps he did not think this privilege unusual for poets. He has to mean something unusual when he tells us, at the start of the poem, that his adventurous song will pursue

> *Things unattempted yet in Prose or Rhyme.* (I. 15)

Modern readers perhaps assume that he is boasting about his style here and fitting in a claim for Blank Verse, but he was not as aesthetic about a religious poem as all that. He could not want to convey that only unrhymed poets had tried to say the same things before him; and in prose, at least, his nominal theme had been exhaustively attempted. The claim is a larger one; with his eyes sacrificed and his life miraculously spared (the first paragraph is unlikely to have been written first) he was now plainly in the ancient tradition of the bard. He had seen the lid taken off the cauldron of popular heresy and what he calls an outcry against the injustice of God; and as early as *Areopagitica* he was acclaiming this public turmoil for being likely to arrive at new truth. His considered opinion, after taking part in the great debate, might well be something unattempted yet. But the novelty is not evident; so that learned critics can explain he was merely copying out "the hexameral tradition" or even that he was bored with the theme of his epic, like other Restoration figures, by the time he came to write it. I think he was much more likely to be sincere in claiming to attempt some important meaning, and under Restoration conditions it would probably have to be given a protective obscurity. We can be sure what he would most wish to believe: that he had cleaned the Augean stable of Christian theology, that he had succeeded where the Reformation had failed.

It may thus seem trivial of me to have begun this book by saying that the reason why the poem is so good is that it makes God so bad. But that seems to me a basic truth about the poem, which no plan of Milton for the eventual rehabilitation of God could alter. I had tried to make the point in some magazine by saying that the poem is like Benin sculpture, and a rebutting critic said that the views of Empson on Benin sculpture would plainly be irrelevant to the experience of reading the poem even if they happened to be correct. But I was not moving in any private world there; it is a new barbarism to suppose that an appreciator of an artwork is professionally unconscious of its social background. The interesting case of Benin is rather well documented, as British imperialism there for once moved forward on firm moral grounds, almost like the Spaniards against the Aztecs. Far too much human sacrifice was going on; but the dances still being performed before the holy king were as rippingly beautiful (if I remember) as the traditional reliefs. When I first went to teach in Sheffield one of my colleagues kindly took me round a local museum, and we passed through a sheer hall containing nothing but Sheffield Plate. This caused intense depression; then we turned a corner and faced two huge ivory tusks, carved all over for the appalling and splendid court of Benin; not a surprising thing to find there, as Benin artworks were distributed widely over the sack of the capital (1897). They raised my spirits no end. I report this elementary reaction to point out that it is not an affectation or a perversion to feel so; we cannot help doing it; chiefly because we need to feel that, whatever we do with our own small lives, the rest of the world is still going on and exercising the variety of its forces.

The major thing people feel about *Paradise Lost*, if it works on them at all, is the fascination of its barbaric power, which Milton himself feared that being born 'an age too late' he might be unable to recapture. And one does not feel about *Paradise Lost* that its barbaric power comes from living in a malignantly specialized society, as one ought to recognize about the art of Benin. The Puritans do indeed give that impression, but their minds were working on very central matters for Europe; and Milton has stretched his historical imagination very far. The poem really does survey the Western half of civilization and express the conflict which arose from the introduction of Christianity into this great area, as a by-product of offering a solution to it which seems to him tolerably decent. The root of his power is that he could accept and express a downright horrible conception of God and yet keep somehow alive, underneath it, all the breadth and generosity, the welcome to every noble pleasure, which had been prominent in European history just before his time. Unless you look at the poem like that, so that you are undisturbed by the twentieth-century complaints about its argument, I warmly agree that it feels bad. If you praise it as the neo-Christians do, what you are getting from it is evil.

INDEX

INDEX

INDEX